"Oh but that ain't America
For you and me
Ain't that America
Somethin' to see baby
Ain't that America home of the
free
Little pink houses for you and
me."

"Pink Houses"
John Mellencamp
Uh-Huh

Declaring myself an expert on all things disability is far from what the purpose of this book. Just because I have cerebral palsy does not mean I know everything about the disorder. I wanted to write this book to demonstrate for current and future generations to come that living with a disability should not, and cannot, define who you are; if you are parent with a child with a disability, the same holds true: don't let it define you. I know, I know, many of you are saying it's easy for me to say when I don't have a child that demands all the strength out of you 24 hours a day, every day. I read several Facebook posts from parents, on their last thread because they don't have adequate supports. I read posts from individuals with disabilities who might be struggling with some kind of issue. I wish I could fly out to each and every one of you out there and give you a hug and tell you you're doing all that you can do. I wish I could give you a helping hand. Maybe I don't know your struggles first-hand, but I have tremendous empathy for those who try their hardest every day.

The title, "What If Nobody Finds Out Who I Am", is a lyric I took from Billy Joel's "Big Man On Mulberry Street". I believe it is the human condition for most people to want to have somebody to really know who they are through and through— what makes them tick. Maybe people see this 'want' as a sign of seeing themselves better than others. This is not my intention. My wish is to demonstrate for whoever reads this book that people with disabilities are just that—people who have disabilities, whether the disabilities are physical, intellectual, or other disabilities. Many people who don't have the ability to communicate for themselves have a difficult time getting across who they are on the inside, rather than just being represented by their appearance.

So, what if nobody finds out who I am? Would it be all that bad if I go unnoticed? Of course not. It would be irresponsible of me to go through my life, with all of the gifts and abilities that I have been given, not to use my gifts, not to share my experiences and thoughts to assist many people who might be struggling to navigate life with a disability. I need to demonstrate that people with disabilities can have happy, fulfilling and successful lives. The journey will have its challenges, like many lives do. And like most individuals, it is their choice how they want to live their lives. This book represents my life.

For a long time, I was planning the title to be, "Round Here We're Never Sent to Bed Early and Nobody Makes Us Wait". It is a lyric from Counting Crows' "Round Here". When I first heard these lyrics, they spoke to me. I thought, *yes, that is what I want to convey about my life.* Nobody, especially an adult with a disability, should be sent to bed early, and nobody with a disability should have to wait. When I speak about waiting for something, I don't mean things we all have to wait for, such as a promotion, a bus or a concert two months into the future. I am talking about the essential stuff like going to the bathroom, getting out of bed, getting a drink of water. If somebody has a physical disability, I'm sure that a majority have waited for any one of these essential activities of daily life. Sometimes situations happen. But when somebody specifically avoids helping the physically dependent with these vital activities, it is considered abuse. I have witnessed in my formable years caretakers turning forward the clocks an hour within our unit to fool eight of us it was bedtime. I thought it was funny then but I don't think it is funny now. One time, for fifteen minutes, I waited in my bathroom to be showered while my PCA purposefully chatted on the phone with one of girlfriends about a party they went to on Saturday night. I had little respect for her after that, if at all. There have been other times I have been forgotten on the toilet for one or two hours and have been hysterical about it because it was a "blonde" moment. We can still laugh about it today.

The phrase, "Don't Settle" should be a universal mission statement. Unfortunately some don't learn about the idea of not settling early enough. Some people's life circumstances don't allow themselves to advance their lives from what they know due to a variety of reasons such as finances, education, race and disability. This is very sad to me because I live in the United States, the land of opportunity, the land of the free, and still many of our citizens don't get the chance the invoke the idea of not settling. I understand that not everybody is cut out for higher education, and some people enjoy sitting in front of the television all day long. Some people just have the capacity to such things due to a disability. Many who don't have a disability watch television all day. Even if I can't walk or talk with accuracy, I am a very driven person. I have been driven all of my life.

Lastly, I want my book to be the voice of so many who can't express themselves adequately due to a disability. Still, in this day and age, non-verbal people are stereotyped as having intellectual disabilities. This is seldom the case. It is also stereotyped on occasion that people with disabilities are unable to feel pain or emotion. I'm here to tell you that this is never the case. Every human being on the face of this Earth has the capacity to experience love, sadness, happiness, anger, excitement, disappointment, acceptance, rejection, joy, fear, pain, relief and every other feeling known to the human experience. People with speech impairments express themselves in a whole host of different ways, from facial expressions to eye moments, from sign language to using augmentative speech devices, from vocalizing sounds to body movements. Some non-verbal people have an uncanny ability to verbalize one or two specific phases such as "I love you" or on the opposite spectrum, "go to hell".

I would also like this book to be a "guide", if you will, for parents of children with disabilities and/or young adults with disabilities. Like I said before, I don't consider myself an expert. I can only relay my experiences throughout my life, whether or not they are positive or negative, to give you some kind of idea what to expect as you weave your way through this journey.

If you are a parent, know your child. That concept is

very obvious to parents across the board. You know their personalities, their needs and their likes and dislikes. Just as you advocate for a non-disabled child, advocate the same way for a child with a disability. It might take more time, more steps to advocate for a child with a disability and that is okay. If you have more than one child, depending on their age, include them on understanding the advocacy process for the sibling. It might give them a sense of helpfulness and bonding time. Demonstrate a balance between advocating for them and advocating for the sibling with the disability whenever possible. I believe a family who works together on a common ground builds strength.

For those young adults with a disability, know yourself. Know all of your needs, wants and aspirations. You are your destiny! With age comes wisdom, and boy, is that true. When I was a child, I was fascinated with being a doctor to the extent where I had stitches in my Raggedy Ann and Andy dolls. I explored and found cotton. I used to use my Mom's ironing board as an operating table because it had a wire-twirling thing that rotated up to hold the electrical cord out of the way. It made an awesome IV pole. Oh yeah, I was medically crazed as a child.

Several years later, our class watched a television movie where Leonard Nimoy played a neurosurgeon who had to save a woman's life by cutting out some of her brain. My friend, Paul pointed out something very important. He said for me to be a brain surgeon, operating room nurses would have to tape the different surgical tools onto my headpointer repeatedly over the entire surgery. Never did Paul bring up the very obvious fact that I had athetoid cerebral palsy and neurosurgery may not be the best fit for me. I thought long and hard about having to tape and re-tape surgical tools onto my headpointer, and Paul was absolutely right.

When kids are teenagers, they think you know it all, but they don't for the most part. If you know what your interests are and what makes you excited, speak up and say, "I want to do 'this' when I get older. Please help me to figure out how to achieve my goal." Sometimes people go through college majoring in one subject, and then graduate to only hit roadblocks that they couldn't envision. Many, many people discover their passion or life direction after they are handed the beautiful college degree. It may happen immediately or after 20 years. This happened to me. I didn't become disinterested in my profession; it was mainly because I didn't know where I fit in on the employment scene, and my area of study was too narrow for full time employment.

For both parents/caregivers with children with developmental disabilities and young adults with developmental disabilities, it is always amazing what you can learn from others in similar circumstances. Being able to talk and share common issues gives you a sense of you are not alone in this journey. The act of just communicating to somebody who understands what you go through on a daily basis can be exhilarating. Unless your child or you are affiliated with an educational or recreational program with others with developmental disabilities, finding groups or organizations that specifically cater to advocate for people with disabilities often takes time, especially in rural areas in the country. Twenty years ago we didn't have the Internet as we know it today. Information now can be immediate and worldwide. I have read some poignant and some heartbreaking posts on social media from parents/caregivers who are overwhelmed by the amount of energy is required to care for their loved one. Many children with developmental disabilities require 24-hour care, and too many of these parents/caregivers don't have a minute for themselves. The old adage is definitely true: you can't care for someone else unless you take care of yourself first. An hour or two a day of respite might be all you would need. Don't find yourself on your last thread and contemplating running away. Don't be afraid to express your feelings to family and friends; put them in your shoes to make them understand your daily struggles. Before you get to that point seek out supports you need; seek out supports your child needs.

Supports for children and adults with disabilities differ from state to state. My Mom once told me that if Rhode Island didn't have the supports I needed as a child, she and Dad would have seriously considered moving to a different state. I have investigated which states have the most comprehensive services for children and adults with developmental disabilities. It is never a clear-cut answer. It depends very heavily on the type of disability and the supports needed. Supports vary widely from state to state depending how much programs for people with disabilities are funded. Some states may have excellent programs for children with developmental disabilities while these states don't have the proper programs for adults with disabilities. Some states often cater to one specific disability group while disregarding the autism community. What the hell is this?! Whether somebody has muscular dystrophy or dwarfism shouldn't determine their overall need for individual assistance. I support a uniform policy for every state to have a comprehensive evaluation system for all children and adults with disabilities so that each person can have their specific program to follow for self-achievement. If many people can realize their self-worth and direction, federal and state could save millions of dollars. It doesn't take rocket scientists to figure this out.

Often getting what you want takes self-advocacy. Oddly enough, I didn't realize what self-advocacy was until I was in my mid 30's. I grew up in an age where I listened to authority figures. I was considered a 'compliant client'. Of course when you are a child and a teenager, your role is to obey your parents, teachers, coaches etc. At certain times in these formable years, I tested the waters a little bit, only to realize that my actions were usually wrong. I didn't like to make mistakes; making mistakes made me feel inferior. I didn't want to feel inferior, so I became a follower instead of a leader. This is why I feel self-advocacy should be taught around age 17 or 18 depending on the maturity of the individual. The individual should possess the idea that they are in charge of their lives. They should be allowed to make mistakes, within reason, so they understand consequences of their choices. These are the tools they can use for the future.

To be taught compliancy is to reinforce the idea that the feelings, needs and wants of the individual with a disability are secondary. I believe compliancy training goes against the grain of teaching people with disabilities to advocate for themselves. What does this conditioning do to an individual over many, many years? They feel inferior because they cannot be trusted to make decisions for themselves. Their self-esteem wanes; they feel uncertain about their future because they know they will be second-guessed at every decision they will try to make for themselves. I know this is true because I have experienced it many times through my life. I have come to realize I am the captain of my own ship; I am in control of my own destiny. I will ask opinions of others if I choose to ask.

It is very common for parents to have the need to protect their child, whether they have a disability or not. Sometimes parents want to save their children from feeling disappointment, sadness and hurt feelings. If children and/or young adults don't experience these life lessens, they will find it difficult to cope with these feelings as adults. I was very fortunate to have parents that allowed, and often encouraged me to do things that were a little out of my comfort zone. Sometimes when I asked my parents if I could do things, which I never expected them to allow, they gave permission for nearly everything I wanted to do. A few times, I found my jaw dropping to the floor. *They are really going to allow me to do this?!*

In conjunction with the skills of self-advocacy and self-determination, families should discuss future plans. Many parents I have known, including mine, believe they will be able to care for their disabled child for as long as they live, or as long as they can stay healthy. If their adult child has the ability to do most of their ADLs (activities of daily living) themselves, than this lifestyle may be feasible. When the adult child requires a lot of physical assistance with ADLs, expecting parents to do this physical work is not feasible. Many elders today still care for their adult child due to a number of factors. I never expected to

9

be in the position to have to live with my parents after I graduated college, but I did. Within two years after college, I was eligible to receive supports for PCAs (personal care attendants). Even with these very vital supports, our family didn't discuss future plans regarding my living arrangements once my parents were unable to provide a home.

Yes, it was comfortable living with Mom and Dad after college, but I wanted something more. I didn't want them to spend their later years taking care of me even though they wanted to do such that. In 1995 or 1996, I submitted my name to the accessible apartments at Rock Harbor in Orleans, Massachusetts. When my name came up, I had to make a decision. My Mom didn't like the idea of me living alone. She didn't like the fact that I would have to contend with the possibility of a PCA not showing up one morning, and not being able to eat for a few hours until somebody showed up. I wasn't thrilled about living in Orleans in the dead of winter without much to do. I sought action, and Orleans wasn't the place to be. I thought I would be very isolated. Mom and Dad offered to build an office in the attached garage if I remained living with them. I took their offer, and still my future was uncertain.

If you want an in-depth depiction of people with disabilities in America, I strongly recommend Kim E. Nielsen's *A Disability History of the United States*. The history that I will give will be very brief. State institutions began being built in Revolutionary War times when the Europeans came to these lands. The journeys across the Atlantic were brutal on the passengers. Ships were unequipped with proper sanitation, which resulted in sickness and disease. Many perished before they landed on American shores. The diseases often couldn't be treated effectively. If a person was deemed 'crazy' or 'dangerous to society', often they would be passed from county to county, or across state lines. Many of these people were locked away in somebody's cellar. Many were homeless. These circumstances spawned the creation of institutions.

Let us move ahead one hundred years or so. I have heard first hand accounts of people with developmental disabilities entering institutions at very young ages. Many state institutions were started with the idea to teach and train their students to work. As time went on, as directors and executives changed, state institutions lost their original mission, and became warehouses to house people with intellectual, behavioral and often, people with physical disabilities. It was very common for physicians throughout the early 1900's through the 1970's to counsel parents to institutionalize their child so they could have a 'normal' life. Without fully understanding the essence of being a mother myself, I couldn't imagine handing my child over to strangers for the rest of their lives, unless it was the process of adoption, or a similar circumstance. The children who were institutionalized during this time spent their days and nights in bed dressed in only diapers. I can't imagine what it would have been like lying in bed all day in a large room with 20+ other children in the same predicament, waiting to be fed, waiting to be changed, and waiting to be bathed. The society as a whole didn't want to be reminded that people with disabilities existed, so they isolated them away.

The disability movement was slowly growing during the 1960's and 1970's, especially when disabled vets were returning from Vietnam. The disabled community found many voices; they wanted change, they wanted to be looked upon as equals and wanted opportunities like all Americans. Gradually state institutions were being closed, and community-based group homes and day programs were being developed. The Rehabilitation Act of 1973 was enacted on September 26th, and signed by President Richard Nixon. This Rehabilitation Act of 1973 replaced the Vocational Rehabilitation Act, extended and revised grants with special emphasis to serve people with severe disabilities. This Federal Law put responsibilities on the Departments of Health, Education and Welfare to develop and maintain programs to assist people with disabilities.

With community-based group homes growing in numbers, people in sheltered workshops grew as well. Sheltered workshops came into existence in the 1840's, and their function was to provide people with disabilities a place where they work, isolated from society, usually doing piecework. Unfortunately, sheltered workshops still exist today although in far lesser numbers. It has been a widely accepted practice and Federal Law, Special Minimum Wage Certificate (1938), permits sheltered workshops to pay workers with disabilities sub-minimum wages. Their hourly wage was often determined on the level of work output. Later, I will give you my thoughts about the sheltered workshop.

With the closing of many state institutions around the country, people needed places to live. Besides group homes, independent living apartments and complexes were being erected. Still today, there are not enough affordable and wheelchair accessible housing being built for the thousands on waiting lists. The sad result is people with the most physical limiting disabilities usually find themselves waiting out the process living in institutions or nursing homes. This process can take several years, which can be devastating to the human spirit.

In the last seven years the Department of Human Services, probably in all 50 states, have endured severe budget cuts, directly affecting the lives of people with disabilities. When the economy is on the downturn, it is always human and social service programs that take the brunt of the budget cuts. Vital supports are cut, such as transportation to work, recreational activities and even hours are cut for ADLs. Many times during rallies and protests at State House, I cannot help the fact that a good percentage of the representatives and senators that serve in this grand marble building see people with developmental disabilities a "financial drain" on state and Federal budgets. Some representatives and senators understand fully about the plight. I often wonder if people in our government can really see the big picture. When our state and Federal governments cut budgets for programs for people with developmental disabilities, they perpetuate low incomes of those and the people who work as caregivers. Many caregivers barely earn $25,000 annually. It can be very physical work; many people love their jobs and can't see themselves doing anything else. New hires at McDonald's commonly earn a higher hourly rate than caregivers who have been working more than three years. Yearly state budgets for programs for people for developmental disabilities don't give cost-of-living adjustments, perpetuating low incomes of caregivers.

Over the past 200 years, people with disabilities and their advocates have risen up and made their voices be heard. But much more has to be achieved. If a child is born with a developmental disability, or if it is shortly onset after birth, early invention is key. Early intervention consists of proper diagnosis, treatment for their disabilities, whether it will be physical and/or occupational therapies, speech therapies, behavioral therapies, educational therapies, or a combination of these therapies. When the child reaches school age, education goals should be reassessed at least on a yearly basis. Individual Education Programs should be written with the emphasis on achieving the most reachable educational goals. The child should be mainstreamed into public or private schools if feasible. When assistive technologies are needed, the child must have a thorough evaluation with an assistive technology specialist to equip the child with devices that will advance the child to their fullest potential.

In 1975, Congress passed The Education of All Handicapped Children Act (EHA), renamed and tweaked in 1997 as The Individuals with Disabilities Education Act (IDEA). This Public Law 94-142 mandates children with disabilities attend an education institution from age 3 or 6 to 21. It also mandates children with disabilities receive physical, occupational, speech and/or behavioral therapies when required. If an educational institution cannot provide these therapies onsite, transportation must be provided to these therapies. Through the 80's, 90's and

2000's, much more emphasis has been put on total inclusion than ever before. Studies have been conducted and the results have proven that when a child with a disability is immersed in total inclusion, their personal success is greater. Their social skills are honed. Their self-esteem rises. It is also proven that non-disabled children have greater success when exposed to their peers with disabilities. Total inclusion is the ultimate goal for people with disabilities; total inclusion is the ultimate goal for all mankind.

As with education, total inclusion with regards to employment must be achieved. I believe all sheltered workshops should be closed immediately. The general definition for 'shelter' is: "protect or shield from something harmful; prevent (someone) from having to do or face something difficult or unpleasant." Within the term 'sheltered workshop', you have to ask yourself who is being protected—the people with disabilities inside the workshop, or the people outside, the 'normal' people? This question has different arguments depending what time period you are referring to. Very recently, stories have been uncovered about inhumane conditions at certain sheltered workshops. People working in rundown buildings without heat and proper ventilation were common problems. Often sheltered workshops have difficulty obtaining and keeping contracts to provide actual work. In these cases, workers spend their workdays playing games, or doing nothing at all. Reports of sheltered workshop CEOs earning $500,000 or more, while employees with disabilities earning less than $.50/hour have increasingly eroded the foundation of the sheltered workshop. These practices went on for decades because many workers in these workshops have significant intellectual disabilities, which may not allow them to advocate for themselves.

Similar studies to those of inclusion with education have been conducted to prove that people with disabilities became more successful working in their communities. Their self-esteem flourished and the social skills increased. They realize they have a purpose, and that is gold. If society cannot

14

understand that feeling is universal, the feeling that every human being has a need to feel useful, then we should go back to bed and not get up again until we do.

It is from my own experience, and many other people with disabilities, becoming a wage earner can be exhilarating and terrifying at the same time, especially if the individual depends heavily on PCA services, medical equipment and insurance. If an individual earns too much income, and if they are a recipient of SSI/SSDI, the Social Security Administration will begin decreasing or ceasing your financial benefits, depending on your earned income. That's all fine and dandy, but when an individual reaches that threshold of earning substantial income to not qualify for SSI/SSDI, the individual usually doesn't qualify for medical assistance and/or the Medicaid Waiver Program. If a person is earning $40K annually working, most of their income will be dried up paying for PCA services, medical equipment and insurance, leaving nothing for shelter and food. People often question whether working is worth the tremendous insecurity of not having these critical supports in place just to survive day to day.

This system must improve. I propose that we work out a manageable system where individuals with disabilities are working, and are earning income that exceeds the Social Security Administration threshold, the individual must be evaluated to determine what supports he/she needs to maintain employment. If their needs, especially physical needs, are substantial, Medicaid needs to maintain these supports Depending on the individual's earning, a monetary scale should be devised where the individual is required to pay into the Medicaid system based on their earnings. Individuals who earn just over the Social Security Administration threshold should pay the least, depending on their needs. Individuals with the same needs, but who are earning substantially more over the Social Security Administration threshold need to pay more into the Medicaid system. I am not a numbers expert, but I feel this is very workable. When people with disabilities have the ability to

15

work, and are not collecting SSI/SSDI, millions of dollars could be saved.

Education, work and the general living experience should be inclusive. We are living in the 21st century where in 15 more years, cars will be able to drive themselves. Nearly fifty years ago, we put men into space, but today, we don't have enough accessible housing for the ones who need it. We have people with disabilities who want to work but who can't find appropriate employment for diverse skillsets. I live in the greatest and richest country in the world; our nation was made on innovation and hard work to achieve a better future. Why is it that more than 200 years after its birth, very few have come together to ask, "what can we do to make people with disabilities seamless with their non-disabled counterparts?"

"Oh, are we locked into these bodies?"

"The Distance"
Live
The Distance to Here

Cerebral palsy occurs in 2.5 in 1000 births, making it the most common of all developmental disabilities which occurs in early childhood. Cerebral palsy is a collective term that encompasses the four different types of the brain disorder. Let me clarify this again: cerebral palsy is a disorder and not a disease. Sometimes the lines get blurred comparing a disease with a disorder. Cerebral palsy, in itself, is not progressive. Once the onset of the occurrence of cerebral palsy takes place, the brain damage is done. Each case of cerebral palsy is as diverse as a fingerprint. The spectrum of physical and intellectual impairments is vary widely, from very mild to very severe. Cerebral palsy can affect a single toe for some, while others have extremely limited movement, confined to a wheelchair.

The most common type of cerebral palsy is spastic cerebral palsy, occurring in 70% of all cases.[1] Some studies put the number of spastic cerebral palsy at 90% of all cases, but not confirmed. Spastic cerebral palsy is characterized by hypertonic muscle tone/muscle stiffness. Although initially caused by brain damage from the occurrence of an upper motor neuron lesion, spastic cerebral palsy is considered a classification of orthopaedic and neuromuscular challenges. Depending on the specific location of the upper motor neuron lesion, it can have subsidiary affects of the corticospinal tract or the motor cortex of the brain. These subsidiary influences can impede the amount of gamma amino butyric acid (GABA) nerves receptors can receive, resulting in muscle hypertonia.

Spastic cerebral palsy can range from mild to severe due to the severity of the onset damage. Spastic hemiplegia is characterized by one side of the body, usually one of the upper extremities, being affected. If the initial damage occurred on the right side of the brain, the left side of the body is affected, and visa versa. People who have spastic hemiplegia possess the

---

[1] Stanley F, Blair E, Alberman E. Cerebral Palsies: Epidemiology and Causal Pathways. London, United Kingdom: MacKeith Press; 2000.

ability to walk. If they do have weakness or spasticity in any of their lower extremities, a limp may be present.

Spastic diplegia is characterized by the lower extremities only being affected in most cases. People with spastic diplegia typically have the ability to walk, although each case is different. People who ambulate have a mild to pronounced "scissor-gait" walking manner. The muscles on the inside of the thighs, called abductors, remain the contracted muscles in the lower extremities, bringing the knees together and the feet further apart. The ankles are slightly inverted while the hips and knees remain somewhat flexed. People with spastic diplegia predominantly walk by swinging their hips while the legs remain in a static position.

Spastic monoplegia affects only one of the four limbs, while spastic triplegia affects tree out of the four limbs. Spastic quadriplegia affects all four limbs, and again with all types of cerebral palsies, can range from mild to severe depending on the severity of the initial onset brain damage. People with spastic quadriplegia are the least likely to have the ability to walk.

Athetoid or dyskinetic is the second type of cerebral palsy, occurring in 10% to 20% of all cases. Its characteristics are the inability to control one's muscles, especially when it comes to fine motor control: the inability to pick up objects like a spoon and a pen with the index finger and thumb. People with ADCP usually have hypotonia, low muscle tone, resulting in poor balance and poor muscle coordination. Unlike spastic cerebral palsy, damage to the basal ganglia in the brain, which controls motor control, is often seen in people with ADCP. ADCP is a non-spastic cerebral palsy. It can be divided into two different groups: choreo-athetoid and dystonic. Choreo-athetoid cerebral palsy has the distinction of involuntary movements typically in the face and extremities. Dystonic cerebral palsy has the distinction of slow, but strong contractures, affecting one area of the body, or the entire body.

Ataxic is the third type of cerebral palsy and the least common, occurring in 10% of all cases of cerebral palsy. Ataxic cerebral palsy is the result of damage to the cerebellar structures of the brain. Characteristics of ataxic cerebral palsy are poor balance, poor muscle coordination, and frequent tremors, especially when people are trying to grasp an object or performing tasks with their hands.

Lastly, the fourth type of cerebral palsy can be a combination of two or more of the three types, referred to as mixed cerebral palsy. Different degrees of the two or three type can manifest at different intensities. For example, someone can exhibit more spasticity than involuntary movements, or visa versa. Some people can exhibit all three types equally, or have varying degrees of each. Hence, each case of cerebral palsy can be as different as a fingerprint.

Cerebral palsy occurs before birth, during birth, or in early infancy. The lack of oxygen to the brain is very significant to the development of disorder. The causes of cerebral palsy are not always known, but premature infants are vulnerable to developing the disorder. Periventricular leukomalacia (PVL) is a type of white matter injury, characterized decreased blood flow and oxygenation to the near the lateral ventricles. PVL is most prevalent in premature infants and it is estimated that 20% to 75% of all PVL infants will develop cerebral palsy. Seizure disorders are predominantly associated with PVL. Infections, especially intrauterine infections, during pregnancy can cause disruptions in the fetus' brain development. Diabetic expectant mothers at more at risk of having a child with cerebral palsy. Injury or fever to the expectant mother can also cause cerebral palsy in some cases, especially if the injury induces premature labor. Rupture of the placenta also carries the risk of premature labor.

The occurrence of multiple births: twins, triplets, quadruplets, etc. raises the risk of a child or children having with cerebral palsy. I have known cases of twins both having cerebral palsy at different degrees. I have known cases when one twin dies, where the surviving twin has cerebral palsy. I have seen where only one twin has cerebral palsy. Different medical complications have varying degrees of results.

Complications can also arise during birth with a near or full term fetus. Hypoxic-ischemic brain injury is when oxygen cannot perfuse to brain cells resulting in brain cells dying. Lesions are created after this period, which cause injury or infections leading to the development of cerebral palsy. Hypoxic-ischemia/asphyxia was thought to be the leading cause of cerebral palsy but in actuality these account for 10% to 27% of all cases. Also, high production of the substance, bilirubin, in the gray matter of the central nervous system can cause cerebral palsy, especially ADCP.

Causes in the occurrences of cerebral palsy after birth include choking, near drowning, strokes, trauma and infections such as meningitis.

There is no cure for cerebral palsy. The bulk of today's research is concentrated on the prevention of cerebral palsy and the childhood treatments. Several studies have been conducted in the administration of antenatal magnesium sulfate to high-risk preterm labor for women before 34-week gestational period to reduce the overall rate of cerebral palsy. Results show antenatal magnesium sulfate does reduce the onset of moderate to severe cerebral palsy in a small percentage in cases, but these studies also show no reduction in the infant mortality rates. More studies are needed to determine the proper dosage of antenatal magnesium and the most appropriate time to administer the drug for greater results.

Stem cell therapies are being aggressively researched, especially in European countries to treat spastic cerebral palsy. Studies with rats show promising results. Stem cell therapies are several years away from becoming viable, common treatment.

There is no concrete evidence hyperbaric oxygen therapy for children with cerebral palsy is beneficial with increasing motor function. One of the side effects of hyperbaric therapies is inner ear pressure disturbance, which can lead to the need for ear tube placement.

Traditional therapies for cerebral palsy include physical, occupational, speech, drug therapies, and surgery. Physical and occupational therapies work on developing muscle strength, tone and coordination with completing everyday tasks such as crawling, sitting, standing, walking, feeding, dressing, and a number of other important tasks. Physical therapy is also important with stretching muscles, especially with spastic cerebral palsy. People with spastic cerebral palsy can have severe muscle contractures, which can render joints static. Contractures and muscle spasms are often painful and require drug therapy or surgery to cut the tendons at issue.

The procedure, Selective Dorsal Rhizotomy (SDR), has been preformed on some children and adults with spastic cerebral palsy since 1980. Personally, I have never known anyone who has had this surgery. The objective of SDR is to identify the nerves that cause spasticity and destroy them. The result is when the specific nerves are destroyed, spasticity will end in the corresponding muscles. SDR sometimes is seen as controversial risky because post-op complications may develop. Complications from SDR range from 5% to 10%, and may include permanent paralysis, incontinence, permanent impotence, infection and/or spinal fluid leakage at the incision site just above the waist on the back. Results from SDR can be very positive, especially with candidates who were somewhat ambulatory prior to surgery. Within a year or two post-surgery, these candidates had a moderate to significant increase of mobility and a decreased occurrence of contractures and pain. The optimum age for this surgery is 2 to 7 years, because contractures that disrupt or deform joints can be maintained adequately in early childhood. If children do present with contractures, more surgeries will be needed to correct these deformities. SDR has been performed on suitable candidates over the age of 20 with some positive outcomes.

Along with cerebral palsy, some secondary disorders may arise. These include but not limited to learning and intellectual disabilities, seizures, scoliosis, hearing, visual and speech deficits, sensory impairments, feeding difficulties, bladder incontinence and depression. Learning, intellectual disabilities and/or seizures occur in about 30% of cases of cerebral palsy. Children may outgrow seizure disorders with age. Seizure disorders most often can be controlled by medication.

The major theme of this book, my story, is concentrated around cerebral palsy, because whether or not I like it, cerebral palsy is my lifestyle. I embrace this lifestyle. A lifestyle can be defined in so many ways. My lifestyle parallels many different lifestyles, like diabetes or blindness. You can't disregard many afflictions because some are physically debilitating to affect your every day life. For me, I just can't wake up one morning and say I am not going to have cerebral palsy. Am I going to get up on my own two feet and walk to the bathroom? It is not going to happen. Even though this book is so heavily centered on cerebral palsy does not mean that I have no idea about other disabilities such as muscular dystrophy, spina bifida, Down Syndrome, autism, and similar disabilities. I was always was told to write about what you know and I know about cerebral palsy.

I would like to dedicate this book my Dad, Tom, to my siblings, Peter, Martha and Paul, and to the memory of my Mom, Hope, who was my biggest advocate and fan. Without their love, devotion, parenting skills, advocacy and belief that I could probably do anything I had my mind set on doing, this book wouldn't have been possible. I would also like to dedicate this book to the memory of the handful of friends who didn't get the chance to live out their lives due to their disabilities, especially Paul James and April Green. To all these people looking down at me from Heaven, I dedicate this book to all of your memories.

*"Maybe just light a candle
and take a seat for the ride."*

"The Ride"
Live
V

Over my many years, not a lot of people have asked me, "Hey, what's it like to have cerebral palsy?" Hey, I haven't asked many people what's it like to walk. I never felt the need to so. I have athetoid cerebral palsy, which makes it very difficult to control my muscle movements, especially fine motor skills. It's impossible for me to pick up a pen with only my thumb and index finger. I don't have the ability to pick up a spoon to feed myself. Grasping the spoon would be one thing, but loading it up with food and bringing up to my mouth would not be a pretty sight. I don't possess the muscle coordination to accomplish such an ordinary daily task the majority of people would take for granted. Having athetoid cerebral palsy is very much like having all of your fingers and toes, arms and legs, neck and facial muscles being controlled by an invisible puppeteer over your head. If I reach for something with my right hand, the invisible puppeteer yanks back on the string that is controlling my right hand and says, "Not so fast, Missy". It's like playing tug-of-war with your own hand. The puppeteer can also be below me, to either side of me, in back of me pulling on how many strings the puppeteer wants. She, the puppeteer, likes to have my hand smash into a table edge, smash my toes into a nearby wall, or smack myself in the face with my own hand. I like to sleep with a pillow resting on my left hand and heavy blankets on my feet to subdue the activity. Weight on my extremities certainly helps me to sleep. It's my lifestyle; I accept it. I feel defeated by the puppeteer when I involuntarily hurt somebody with one of my muscle jerks. The miscalculation stays with me for a period of time, sometimes, even years. I know it is not my fault, but I still feel guilty. I have learned to keep these incidents at a minimum by hooking my arm underneath an armrest, or keeping my feet tied secure.

Since my hands and fingers are so unpredictable, keeping my fingernails short is a necessity. There has been countless of times, especially on my left hand, that I have drawn my own blood from other fingers, involuntarily, with my thumb and index fingernails. Also, when my fingernails are getting long, if I make a fist, my fingernails create indentations in the palms of my hands. If the pain is great enough, my natural athetoid reaction is to tighten my grip, until the grip hits its breaking point, or if I'm able to reposition my hand so it will open up to relieve the pain.

Keeping my toenails short, or moderately short, has more to do with preventing broken toenails when I crawl barefoot. When I crawl, my toes take the brunt of the uncontrolled impact with my feet to the different, but relatively soft surfaces I crawl on. My feet have a tendency to whack on the doorjamb between my bedroom and bathroom. When I'm in the process of crawling backwards, my toes might bend in awkward angles or get wedged between two objects.

Have you ever had your eye pressure tested with an old fashioned tonometer? A tonometer looks like a miniature corkscrew opener. During this test, the ophthalmologist needs to probe the surface of the cornea with a needle to measure eye pressure. In 2001, I was subjected to this particular test. When I saw this tool coming towards my eye under the control of an intern, I became very weary of this test. It was obvious that this young intern hadn't had any experience with somebody with athetoid cerebral palsy.

People undergoing this, seemingly ancient, eye test must have the ability to sit perfectly still. When I heard the intern announce this, I wanted to yell out, "Do I look like I can sit perfectly still?!" He made a few attempts with shaking hands. I looked over at Martha, who was sitting beside me. I grew increasingly anxious and irritated. Once the intern announced, "If you move during this test, there is a strong chance I will scratch your cornea." Right there and then, I refused this eye test. Come to find out, ophthalmologists have access to eye pressure machines that do not come in contact with the eye surface. Hello?! Get one!

The Art of "W" Sitting: Physical therapists really frown upon the sitting position referred to "W" sitting. It is when an individual sits on their bottom with their knees bent and rotated on the floor behind them in the shape of a W. This sitting position has resulted in orthopedic issues in some. When a kid has cerebral palsy, especially athetoid cerebral palsy, when spasticity is not chronic and when the ability is there, he/she will fall in love with this sitting position since it provides unprecedented stability.

If my parents and I listened to all the therapists who "frowned" upon "W" sitting, I wouldn't be the person I am today. There is something quite spectacular about "W" sitting that is best explained by the people who sit in the "evil" position. When I was younger, I enjoyed drawing and coloring. If I sat in my wheelchair or in a regular chair at a table, I didn't have the ability to grab the crayon off the flat, hard surface. Barring the fact the table was at the wrong angle so my wrist would be supported once I grabbed it was only part of the battle. When you have athetoid cerebral palsy and everything is moving all at once, it's nearly impossible to do anything with your limited fine motor skills you do possess. Crayons and pencils roll, and then it becomes a mind game to grab the object before it rolls off the table and onto the floor. Before it actually rolls off of the table, my movements become exaggerated because I am certain I won't be able to grab that object before it hits the floor. When it drops to the floor, I've failed.

When I "W" sit on a carpeted floor, I am as steady as a surfer surfing on terra firma. With my back legs beside my hips, I won't fall to the left or the right; I definitely won't fall forward. Falling backward is often a chance, but it is a slim chance, especially I lean against something. The floor was my canvas growing up. I could do tasks, which I couldn't do anywhere else. I could grab that crayon with confidence, because it wasn't going to fall; it was on the ground and I was on the ground. To make it easier to grab an object, I push the object where I extend my arm out straight and grab it. Extending my arm straight affords me the greatest control over my hand. Without having movement in my elbow frees my concentration to control my hand. When I am confident the object is in my hand the way I want it, I use the floor to stabilize my wrist in an extended position to hold onto the object. If my wrist enters the flexed position, my hand will open, causing me to drop the object.

These days, my "W" sitting is relegated to 30 minutes to two hours on an average day at home. I am in my power wheelchair most of the time. The time I do "W" sit comes later at night, when my allotted PCA hours are over. There's something quite refreshing about getting out of your wheelchair and possessing some kind of adequate mobility to get around on your own steam power, and do things for yourself that are impossible to do in your wheelchair.

I continually played on the floor as a child. I played a lot with Hot Wheels and Matchbox cars; I liked pushing around big Tonka ambulances around the house; I had many, many Fisher Price Adventure People play sets. Once, Martha built an entire play city for me upon a 4' x 6' piece of plywood. It had roads, it had streetlights, it had trees and bushes, it had stores, a bank, a schools, and it even had a McDonald's, with the Golden Arches! It was so, damn perfect that I didn't dare play on it. One false move by either of my athetoid arms could spell disaster. After "Scooby Doo", Paul and I used to enjoy those cheesy, black-and-white, Godzilla-wipes-out-Tokyo movies. I didn't want to be Godzilla that wiped out my own town. So, I just admired my groovy, little town along its outskirts. I used my imagination to create the activities that may have been going on within my town. My tiny town survived a few trips coming in and out of the house, but soon, it started to fall apart.

Another favorite, childhood toy of mine was the Etch-A-Sketch. I positioned it near my right leg, as I "W" sat on the floor. My right hand offered me enough control to operate both dials, but of course, separately. I used the outer edges of my right fist to turn the knobs. I couldn't create diagonal lines on the Etch-A-Sketch, but in all reality, only the very talented Etch-A-Sketch artists managed to draw great diagonal lines. My Etch-A-Sketch drawings mostly consisted of hospitals, including multiple floors, windows, staircases, elevator shafts and ambulance bays. When I wanted to begin a fresh sketch, I flipped the Etch-A-Sketch onto my lower, right leg. I had the ability to hold the Etch-A-Sketch in my right hand. Holding it snuggly against my ribs, I shook it until it came clean once again.

Many people with moderate to severe athetoid cerebral palsy have the condition known as Dysarthria. Dysarthria is a motor speech disorder, mainly affecting muscle coordination for articulating speech. Dysarthria can also affect eating, swallowing and breathing depending on the severity of the disorder. The easiest way to describe the most common difficulties of Dysarthria is slurred speech, very much what an extremely intoxicated person would sound like. Again, depending of the severity, speech may be mildly or severely affected to where individuals can't verbalize at all due to the intense lack of muscle control within the facial area, mouth and throat. Dysarthria is not a cognitive disorder; it is strictly a muscular disorder.

I became familiar with this term in 2007, when I went for a speech evaluation to obtain an augmentative/alternative communication device. First, the speech therapist asked me to eat some vanilla pudding. She observed me swallow. Next, I ate a cracker and drank some water. Again, she observed. Before age eleven, I was able to get the hang of drinking from a straw. I recall just trying the straw one day, and I developed my own way of drinking from a straw. That was quite an accomplishment that no one predicted would happen. I have seen many individuals with varying degrees of Dysarthria. One extreme case was a young man who required his food be pureed. He also required someone to physically hold his jaw closed in order to swallow the food.

My Dysarthria isn't that extreme. I do have difficulties swallowing foods like rice, corn, peas and foods small in nature. If I inhale when I have small particles of food in my mouth, chances are greater of things going down the wrong pipe, causing coughing. Also, I stay far away from lettuce because it is so difficult to chew, and if big pieces are not chewed properly, lettuce becomes a serious choking hazard. I also have some difficulties with swallowing anything that might be a little dry, for example overcooked meats or fish. I'm one of those people who love their hamburgers still mooing. The more liquids I can get into my foods, usually the better.

Eating acid and tart fruits exacerbates the involuntary muscle movements within my jaw area. I stay away from tarty fruits and similar foods. I can have a tremendous gag reflex at times. Fruits, hunger, fullness, feeling cold and additional jaw muscle activity can bring on gag reflexes.

I consider my speech articulation right down the center of good and bad. People who know me well can understand me about 90% of the time, while people who don't know me at all cannot understand much that I verbalize. People who know me really well also have a clear understanding of my humorous personality, which also is very helpful in understanding my speech. Barring her hearing difficulties later in life, my Mom might have been the best at understanding my speech. Mom nurtured my speech when I was a toddler, so in essence, she kind of co-owned my speaking ability. There was one time a new speech therapist arrived on the scene when I was about 21. I had never met this woman before, and she stopped me when I was going somewhere. When I try to talk to someone I have never met before, or someone who doesn't know my speech very well, I usually become tense, as I try to pronounce my words clearly. I also don't want to waste anyone's time as they try to catch what I'm saying. This speech therapist asked me a question. I answered, and she understood every word I said. It was completely mind-blowing.

This might sound strange to most people, but when I speak, what is coming out sounds rather normal to me because I know what I'm saying. Of course I recognize when I don't say a word very clearly, or if I stumble on a word. I speak in my head constantly, and what's spoken in my head is good, ol' American English. I can't verbally do a British or an Australian accent, but I can certainly formalize different accents in my head. Yes, I hear voices in my head, but they are all my one voice. I hear every word I write.

I also imagine in my head, myself speaking normally, with all the gestures that I might do if I didn't have cerebral palsy. I tend to play out many conversations in my head. It is just my imagination at work. In my head, I communicate without impairments and with a lot more physical gestures than I can do in reality. My inner brain is my stage and I like to perform.

I have a very expressive face that usually helps people understand what I am saying. Sometimes I don't need to say anything at all, because some facial expressions say so much. I like to make people laugh if the occasion calls for it. It's just the kind of personality I have.

Some people don't have much of a filter when they talk; they just say the first thing that comes to mind. Most of the time, I have a very concentrated filter, where I think about the next words that come out of my mouth. Mainly I do this out of necessity, as I sift through words that are easily understood. For example, I would typically say, "How are the kids?", rather than, "How are the children?" I don't think anybody would understand 'children' on the first, second, third or forth try. I would need to spell it out. It's not the kind of word that easily rolls off my tongue because of the complex phonic combinations. I try to keep my words as simple as possible.

I can repeat myself over and over again, until I am blue in the face, only if the other person is truly giving their all to understand what I'm try to say. If someone pretends to understand me, I get very frustrated and usually stop talking to them all together. If they can't respect me enough to tell me that they cannot understand me but pretend to, I figure why waste my energy. Don't patronize me; don't disregard what I'm trying to say just because you aren't willing to give a little effort. A little effort goes a long way. Usually I am close to a computer where I can type out what I'm saying. In the realm of hiring people for personal care attendants' positions, if they are patient enough to listen to any person who has speech impairments usually signifies they might be a good asset.

Another thing that really gets under my skin is when an individual asks me a question through a friend that is accompanying me. Usually my friend will respond with, "Ask her," pointing to me. This is the correct action to take. It might make the person uneasy for a minute or two, but the experience can be valuable. Many people who haven't had any experience or knowledge of people with disabilities will often act like I am invisible, which usually indicates they assume I cannot comprehend anything around me. They may assume I am deaf or have intellectual disabilities. This is very degrading, especially if it is followed up by a pat on the head. I'm not five years old!

One of the greatest depictions of a person with a disability, namely with athetoid cerebral palsy, on network television, was the *ER* episode during season 4, where this gentleman was brought in following a pedestrian accident. He wasn't hurt, but his PCA was injured. His wheelchair was beyond repair. The doctors had him on a hospital bed, somewhat sitting up. It was the usual first impression: doctors and nurses began to assume that this guy didn't understand anything they were saying because he had funny jerks; he might have been deaf because he couldn't verbalize. These attitudes makes the gentleman frustration and angry.

When this gentleman began to bang one of his legs repeatedly on the bed, the initial reactions of the medical staff was this individual must have some cognitive disabilities, until Dr. Carter picked up on this gentleman's pattern of banging his leg. Dr. Carter looked directly in his eyes and inquired if the gentleman was trying to communicate a phone number. The gentleman smiled at Carter; his eyes spoke, "thank you". As the episode concluded, the person who came to the hospital to assist the gentleman explained to Carter that this gentleman was a renowned scientist in his chosen field. It was just an incredible episode that I will never forget. I hoped many saw that particular episode.

As I said, my speaking abilities are co-owned by my late mother and myself. I am an individual who has always loved to sing. I can't carry a tune to save my life, but I just love to sing. My favorite show as a child was *The Partridge Family*. Give me a break—I was five, six, seven tops. Even if I didn't have cerebral palsy, I would probably still love to sing. I think I got it in my head at a very early age that singing was some kind of a release. Looking back, I truly believe singing aided in my speech development. I know singing wasn't destructive to it. How could it be?

There is something very fundamental about singing along to lyrics. For me, I think it was the discovery that I pronounce words better while singing than just talking. I cannot specifically pinpoint why this is true. Maybe it has something to do with the rhythm of the lyrics. It may be the fact that I love to sing so much that I was so driven to pronounce every word as clearly as I possibly could. I get such a thrill out of pronouncing words as I sing. I get such a thrill hitting those high and low notes to the best of my abilities. I get such a high holding notes for as long as I can. I was unknowingly exercising my diaphragm and my sound capabilities. I was exercising my mouth and throat muscles. I was unknowing learning how to articulate better. I was kicking my Dysarthria right in its ass!

Whether this was my own phenomenon or a true finding, I didn't know for the longest time. After watching Gabby Giffords speech therapy sessions weeks after her brain injury, for her, stringing more than three words together was very difficult. When her therapist had Gabby sing a familiar song with accompaniment of a guitar, she sang all the lyrics without hesitation. I found this fascinating. It has been studied extensively that the area of the brain that controls speech and language is in one, localized area. The activities of music are controlled by many parts of the brain, and this is why Gabby could sing lyrics flawlessly. I am not comparing Gabby's brain injury to mine in no shape or form, although I have to wonder if my ease of singing is controlled by different parts of my brain. Of course this doesn't negate my disorder of Dysarthria, but something should be said about the power of music.

The other trying effect of having cerebral palsy is the startle reflex. Some people with cerebral palsy have a certain sensitivity to sudden, semi loud noises. Some people are more sensitive than others. I have a high sensitivity to sudden noises. Hate parades—love rock concerts. Figure that out. Luckily, I have an explanation. Parades with just band music are quite all right, but when guns and cannons are involved, I want to be as far away from the kabooms as possible. As luck would have it, the Gaspee Day Parade passed right down Fair Street, heading back towards Pawtuxet Village. Oh yay! I hated to sit through a parade with guns and cannons, or anything with guns and cannons. I had to have somebody hold their hands over my ears to buffer the sound. If I knew a kaboom was coming, I would hold my breath, as I tried to anchor myself to my wheelchair like a dingy to a mooring in choppy seas. Why couldn't they turn down the decibel level on the guns and cannons, I asked myself. *Do they really need them that loud?* It wasn't like anyone would mind the lower decibels. Boom! I still jumped sky high. Every muscle contracted. Firing guns and cannons are my torture. I might deal with one round of waterboarding somewhat better; definitely I could have dealt with Chinese water torture over the blasting of guns and cannons.

A door slam, a dropped pan, a sudden dog bark, a car backfiring, and very similar events, which always make me startle. I also made myself startle if I bite my tongue or cheek, or if I stabbed a fingernail into another fingertip, usually on my left hand. I startle if things sneak up on me, such as spiders and silent intruders. A great number of things can make me startle. I believe Mom and Dad thought I could control my "jumping", but I really have no control over it. Sometimes I felt guilty that I couldn't control my startles. The only thing that might have curtailed my "jumping" would have been if the doctors would have prescribed 20 milligrams of Valium. Twenty milligrams would have put me in a comatose state. Nobody would have tolerated me in a comatose state, especially me.

Unlike guns, cannons, slamming doors and creepy spiders, I tolerated live marching and rock bands extremely well. Constant, rhythmic sounds are almost soothing, especially if I recognize the tune. I love music, and loud music is comforting. I can live without rap and bang-your-head heavy metal music. If I know what noise was coming and when, I hardly jump. If I have background noise on, such as music or an audiobook, it tends to calm me, drowning out other noises that might startle me. I don't like being at silent events such as funerals or churches because I'm usually the one who makes the sounds that throws the attention right back at me. I fight my body so hard that it typically backfires. I feel more at ease at outdoor settings where sounds don't ricochet off of walls and ceilings. Bring me to a musical concert, and I am in my glory.

*"I'm talking about my world,
my love, my life"*

"My World, My Love, My Life"
Roxette
Room Service

37

I consider myself to be a very simple, and laid back person. I can be a very sensitive person at times, although I am a very strong. Above all, I am a very family-oriented person. I love my family most of all. They have been by my side through thick and thin. They are very impressive individuals who were raised in a family that was a little skewed because they had a different kind of daughter, sister, niece or cousin who couldn't walk or talk like the rest of the average population. They had to accept our parents having to give me more attention. They had to accept the fact that they had to help with some of the physical assistance I required when Mom couldn't lift me out of the school bus or into the bathroom. They handled all of it with grace and a very respectful attitude. And with this book, I thank them from the bottom heart.

Like my family, I have a group of very good friends. I won't lie, there have been times when I have been burned by people who I have thought were my friends but turned out not to be. I think this is one of the reasons I am strong. Luckily, not many close friends have burned me, but the ones who have, I probably won't speak to again. When you have a disability, it is always a gamble who you allow to see the real you, and who you can ultimately trust. I have to admit most of my friends I have met were because I have a disability. I can say about 90% of my friends have seen me naked because at one time or another they have physically taken care of me. Isn't that fact a real kick in the head? More people have seen me naked than your average Playboy Bunny. My friends, old and new, are the greatest.

If you have gotten this far in this book, you might have already gotten the strong impression that I kind of love music. Love might not be a strong enough word, but we will describe it with love. I would say that I am infatuated with music. Once, I went six weeks without having a stereo receiver hooked up to my 200 CD changer and nearly lost my mind. I have discovered I have much more focus writing listening to music than listening to silence. Music closes me into everything that I am supposed to do. Music opens up my mind and pumps up my heart, especially when I get to sing. Music is my religion; listening to music is when I feel the most spiritual and I feel closer to God.

A lot of kids get this feeling of what they were born to do early on. I had that feeling with my love of music. It was my fifth birthday when I asked for a toy guitar. I knew that I probably would never be able to play a guitar or any other musical instrument; I just wanted to emulate David Cassidy. I had the ability to get my left hand wrapped around the neck of the guitar while I essentially pounded the body of the guitar because I couldn't do a strumming motion. Boy, did I feel like a rock star when I could hold, bang and sing simultaneously, which not an easy feat for someone with athetoid cerebral palsy.

At age ten, my music tastes sophisticated ten fold when someone exposed me to the legendary, Billy Joel. After the likes of the Cassidy brothers, Captain & Tennille, Debbie Boone and Albert Morris, Billy Joel was like a brilliant light that lit the way out of my musical trenches. The first time I heard *The Stranger*, I couldn't get enough of it. It captured my attention like nothing ever did before. I owned the cassette and made sure I had it everywhere I went. Peter's stereo was downstairs in the dining room in the wooden étagère he made in high school. Mom would pop the cassette in and place the headphones on my head and just listen to it over and over again. Listening to anything with headphones is better than any other way. I sung to *The Stranger* many, many times in that corner of the dining room. I loved every moment of *The Stranger* and I still do.

I could write an entire book on how music excites me, but for now, I'll stick to the highlights. I am very confident that if I didn't have cerebral palsy, I would have been a musician in some capacity. I probably would have begged my parents for piano and/or guitar lessons. I think drum lessons would have been out of the question. We kept Aunt Pat's upright piano in our living room while she worked in Chicago for American Airlines. I was always fascinated by it and the sheet music that rested on its stand. What did it all mean? I did not know. Sometimes I would sit at the piano and just bang at the keys, knowing I wouldn't have the physical ability to play it like it was supposed to be played. I lived vicariously through Paul when he got his electric guitar at Axelrod in Downtown Providence. He mastered *Stairway To Heaven* and *Smoke On The Water*.

The last stair of our stairway up to our second floor, decked out in gold, shag carpeting, became my pretend piano of choice. Dad had transformed a gooseneck lamp into a mic stand for my toy microphone. With my Panasonic tape recorder by my right side, I pushed play. Billy Joel started to play, and again, I emulated. My left hand, oddly enough, could open up easier than my right, prominent hand. I thoroughly enjoyed pretending I was Billy Joel. By this time, I had *Piano Man*, *Streetlife Serenade*, *Turnstiles*, and *52nd Street*. I practically knew every word to every song. I was born to embrace music.

For my 11th birthday I was blessed with tickets to my first concert, my first Billy Joel concert. He played the Providence Civic Center. I don't think I ever was so excited in my 11 years. Martha took me and we sat in two regular seats. I must give Martha a lot of credit carrying me down and up about seven or eight steps to our seats. The flip-up seats were perfect for me to sit in, because it kept my skinny, little butt in back of the seat. I liked to straddle the seat for more balance, as I wedged my fists down next to my hips.

As I looked out over the expansive space of dim light and bustle, my excitement grew by the minute. The stage was awesome with his piano set to the right of the stage. I kept looking at the large digital clock over my right shoulder. It wasn't moving fast enough for me. Finally, the struck 8 o'clock. *The concert can start now. Come on, come on, come on!* After seeing Billy Joel two or three times, you learn that Billy Joel is always, punctually, 30 minutes late. When that clock hits 8:30pm, you're in darkness and the crowd roars. He might have opened with "Big Shot" that night, as he told a stage security guard to leave some guy alone, disrupting the lyrics. It was

40

definitely loud but I loved every damn second. I sang along at the top of my lungs like many others. Nobody cared if they were off key—everyone was there to see Billy Joel. At age 31, Billy could run around that stage like he was five, running around a playground. The stage was his playground. I wanted to be the one on stage.

With the beginnings of *Solid Gold* and MTV, music became visual. I'm not the type of person who can sit quietly in front of a television and just watch. I need to be doing something else while I watch. There seemed to be a surge of new musical artists that sprang up in the early 1980's, such as Rick Springfield, Pat Benatar, John Mellencamp, REO Speedwagon, and Quarterflash. I was enthralled with Rick Springfield, John Mellencamp, and Quarterflash, but Quarterflash set the stage up for me to really to study the art of drumming, in particular, air drumming. Peter picked me up some drumsticks at Ladd's Music, and I air drummed for the next 30 years. With the video tape recorder we owned, I recorded my favorite songs on videotape. Brian David Willis caught my attention as the drummer for Quarterflash, as he just whaled the hell out his drum kit. From the mid 80's on, it was David Uosikkinen of The Hooters that spurred me on. I wanted to do that. So, with repetition of watching the same songs over again, I picked up some drumming skills. Drumming became more of an endurance test and an accuracy game. Every time I drummed, I wanted to stay in rhythm and hit everything that he hit with the same passion. It usually took me a few minutes to calm myself down and feel that control I had over my withering body. It was euphoric—*take that cerebral palsy!*

The true obstacle was to figure out how to keep the drumsticks from flying out of my hands. I couldn't grip the drumsticks in the proper way, so I found holding the drumstick between my index and middle fingers worked extremely well. The next thing was to figure out how to keep the sticks from not sliding out of my hands, especially when my hands became sweaty. We tried golf gloves, we tried to devise a hand harness made from shoestrings, and a few other ways. Since it was easier for me to grasp the skinny part, the top of the drumsticks, I held the drumsticks upside down. We came up with the idea that we built up the tips of the sticks, they wouldn't slipped out of my hands easily. At first we used string or twine with a whole lot of glue to build up the ends. Years later, I surmised that rubber stoppers would work a little better, and in fact, they do. With a hole drilled through the center, and some grinding of the rubber's edges, the stoppers work very well. Another advantage of holding drumsticks upside down, especially for somebody with athetoid cerebral palsy, is that you can't really poke your eye out because the butt of drumsticks are thick and rounded. Of course, you can whack yourself in the eye with the butt of the stick, which I have done a few times, but no harm came from it. Besides leaving a few bruises on my legs frequently, I haven't significantly maimed myself while drumming.

Air drumming is another one of those activities I can do while "W" sitting on the floor. If I drop a stick, I can pick it back up. I also like to wear wrist weights. For some people with athetoid cerebral palsy, wearing weights on certain extremities helps with muscle coordination and/or to lessen involuntary movements. Using weights to help with these particular reasons have their proponents and opponents. For this discussion about my air drumming, I'll stick with what I know to be true. I only wear wrist weights when I drum. The first time I wore weights, I couldn't believe how much more control I had over my arm movements. With any introduction to weights during exercise, one must take caution not to overdue. Well, I was so happy with the control I had, I just continued. My upper arms were a little sore, but gradually I worked to where my muscles weren't sore anymore. Usually air drumming last on the average an hour, depending on frequency of drumming sessions. Drumming, for me, is a tremendous workout, although with age, muscles and joints take longer to bounce back.

Dogs, Labrador Retrievers in particular, have been tugging on my heartstrings for the last 16 years. Labs, along with many large breed dogs, have a predisposition to accept the rigors of being manhandled by rambunctious children. Large dogs can easy shrug off a tail being pulled, an ear being tugged or an eye being poked. Labs are the most forgiving creatures on Earth. For somebody who has athetoid cerebral palsy with a heavy hand, Labs tend to enjoy any human attention. Of course I am as gentle and careful so I don't cause physical pain, but I am confident my big dogs I know are gentle giants. I am uncomfortable patting a small dog because I could possibly injure them with my heavy hand. If I am in contact with small and delicate dogs, I will only use my head or face to pet them. Small dogs are impossible to reach if you are sitting in a wheelchair, especially if you have a limited reach.

Growing up, we had three Springer Spaniels at different times. I liked them a lot even though we had each of them a relative short time due to a number of various factors. I think something changes a person once you have the responsibility of caring for your own animal, or as much one is physically able to. On November 16, 1998, I received quite a surprise Christmas present. It was a Saturday and my parents went out, which wasn't that unusual. My PCA was with me for the time my parents were gone. I had somewhat a clear vision of the front, side door from where I sat on the floor in my office. Mom and Dad returned, and when Mom came in, she announced that they had brought back my Christmas present. In my head I was thinking it had to be a piece of furniture or something like that. With my humorous personality, I kiddingly, oh so very kiddingly replied, "It's not a dog, is it?" In no way, shape or form did I expect my parents to buy me a dog, let alone, a puppy. The next thing I knew, this brown, cute 35-pound puppy was dashing towards me. She stood upon my lap and begun to lick my face. I was completely speechless that we had a puppy in the house, and she was mine. I think it was one day later I named her Murphy, as in Murphy Brown because she was a spunky, Chocolate English Labrador Retriever.

43

My parents and I sort of learned as we went along with taking care of Murph. Mom and Dad knew the basics, while I knew very little. Who knew that this cute, little, Chocolate puppy would grow to 90-pounds? The vet knew. Murph had massive paws that she had to grow into. Mom chose this particular puppy because Murph had the same birthday as she did. She also had pretty gold eyes. I always remarked that she was the Cindy Crawford of dogs because she was beautiful.

I don't know what it is like to be a parent, but I'm well aware it drastically changes your outlook on life. Parents go to extraordinary lengths to protect and give everything they have to their children. Your mindset is very similar for those who own pets, but with one very different aspect: common pets have very short lifespans. Giving their short lifespans, we love them like they love us: unconditionally. Early on when I had Murphy, I decided that when Murphy got to the point where she was struggling to do the simple doggie things, if she became very ill or got badly injured, I would not let her suffer. On September 8, 2009, I had to stick with that very difficult decision. I was unaware Murphy had hemangiosarcoma, a common type of cancer not detected until it is in its advanced stages. Surgery was expensive and with all indications, would only prolong her life by a few months. Even though it was a sad occurrence, I felt peaceful knowing Murphy wasn't going to suffer.

Seven weeks later, I sacrificed a trip to New York City to bring home another chocolate, gold eyed beauty, Rees. What can I say? I love dogs.

"There will be other words
Some other day
But that's the story of my life."

"Famous Last Words"
Billy Joel
River Of Dreams

This autobiography has been a monumental task to complete. In the past several years, I have made a few attempts to start writing my autobiography, in the hopes that it would be perfect from start to finish right out of the gate. These few first attempts were complete failures, mostly because I didn't possess the true focus I needed so desperately. I have learned that if a writer has a project formed in their minds, that project needs to be detailed in an outline. It wasn't until the end of December 2013 that I had created a 5-page outline for this autobiography. Once the outline became my guide, and my anchor, the writing process became fluid. Without that 5-page outline, my writing was going round and round in circles, creating the illusion that my words were on the correct path, but they weren't.

Also, during the process of writing this project, I was thrown into a period of sadness when I endured some losses of very dear people in my life, including my Mom. The lost of Mom knocked me to the ground. My focus was shredded to where I didn't have a plan set out in my head what I would do every day. It was like me to not have a notion how I would spend my day, but for a period of time, I didn't have my usual determination. It was a transition period into my new reality.

Like the movement of the sun around the Earth through a very cold winter, gradually my focus returned. Focus lasted longer, providing me with a brighter day. It was my purpose to give myself room to breathe; it was my purpose to construct a plan that would lead me to feeling as though I had a significant purpose to everything I do beyond this very moment. I knew it was time to rise up and demonstrate that I, indeed, am somebody. Screw cerebral palsy—I am somebody!

My writing this book is a dedication to Mom, and many others, who believed wholeheartedly that I had the prowess to write non-fiction. Many people have pleaded, almost down on their knees, for me to write a sequel to *Always A Place*. Early on in the process of writing this novel, I decided there would never be a sequel. I didn't see the point. Writing *Always A Place* was something to preoccupy myself with while hoping to find a job. Writing a sequel to *Always A Place* would be so easy to do; I have learned over the course of writing this autobiography that writing fiction is a hell of lot more enjoyable, and it allows you to imagine anything and then put it on paper. Writing non-fiction is dramatically different, especially if it's your autobiography. You have to rip open your chest, take out your heart to smear most of its contents over three-quarters of all the pages. I laughed a lot, and I also became very emotional writing parts of this book. This will be my one, and only, autobiography. After I spend some time composing an abundance of new music, most likely I will put my fiction hat back on, and write something other than a sequel to *Always A Place*.

"Well, sometimes you may find them Like a wolf in sheep's disguise Sometimes they're just hiding
Right before your very eyes"

"You Never Know Who Your Friends Are"
The Hooters
Zig Zag

Given the lifestyle that I have, I have met many, many people. Everyone has a different personality. Some are easygoing, and some are high-strung; some are funny while others are serious; some are worriers where some take everything in stride. Some people are on the same page while others have their own agendas. I always found it a lot more challenging to adapt to a certain number of austere people who only saw a single side of the coin. I don't recall despising anyone in my life. That's not who I am. I try to see the good when their good is like trying to find a needle in a haystack. I try to bring out the very best in people.

People, in particular, people of authority, could easily intimidate me. Very few made me feel like much less of a human being. I avoid conflict although avoiding conflict may not be the best path to take. I have voiced my opposition a number of times, usually with writing strong letters. Some were successful and some were not. Being exposed to many people, I have a well full of empathy. Maybe I have too much empathy at certain moments. People struggle with all types of personal issues, from struggling to support their family, from having illnesses to fixing their car to go to work, from struggling with serious family issues, to trying to be their true selves. I have known two people who have been tragically murdered. I have to laugh when the people of authority tell caregivers not to get too close to the people who they care for. The human condition will eventual win out.

Empathy, whether it is ingrained or learned, is a virtue. I witnessed empathy from Mom. Our doorbell rang one evening. The woman looked to be in her mid 50's. She told Mom she was lost but Mom knew she was intoxicated. I sat at the breakfast nook because Mom was going to feed me dinner. I had a line of sight to our front door; I watched Mom invite this woman inside. Nobody else was home at the time. Mom directed the disengaged woman into the kitchen and introduced me. Continuing at the task at hand, Mom prepared my dinner on a plate and sat down on the nook bench. The woman sat on the opposite side. It was my first time I smelled someone of alcohol, a dirty, antiseptic smell. I was the elephant in the room, and soon the woman started to asked questions about my condition. Mom told her about my cerebral palsy. I remember looking at my Mom's eyes for reassurance. Her eyes didn't waiver. Watching Mom feed me, the woman wanted to try her hand at it. I was unsure but I allowed her to feed me. She fed me three or four bites of food. Mom offered to allow the woman to rest upstairs. She slept for a while, as Mom fed me the rest of my dinner. I recall waving goodbye to the woman from afar once Mom deemed her fit to leave. We don't know what became of the woman, or even if she remembered her time with us. That evening will always remained with me.

Of course you will like some more than others, individuals and caregivers alike. Some relationships you will form right away, and some take time to grow. Some relationships dissolve with time where some don't develop at all. I wasn't everyone's favorite individual, but that's not to say I wasn't well liked. Many people love me and I love many people. What you see is what you get with me. I don't use my disability to manipulate people into handing me things on a silver platter. For those who do, I feel they don't accept their circumstances.

I was one of those kids who caregivers enjoyed bringing home. I guess the dangers of today existed 40 years ago, but people seemed to trust each other more back then. My first sleep over was with my speech therapist, Barbara, when I was six. She and my Mom talked often about my speech development, and were on the same page. Barbara had a yellow Volkswagen Beetle. Through these very formative years, I made it a point not to gloat about my favoritism in front of the other kids. I knew I was fortunate in all the opportunities I had.

For a number of years, I was a student at residential school far from home. At one point, in my teenage years, I was kind of being pulled in two different directions. One party, Suzy, wanted me to stay very sheltered and innocent, while the other party, Seashell, observed me from a distance and thought I should be allowed to spread my wings a bit. I must admit I felt smothered by the Suzy quite a bit, and Seashell's side was very tempting. While I was under the umbrella of the entire school's staff members, no one particular unit "owned" me. On or around my 14th birthday, myself along with another student, went with Seashell and another staff member, to dinner where I had a small glass of beer. After dinner, we went to see *Porky's*. It was my first R-rated movie, but it wasn't my first taste of an alcoholic beverage. What Suzy didn't realize was that I wasn't as innocent as I appeared to be. At the time, I had very little inkling that this conflict was going on, but I did sense some tension between the Suzy and Seashell. Eventually Seashell won out. Ironically, Seashell became my new "possessor" a few years later, and what started as a very self-determining atmosphere, ended up as a very restrictive, stressful atmosphere.

Doubts: everybody experiences doubts at some point in their lives. Doubts are another one of those human conditions that we cannot deny exists. Throughout my life, doubts became regular feelings. Would I succeed being mainstreamed into high school? Would I be able to handle college? Would I find a job? Will this book meet my high expectations? Doubts chase me around every corner. I cannot speak for every person with a disability, but I feel that doubting yourself comes more with the territory when you have a disability, especially when you have a speech impairment. I never was the kind of person who would walk away from a challenge, but there have been times I needed some prodding. The best way to conquer doubts at a particular moment is to take on your doubts head on. You never know what you can or cannot do unless you try. If you fail, get back up and try again.

Doubts also come when you are in relationships. I have had three serious relationships. The first two relationships were very traditional, which occurred in my teens and early twenties.

The third one was a very unconventional, occurring in my early thirties. All of them ended due to very different reasons, and I will talk about all them in more detail later. My first serious relationship was with Ken, began when I was 15, on a strong recommendation by our mutual friend, Paul. At 15, everyone thinks they know everything about everything, but they don't. We actually had a very happy relationship for a year. The unraveling of that first relationship was a combination of very difficult issues we had to face, including Paul's death. I squarely put the blame on myself because I was too strong, and I didn't show vulnerability in front of him. It is one of my biggest regrets of my life. There was this magnetism I had with Ken that I couldn't give up. Certain circumstances created a new environment where did carry on a secret relationship for several more months. I'm not really sure why we hid it away from everyone. I don't think we were very good at keeping our relationship hidden. In that time, my feelings grew for him. He was going back to finish high school in his hometown. I was very unprepared for the moment he declared our relationship was over. It took my breath away. I don't think he had any other choice. I must admit it took me a very long time to emotionally let Ken go. We remain friends today.

My second relationship, with Charisma, also started by a strong recommendation by a mutual friend, but this time I hesitated to accept. My personal confidence was not that strong after I fucked up my relationship with Ken. I must say Charisma was persistence in his pursuit. I kept making up excuses, pretty lame excuses, why I couldn't date him, even going to the extreme by falsely proclaiming I was lesbian. Nobody bought that bold excuse. He wore me down and we started dating. I had strong reservations that I was not enough for him, not good enough. He was very charming. I must say that I never was so in love before; it was a great five months. After five months, he became more distant. I tried to get him to open up to me like he had done in the past. I waited him out, waited to see if we could get back to that extraordinary place we were in. I observed him from a far getting closer to another girl, a staff member, which was against school policy. When I inquired about her, he denied anything was going on. Being caught with the staff member revealed the truth. Soon, he graduated and left the school, but she kept her job. I got the undesirable privilege of seeing her almost daily in the school halls. Every time I saw her I would immediately want to go the opposite way because this feeling of being inferior engulfed me. *What did she have that I have?* It was a reoccurring question I could not answer. Obviously it wasn't her intelligence because she wasn't bright enough to not get caught. I avoided being 50 feet of her.

Somehow I reconciled Charisma for a longer period of time. Things would never be the same after his initial betrayal. He was a complicated young man who scared me on one or two occasions. He didn't have much of a relationship with his parents, and lost his only brother in a motorcycle accident. He had an unhealthy relationship with alcohol. I didn't particularly want to stick around and witness him be destructive to himself. Also the fact that we had difficulties, due to our disabilities being intimate, didn't help either of our confidence levels. Funny, as our relationship ended, we were able to stay friends until I left the area.

In between my relationship with Ken and Charisma, and shortly after my reconciliation with Charisma, I very much admired four different guys who all possessed hearts of gold. Another funny thing was that they all had the ability to play guitar. The Artist, was a staff member, and I knew he was completely off limits. I could stare at The Artist all day because he was so sweet looking. I definitely clammed up when I was around him. One of my counselors, Maura, was friends with The Artist and game him some of my lyrics to set to music. He did an extraordinary job. Before he left the school to move on with his career, he drew me this very colorful, abstract pieces contained within a circle.

Brown Eyes was a fellow classmate that I met when I started regular high school. We took Western Civilization together. Sadly, during that first semester, his then girlfriend passed away very unexpectedly. He was very helpful to me during the three years. We became friends. Brown Eyes and any young man who could play a musical instrument were very popular in school. I admired his friendship. He wasn't off limits, but I totally avoided the possibilities. Before graduation, I wrote Brown Eyes sort of a deep-hearted appreciation letter for his friendship. I told him what a great guy he was, wishing him a successful future.

The Ex Marine, who worked with me directly, was a bit of a surprise. I was on the reconciliation period with Charisma when Ex Marine informed me that I was extraordinary person, and if we weren't already in other relationships, he would have scooped me of my feet. I was blown away. He was, himself, an extraordinary person, and today, has two daughters with his wife of many years. This makes me very happy.

Placid came into my life directly following the exit of Seashell from my environment. It was such a dramatic change of existence, from being judged and put down at every turn, to breathing air into your lungs again—feeling excruciatingly happy and relaxed. Placid was an extra breath of fresh air. He was doing an internship at the group home where I was living until I graduated from my two-year college program. We had so much in common, especially our love for music. He did solo gigs around his hometown of Sommerville on occasion. He loved the music of Tracy Chapman. Sometimes we spent hours just talking. He was a deeply engaging and caring individual. Our relationship remained purely a friendship, but he would have made a great husband. Just I did for Brown Eyes, I wrote Placid a very heartfelt letter, and essentially told him I know he would be a husband to one lucky lady. We did keep in contact through letters for about a year. I often wonder what he doing today.

For all those who may be reading this might be asking yourselves why I gave up so easily on Brown Eyes and Placid. I am a very pragmatic person and I knew these guys were heading

What is new, someday, will be old. Some people really enjoy the things from the past, such as record players. Vinyl seems to be popular with many. I guess those little bits of static are tantalizing to the ear. I had vinyl LPs and 45s as a kid; you have to be so delicate and precise to place that needle. Delicate and precise are adjectives that I wouldn't use to describe a person with moderate to severe athetoid cerebral palsy. Maybe a better description would be a bull in a china shop.   One false move and a record is ruined. Turning the record over has its share of more obstacles. I have broken my share of records—the vinyl kind.

I seek out ways to make different tasks easier. Thankfully I moved out of the stage of playing video games long before I hit 20. I had the very popular Atari game console. My very creative Peter adapted the Atari controls on a carpeted piece of plywood, and secured them down. I "W" sat on the carpeted board and played Atari for hours on end. I was very skillful at the games that didn't require me to press the red button to blast asteroids or to shoot down UFO's in Missile Command. I excelled at games like tennis, skiing, and of course everybody's favorite, Pac Man. I beat everyone in Pac Man; I was the Queen at Pac Man, and soon, Miss Pac Man. Consoles, such as Nintendo and XBOX, had very complex game controllers that I couldn't possibly use. I haven't had the chance to try a Kinect game, but using a Wii controller is very difficult because I can't hold onto the game controller, direct it and press the various buttons. Give me my Atari back!

The next significant upgrade to computer between the 80's and 90's was the introduction of the hard drive. I used to have an Apple IIe with a 5.25" external drive where you had to take these floppy disks and shove them in and out. Try doing that with a headpointer. I got very proficient at this task. It helped a lot if the floppy laid on a soft surface where I could stick the end of my headpointer into the hole of the 5.25" floppy to lift up the back end to start it into the external drive. Once it was in the drive and was horizontal, I took the end of my headpointer out or the center and pushed and wiggled the floppy the rest of the way in with my headpointer. If I was unable to close the spring loaded door downward all the way with my headpointer after two or three tries, I whacked it down with one or more of my knuckles. I don't recall ever damaging a disk so severely under my own usage. The instructions stated the exposed film shouldn't be touched; I touched it with my headpointer. The instructions stated the disks should not be bent; I bent them to a certain degree. The instructions stated the disks should be handled gently; I handled them harshly. Imagine my dismay when the 3.5" floppies were introduced. They didn't have any holes!

Another very significant feature developed into Operating System software was the Accessibility Options, especially the StickyKeys and MouseKeys. With the introduction of the Apple II computers in the early 1980's, there was a quite an obstacle to overcome: how would a person using a headpointer hold down two or more keys at once? It was a perplexing question. Thankfully, the great Adaptive Engineer, Andy, was on the job to make our lives greatly more independent with every gadget he designed. I would like to think Andy and me had similar, three-dimensional visionary, kind of minds because we saw objects on the same plane. For the key issue on the computers, he designed a lever and weight gadget. For students who used headpointers or only had use of one finger, we were able to slide a cylinder, small weight along this three-inch rod. At the end of the rod was a square, narrow dowel that pressed the shift or the control key, allowing the user to press another key simultaneously. Once the weight was slid back along the rod, it would release the key. Genius!

I am a very unforgiving person when it comes to any failures in adaptive equipment. After graduated college, someone in Vocational Services suggested I get this very compact computer keyboard so I wouldn't need to move my neck across a regular sized keyboard. I believe I tried this special keyboard beforehand, in a controlled environment where everything worked flawlessly. Vocational Services approved the purchase of one for my personal use. When it was delivered to my house, Dad and I followed all the directions. As I recall, this special keyboard was plugged into one peripheral ports on my IBM. It did not work very well, if at all. Dad and I spent a few hours trying different things to improve its function, but nothing worked. I was growing increasingly frustrated by the minute. It was wasting my time. I wanted my trusty, standard keyboard back. I have never looked back. Of course I had "buyer's remorse" because the specialized keyboard found a spot in our attic.

It is all about supply and demand, and the companies who manufacture specialized and medical equipment for people with disabilities have a very narrow market to sell their goods to, so prices are high. If the demand was greater, prices would drop. Sometimes my jaw hits the floor when I see the prices of various items. Many of the communication devices on the market can reach into the thousands. With the introduction of tablets and smartphones, communication applications are being created at a fraction of the price of specialized communication devices.

I do applaud when universities and colleges create prototypes of different items, which are intended to advance the lives of people with disabilities. I have been fortunate to be the recipient of various items, which I will talk about in detail later on.

There are a lot of nay-sayers who believe social media sites such as Facebook and Twitter are going to negatively impact our social fabric as we once knew it. I was one of those kids who was raised on televisions which only had five different channels before cable. I watched *Happy Days*, *Laverne & Shirley*, *Barney Miller*, *The Six-Million Dollar* Man, *The Bionic Woman* and *Three's Company* to name some favorites. As kids, we still used rotary dial phones. If someone had came with their crystal ball to show us what technology would be like 35 years into the future, we might have looked upon them with a great deal of skepticism.

We have all seen how social media can give the once oppressed and persecuted a voice to rise up in an attempt to fight for humanity where seldom exists. We are aware of the downfalls of social media: the online bullying, the constant attempts of predators who are looking for their next prey. There is no doubt the world is much more accessible than it was ever before. In my situation, I am in touch with the issues of the day simply because I can click on a story to read instead of physically fighting to read a newspaper. When information is instant to a person with mobility issues, they feel empowered. They feel a part of this collective society. If people like myself, have a significant interest for seeing the disabled community rise up and fight for equality, fight off stereotypes, and to fight to make people aware that regardless of disability, Facebook is the perfect vehicle, and it demonstrates we are all born from the same human fabric.

I must admit I was a little hesitant to join Facebook. Martha continued to urge me to join. It wasn't until Martha bought my parents this streaming device that I finally joined. If my Mom had a Facebook account, then I surely had to get one. At the time, I did have a MySpace account, but to me, it didn't serve any useful purpose. With Facebook, the big concern I had was coming up with something witty or wise to post every day. Mom liked when I wrote witty things. Imagine my surprise and heartfelt delight when saw friends who I hadn't talked to in over 20 years contacting me. I never expected I would reconnect with so many important people that literally shaped the person I am today. I am a very lucky soul to be given such an extraordinary gift.

Facebook is also an advertisement platform that has the ability to reach millions of people. Companies, organizations, artists, writers, musicians, politicians and the like all have a presence on Facebook. I have a Facebook presence. It brings celebrities up close and personal with their fans, and politicians up close with their detractors. Social media emphasizes, in its full glory, what the First Amendment sets out to protect— Freedom of Speech. I'm just another person on Facebook speaking my peace. My disability only appears when I choose. My disability doesn't appear in my posts. I have many acquaintances on Facebook who have cerebral palsy and they use social media to show how a disability does not define who they are as an individual. I admire all of them.

It's always a good night when I can read, and maybe add my two cents, when David Uosikkinen posts a YouTube video of a teenage drum prodigy, and Liberty DeVitto is awestruck at the talent of this young phenom. David is similarly blown away. Did I ever have the notion at 18 years of age that someday I would be reading public conversations between my two favorite drummers marvel over a kid prodigy? Nope.

"I'm talking for free
I can't stop myself
It's a new religion"

"New Religion"
Duran Duran
Rio

Keene, New Hampshire had a newly opened shopping center around 1985. It was an old, brick factory converted into a Davol Square-like mall. It had two floors of various stores in an open-air brick atmosphere. For those who could be trusted going off alone were encouraged to do so. I never was much of a shopper; I was more of a people watcher and an explorer. I roamed the first and second floors without too much interest. When I was in the elevator, I noticed there was a button for the third floor. I wondered what was on the third floor. I dared myself to find out. I returned to the elevator and pressed the third floor button. The doors opened and I saw a lot of white walls and corridors. I figured this was the mall management space. Since it was a Saturday, this space was quiet. I decided to explore a little further and I drive down this single, white corridor. Suddenly I saw this man walking towards me dressed in a white robe with a golden rope around his waist. I swear on a stack of Bibles, this man in the white robe looked just like Jesus Christ, the same image of Jesus Christ we all see. As we passed, we smiled at each other. What else would somebody do when passing Jesus Christ? All I could do was smile. *Oh my God— that was Jesus Christ!* I didn't feel brave anymore, in fact I began to get slightly freaked out. I turned to watch Him walk out of sight. I went back downstairs and told Nestor of my discovery. "I saw Jesus Christ on the third floor!" I don't know if Nestor, one of my counselors, believed me but I put it out there.

A good Catholic—I'm not. Do I believe in God? I believe in God with every fiber of my being. I believe God listens to prayers wherever they are. I don't attend church and rarely ever did. I had private catechism lessons, and I had instructions before my confirmation. I made my First Communion without even realizing I had. Attending church wasn't an important factor in my life. I have always been a free thinker even from a young age. Some people feel I'm not a "good Catholic" because I don't attend church. I don't believe that. If I enter a church, I get the sense that I don't belong there;

the walls might start crumbling down around me, and leaving me with one last breath in my lungs.

"Good" Catholics believe in all of the teachings. I have a very difficult time accepting a few of the vows and/or beliefs the Catholic Church puts forth. Granted, I have never read the Bible due I didn't had the interest. Some people might say I'm a "bad" Catholic for not doing so. I might not be the greatest Catholic, but I consider myself a good Christian. Jesus doesn't have the capacity to hate, but some hate homosexuality. It is my belief that people should not be shamed for loving who they want to love. Isn't the church present to lift up the spirits of people instead of vilifying their true selves?

I also have a difficult time with the Catholic Church's stance on birth control. God has given human beings the ultimate gift of procreation. Couples should be allowed to dictate when to start a family. The majority of couples have plans to have children when they have the financial means to do so. Some couples don't want children; some couples cannot bear children. Does this mean happy couples can't be intimate without feeling some "Catholic" guilt? Does this mean God would rather see unhappy, struggling parents that are not ready for children? Does this mean fertility therapies are frowned down upon because it is not a natural process? God gave human beings the intellectual ability to create medications to improve lives. I am confident that God cannot argue against people helping the barren and the ill.

I am Pro Choice. I believe women should have control over their own bodies, with their partner's knowledge. With that said, I do not believe a child should be aborted unless it is a case of incest, rape, medical complications with the mother or if the fetus has grave abnormalities, period. Personally, I don't think I could have an abortion for any reason. I would have to allow the situation conclude on its own.

64

God. Who is this being that 95% of the world's population believes in? I often equate Jesus Christ with God, and visa-versa. They go hand and hand. If you pray to one, you essentially pray to the other. I envision Heaven has a glass floor, and God, Jesus and all of my family and friends who have passed on are all looking down, and watching out for you. Sometimes I look up and smile.

God is a merciful being; I have seen it with my own eyes. Growing up, surrounded by other children with a host of different developmental disabilities, you certainly get a sense you were put on this Earth to do something special. When you see a fellow classmate struggle with their disability, so much so that waking up is tedious, your heart breaks. And when people's hearts breaks, God steps in and brings them to the Kingdom of Heaven. The first time I saw this, I was ten years old. It was just a month after I entered a residential school. I wasn't scared because I knew this young teen was in so much pain and misery from suffering major head trauma after a severe snowmobile accident. God brought him into Heaven while he slept. God is merciful.

Growing up surrounded by kids who didn't live into their early twenties, you really appreciate life in so many ways. These kids didn't have a chance to realize their dreams, or live their lives without sickness. I have been blessed with a disability I can manage. I live for them. I live for Mom and everybody else who had a tremendous influence on me. All these people wouldn't want to see me curled up in a corner, mourning them. Don't worry, I grieve sufficiently. I also know that all these people are keeping a close eye on me, making sure I am doing what I'm supposed to be doing. I finally know what I am supposed to be doing. When I am called up to Heaven, a crowd will greet me. I used to fear death when I was younger, but not anymore. Of course I don't want to die anytime soon, but I am not afraid of it.

I guess some people see my life as being not easy, challenging due to my disability. It is awfully hard to gauge your existence when you have never known what it's like not to have a disability. Of course people without disabilities have always surrounded me, but I have never been bitter; I have never been angry. Oh yeah, I have been periodically exasperated when I think about the obstetrician who fucked up my delivery. I sometimes wonder what my life would be like if I didn't have cerebral palsy. I can't dwell on what should have or what could have been. It doesn't do anybody good to do so, especially me. I never felt the need to dwell. Some people ask, "Why me? " I say, "Why not me?" This is God's plan for me.

God created all things, all things great and small. He created man. It is my belief, whether it's logical or not, that God created our world as we know it now, as an experiment, if you will, on how well humans can make our existence better for all. I am pretty confident that God despises wars. I am very confidant that God despises when people brings harm to others. I know that God loves all and has great hope with for people. Who knows when this vast experiment will be complete. In the Catholic teachings, it is said that Christ has died. Christ has risen. Christ will come again. When Christ appears, the experiment will be over, and He will demonstrate for all of us how to live without hatred, greed, shame, and poverty. Everyone will be equal; no one will have superiority. There will be no judgment. Everyone will work for a greater good.

Let's talk about judgment. We all make judgments whether we like to admit it or not. I make judgments. As I mentioned, I am often judged on my intelligence by my wheelchair, my strange body movements and by my speech impairment. We tend stereotype people on appearances alone, especially when we don't "understand" the whole person. In too many instances, I have witnessed people who have been judged on the color of their skin, sexual orientation, gender, and disability. Many minds are closed off from appearances. My heart was saddened when a fellow roommate became distraught because that night, she was assigned to the only African-American working on the ward. As I watched, my thoughts were with the staff member. Later, I asked my roommate what was the issue with the staff member. She didn't have any clear explanation for her outburst to refuse care from the staff member. It was particularly a strange occurrence because she didn't have an issue rooming with an African-American.

Once, not too long ago, I dreamt that I was introduced to this young man in a wheelchair. He was a shut-in due to his monstrous appearance. At first glance, I was taken aback. He had three eyes, three noses and three mouths. His seated body was gangly with extra limbs. Once he started to talk, he harsh looks began to fade. He had an exquisite personality with a bubbling sense of humor. His brother was his caregiver because he frightened potential assistants. I really enjoyed his company. My first instinct was to feel sorry for this beautiful man. He didn't want my pity. All he wanted for someone to discover that he was a human begin just like you and me. He was so isolated and damned by a society that wouldn't except him. He had gifts that no average person could ever dream of possessing. His grace was extraordinary, his faith in God was unmatched and his hope for humanity was unrelenting. I woke up from a deeper understanding that we cannot judge anyone on appearances only. We must open up that book and actually read it for ourselves.

With God being so powerful, why couldn't He have created a universe and a world that looked the same, believed in the same things and communicated in the same language? Where is the challenge in that? If we were all the same, what could we learn from each other? My guess is that we wouldn't learn very much. We would be stagnant and dull. God decided to throw a little diversity into the mix. He wanted to challenge us to think beyond our own small worlds. He wanted us to feel empathy for all people. He wanted us to solve problems for the common good. So far, we have failed miserably.

It's all about total inclusion, boys and girls.

*"She came from Providence
The one in Rhode Island"*

"The Last Resort"
Eagles
Hotel California

My parents married on June 23, 1956 at Saint Paul's Parish at the corner of Broad Street and Warwick Avenue. Mom's father helped to build the church, which opened in 1907. Mom and Dad courted for nearly two years after being introduced by mutual friends, Ray and Helen Watson. Their education didn't extend beyond high school. The country was slowly recovering from The Great Depression of 1929, and when somebody had the opportunity to join the workforce, they took it. Mom worked for Narragansett Electric in the billing department with Helen, while Dad worked at the Providence/Worcester Railroad with Ray. Ray was also going to school to become an undertaker. With the stories Mom told me about working at Narragansett Electric with Helen, they had more fun. Mom always told me that if she had an opportunity for higher education, she would have loved working in advertising, or, to become a New York City Rockette; the two occupations couldn't have been more different.

Both of my parents were born and raised in Rhode Island. Mom was the youngest of nine, and was born two years after the market crashed. My material grandfather, along with his brothers, owned their own rigging and trucking company. He also invested in real estate. Times began to get tough for Mom's family. Business in the rigging and trucking company took a major hit, and soon my grandfather was forced to sell off some properties to keep is family afloat. In 1935, he had a massive heart attack and passed away. He was 51. My grandmother had to carry on the best way she knew how. She was a woman of great faith in God. Mom was four years old.

Between the years of 1933 and 1941, Mom's family moved approximately eight times due to necessity. These were very rough times for the family. Three years after losing their father and husband, they lost their oldest sibling, Mary, to a streptococcus infection. Mary was 23. Four years later, all four of Mom's brothers were drafted into World War II. My grandmother's faith was stronger than ever, and that impenetrable faith brought all four sons home safely.

My grandmother lived with us for three years until her passing in 1976. She was a remarkable woman who persevered through so much within her lifetime. She, along with her family, immigrated to America from Ireland, to seek a better life. She had all of the respect of her children and her 21 grandchildren, who were spread out across the country. I have a picture of Nana on my desk. Her surviving children and older grandchildren still talk about her with great respect for how still lives within us today.

My Dad's parents were distant when it came to engaging with their grandchildren. I hardly remember my grandmother. We went to visit grandmother and grandfather occasionally on Sundays. They lived near Providence College. My Aunt Florence lived with them. Her parents were killed in an accident, so my grandparents raised her as their own. Mom and Dad agreed: grandmother wasn't a good cook. Grandpa usually sat in the living room in front of his television, smoking his cigar. He was never a conversationalist. He was Italian and grandmother was Irish. They had three sons: Matthew, Francis and Thomas, my Dad. Francis died at an early age. Uncle Matt, 62, died in May of 1980, just after two months of being diagnosed with lung cancer. He was a schoolteacher and lived with his family in Long Island, New York. He visited us on occasion but not enough that I knew him well. Grandpa died about three years later at age 89.

My parents bought their first house on Estrell Drive in East Providence, off of the Wampanoag Trail. Only having one car, Mom occasionally drove and picked Dad up from work. Once or twice, she didn't bother getting redressed and drove in her pajamas. Later she realized that driving in her pajamas at night might not be the smartest of things to do. Her brother-in-law, Tom, was a Rhode Island State Trooper. Home alone one night, Mom heard something suspicious out in the back of the house. She dialed up Uncle Tom at once. About twenty minutes

70

later he arrived to check out the scene. It was a raccoon rummaging around with the trashcans. That was my Mom.

Their first child, Mary Ann, was born a little after their first wedding anniversary. Sadly, she passed away 15 minutes after from a heart defect. A year and a half later, they were blessed on Christmas Day with their first son, Peter. Two more blessings, Martha and Paul, followed within the next seven years. I was born two years later.

My mother's water broke eight days prior to my birth; she entered Providence's Lying In Hospital. Unlike with Paul's delivery, my mother's obstetrician did not induce labor when I wasn't coming. Instead, he made my mother walk the halls, promising labor would begin. Labor did not begin. She could have walked a mile every day but labor was elusive. Signs began to arise that I was struggling. Meconium, the stool from the fetus, appeared on bed linens. Meconium is normally expelled after birth. My mother's obstetrician still did not induce labor or preform a Caesarian section. Four more days had passed with no progression in natural labor although meconium was still present. It wasn't until the eighth day of my mother's hospitalization that the doctor induced labor. It was a long and difficult birth, as the medical records state. Mom was unconscious. When I was finally born, the umbilical cord was wrapped around my neck, twice, and knotted. I required CPR immediately, which was effective, but I suffered a seizure. When stabilized, the medical staff administered a blood transfusion to offset the lack of blood and oxygen.

My mother often remarked about the obstetrician coming into her room the day after and not being able to make eye contact with her then or in the days that followed. I remained in the hospital for ten days, confined to an incubator, which provided me more oxygen. Whether or not the extra oxygenation was beneficial in my case, there is no way of knowing. By the time Mom and Dad took me home from the hospital, all indications were I was normal, 8-pound, baby girl. The only noticeable issue I had was I was unable to suck from my mother's breast or a baby bottle.

So, what do very capable and loving parents do with this newborn baby girl who can't suck from a bottle. They improvise. Mom used an eyedropper to give me my formula. It took a little longer to feed me by eyedropper because she had to be careful not to cause me to aspirate. Mom said I did very well and it became easier as time went on. To Peter, Martha and Paul, my difficulties were natural by my parents. They never exploited me as anything different from other babies. I just needed more attention. I was their baby sister.

At four months of age, my mother and father noticed signs that I wasn't reaching milestones like my brothers and sister had done. I couldn't roll over or hold my head up; I resembled a ragdoll. It was then that my parents took me to a neurologist who diagnosed me with athetoid cerebral palsy. I am sure my parents were angry and sad over this diagnosis. The neurologist projected that I would never walk, talk and possibly have a low level of intelligence. I would like to how he presumed all of these things would occur. Do you think he had a crystal ball? Do you think he looked up at the stars? How can anybody predict what a person is going to be like, as they get older? Nobody can make those predictions, and nobody should.

In the 1960's, medical malpractice lawsuits were on the increase. Although my parents were confident my cerebral palsy was caused from gross negligence, they didn't pursue it. It was when I was 18, my Mom broached the subject with me. I could bring suit against the obstetrician before it became too late. I decided to do so with my brother, Paul, beside me at ever turn. I must say it was a nerve-racking process, but oddly enough, when we sat in on the obstetrician's deposition, I hung on his every word as my lawyer interrogate my mother's obstetrician. Mom declined the opportunity to sit in on his deposition, fearing she might just "reach across the table to strangle him." Mom wasn't angry that she had a child with a disability, but she was angry that I had to face the limitations through my life. The elderly man wore a minty green suit to his deposition. Of course he defended his actions. I settled out of court for a lesser amount, a guaranteed amount.

I have never been an individual who sought out any special attention as far as going out of my way to coming up with reasons why I needed extra attention from anyone. Even as a child, I knew it was too exhausting. For the majority of the time, I enjoyed my play by myself. Of course it was great when Paul joined in on my play because he could do things that I didn't have the dexterity to do. Of course when he discovered the game of golf, playtime with little sister took a backseat. I always enjoyed going out and watching Paul and his friends play basketball. Some of his friends, especially, the Pratt brothers, were very excepting of my disability and interacted with me like any other kids. At times, Paul excused me of "showing off" in front of his friends. I must admit sometimes I did. Maybe a particular situation called for me to "show off" some of my intellect. I didn't want anybody to assume that I didn't have smarts. I kind of enjoyed the attention of some of his friends, but I never sought it out.

Paul wrote most of Mom's eulogy to read at her funeral. Paul wrote:

> *"Their main focus was their children, providing a warm and comfortable upbringing in Warwick, RI. Of all their children, they were most focused on Maureen, given her physical challenges. They coped with a lot of emotional and financial difficulties in doing so. Their life was centered on Maureen, ensuring that she always had the best available resources. If there is a theme to Hope's life, it was her (and our Father's) dedication to Maureen; yes she loved us all, but Mo was the focus. They sacrificed many things in this pursuit, but we never knew any difference, we were all happy."*

This affirmation brought on feelings of guilt, and then sadness. I never asked to be the child to who received the most attention from our parents, but I did due to my disability. I never wanted to be the "special" one; I didn't want to take anything away from my brothers and my sister. There must have been times when Dad couldn't attend some basketball games at school because of me. There must have been times money was a little tight to take a vacation due to my need for a piece of adaptive equipment I needed that the insurance didn't cover. Mom and Dad wanted to provide the best for their children, not just me. In my eyes, we were that strong family, only with that little twist. I was that little twist. We are all a bunch of high achievers thanks to Mom and Dad, and we all should be proud.

Many parents of a child with a disability take dedication to a whole new level. Some do not. Some even believe that God handpicks particular parents, the strongest of parents, to be blessed with a child who has challenges. There are sad instances when a parent does harm to their children, disability or no disability. It is never easy to parent a child with a disability when you are not prepared for this life-long position. I don't believe God does handpick these strong individuals. God doesn't supply handbooks on how to raise children. He gave us the capacity to rationalize, to make decisions, and to love. Life is just a random set of chances that we are all given.

I asked my mother how she ever fed and held me at the same time. She said she sat me in a highchair and propped me up with towels and blankets. What a nifty idea, I replied. Eventually I was sitting without the help of towels and blankets.

Early on, my parents recognized my intelligence. I was alert and my vision was good. My Mom engaged me throughout my young life, especially with the magnetic, plastic, colored letters and numbers on the refrigerator door. She said I could name all of the letters and numbers before I was three. In my ability to recognize the alphabet and numbers, it gave my Mom the opportunity to compel me to speak in however clumsy it was in the beginning. When she pointed to a letter, I spoke, and she understood what I was saying. She said she talked to Paul and me all day long, while Peter and Martha were at school. Mom said she spent days upon days explaining different things to us.

In the early 70's, my parents enrolled me in an early intervention program for children with developmental disabilities. I received physical, occupational and speech therapies. I also received one-on-one sessions with top neurologists in the state. Mom and Dad often sat in the waiting room for an hour for only fifteen minutes with the neurologist. They weren't impressed and soon discontinued my visits. The therapy facility was doing a satisfactory job.

When I was six, I began my education at the same facility where I received therapy. It wasn't a traditional kind of sit-at-your-desk classroom setting, or at least not at the beginning. I went to school with children who had different developmental disabilities. Some kids sat in wheelchairs, while others had the ability to walk with the aid of leg braces and walkers or crutches. The children able to sit on the floor did so. I also was encouraged to side-sit with my legs to the left as my right arm held me up, but after about 30 seconds, my right hand would fall asleep and I would fall over or I returned to "W" sitting. Luckily therapists recognized I couldn't side-sit effectively, but also saw my efforts to try. On one particular day, I was sitting on the floor with other children surrounding me. Some of the children didn't have the ability to sit so they lied down but had some ability to move around. These were the days of steel braces and leather high-top shoes. This one particular classmate wore shoes with a metal, shark tooth-shaped piece tacked to the bottom of her shoe near the toe. I recall remarking to myself somebody will get hurt on that metal piece. No sooner that thought left my mind, the classmate rolled onto her stomach as the sharp tip of her shoe filed across the top of my left thigh, leaving about a three-inch scrape. It shocked me more than it hurt. Once I brought my injury to somebody's attention, immediately I was whisked up and taken to the therapy section. I was put on a mat and my scrape was cleaned and covered. I don't recall much bleeding. I was returned to my classmates. You can be sure the shark's tooth culprit was quickly repaired.

It recently came to my attention that some of my teachers in these early school days did not believe I could read. This boggles my mind a bit because all they needed to do was place a children's book in front of me and have me read it out loud. My speech was clear enough for my teachers to understand. I have learned otherwise. It was the mission of one select person to prove that I had the ability to read.

This school was the site where an engineer from Raytheon, Victor Almonte, worked with the therapist and me to try to refine an electronic touch board to operate a Teletype machine. At the time, I had been using a Bliss symbol board, although I never bothered memorizing the Bliss symbols when I had the ability to read the words underneath the symbols. I believed everybody was keen on my intentions not to bother learning the Bliss symbols but I guess this was not the case.

I remember using the Teletype device fairly clearly. It was constructed in a manner where it could be used either on a table or on the floor. Of course, I worked best with it on the floor. Its surface area was about 24 by 18 inches, and it height was about 2 inches. Towards the back of this device was a casing that was 6 inches high, running the length. A numeric readout was placed in the center of the casing, visible to me. On the main surface of this device were eight separate squares, which represented the numbers 0 through 7. Each number measured about 4 by 4 inches in size. In two weeks, I had memorized a 64-symbol code for letters, numbers and punctuation. I had a laminated sheet in front of me that I could refer to if the need was there. When I entered a two-digit number, the nearby Teletype machine would print out the corresponding character. I believe I got quite proficient at using this device. The only drawback was I couldn't see what I was typing because the Teletype machine was about three feet off the ground.

Someone thought of building a platform for me to "W" sit that was about 30 inches off the ground. It was like a platform bed with 12-inch high sides so I wouldn't fall off it. I was able to see the Teletype machine better, although I still felt all the parts were too cumbersome for what I was trying to achieve, or in all reality, to prove to the masses that I was able to read.

It was the spring of 1974 that I had a chance to demonstrate working with the device for the actor, Peter Falk. I'm not sure if I knew exactly who he was, or just knew of him. Mr. Falk was very involved with fundraising for Easter Seals, which my school was often supported by. Martha was the true artist in my family, and at 14 years old, she painted a sketch of his character, Columbo. My school's mission was and always has been to involve the family in the developmental process of each child they serve. Martha came to the school and personally gave Mr. Falk her painting.

As I sat on the floor, pressing numbers on the wooden, electronic board, Mr. Falk crouched down behind me to watch the process. I don't remember what exactly I typed, but it was probably something along the lines of, "Welcome to Rhode Island, Mr. Falk." As I sat keying in all the numbers in to type the sentence, someone was explaining to him the process, and the codes, I was using. A few years ago, after bumping into my friend and classmate, Lois, she had a picture of our small group with Mr. Falk. I scanned the picture and now it hangs proudly on my refrigerator.

No one knew the impression I made on Peter Falk until he appeared on Johnny Carson not too long after his visit to

Rhode Island. My Dad got home from work and he fetched me
from my bed from across the hall. It was 11:30 and I was
awakened from a sound sleep at Mom's request. I lied on my
parents' bed and we all watched Johnny Carson. I was trying to
stay awake. My parents had no idea that during Johnny and
Peter's conversation that Peter would reference me. Somewhere
along the lines, Mr. Falk said, "I met this girl—she's smarter
than you and I put together." I smiled and fell back to sleep.

      During my last two years at this particular school, I was
introduced to the headpointer. From my research I attempted, I
could not find any information on when or how the headpointer
was developed. I can surmise with certainty that the headpointer
was developed after the mouth stick. I don't recall trying a
mouth stick. It would have proven ineffective because of the
extreme involuntary movements in my jaw muscles. I don't
imagine I would have felt comfortable using a mouth stick due to
cleanliness. It's fine for some people but not for me.

      The occupational therapists were able to fabricate custom
headpointer using malleable plastic, which hardened while
cooled. They would cut out the white plastic material when
warmed, cut it and than molded it to my head. They fastened a
Velcro strap in the back of the headpointer to adjust its fit. Next,
the occupational therapists attached a narrow, wooden stick to
the front. Headpointers were very rudimentary adaptive
equipment in the 70's, but served their purpose tremendously
well. I like to refer to these types of headpointers as "unicorn
headpointers", because users resemble a unicorn using this type
of headpointer. I used a unicorn headpointer, effectively, for 30
years, although I had the occasional neck pain and/or stiffness.

      With years came hindsight. In 2007, as I was getting
things adjusted with my new Permobil power wheelchair, my
wheelchair technician showed me a different headpointer in a
catalog. After seeing it, I knew it would be great for my neck,
but it cost $200. His brother owned his own medical equipment

business. That Friday evening, his brother was walking through one of his storage rooms. All of a sudden, this thing fell off the top shelf, causing him to nearly fall over it. He wanted to kick it and throw it away, but for a moment thought my technician might be able to use it. Monday morning, it was sitting on his desk. It is exactly the same headpointer that he showed me on the previous Thursday afternoon. He had it in his storage room for 15 years. I believe that it was divine purpose.

It was divine intervention and/or purpose because the unicorn headpointer took a toll on my neck muscles. I am very fortunate to have still strong neck muscles to accomplish all I want to accomplish. From 2007 through the present, I have been using the same clear view headpointer where the pointer extends from my jaw level, giving me better positioning of my neck and a constant line of sight to my computer keyboard and screen with only eye movement instead up and down neck movement. I don't believe the clear view headpointer was available in the 1980's and 1990's. If I was asked to recommend to a child with a disability who is a candidate for a headpointer, I would strongly recommend a clear view headpointer to maintain strong neck muscles and to have a continuous view on their tasks.

With the introduction of the headpointer to my repertoire, I could now type on an electric typewriter. Most of the Smith Corona electric typewriters at the school had key guards. Key guards were steel, metal frames fastened securely over the keys, providing physical separation between all of them. When I first started typing with a headpointer, I exceled with the key guards. Soon, I tried typing without a key guard and I liked it, I liked it a lot. My WPM rate improved greatly. I didn't need to extract my headpointer out of the guard and plummet it into a different key well. I was able to glide over the typewriter keys like a hawk sleuthing over the ground. I never wanted the assistance of a key guard again. Of course I hit a wrong key occasionally but not enough to warrant the use of a key guard, especially after correcting tape became available to erase typos.

*"High above the winding road
That brought me to my
mountain"*

"Bottle Anything"
Ed Kowalczyk
The Flood And The Mercy

Before the age of ten, it was clearly evident that I was outpacing my fellow classmates within the school's curriculum. I, myself, often became bored in school. I, along with my parents, were often called upon to promote the school's mission, many times in front of television cameras. My parents became tired of this constant promotion, especially when the school's education curriculum wasn't meeting my needs. My Aunt Anne was the first grade teacher at St. Peter's Parish in Warwick. She along with most of our extended family who lived in Warwick were parishioners of the church and essentially everybody knew each other. Martha and Paul also were students at St. Peter's. Monsignor Cox was the one who suggested to my parents look into this renowned residential school for children with developmental disabilities in northern New England. I'm not sure what Mom and Dad's initial thoughts were about sending me away to school, but I'm sure they had serious reservations. Serious reservations gradually turned into just reservations as they investigated the school with I imagine would have been intense scrutiny.

It was the responsibility of the Warwick School Department to see to it that I receive the proper education needed for my success. Luckily we had a very strong advocate on our side within the Warwick School Department, Mr. Jeff Sharkey. Mr. Sharkey believed that the residential school would meet all my needs. For eleven years, the Warwick School Department paid for the tuition for the residential school in northern New England.

I thought it was kind of funny when my parents signed me up to go to summer camp for a week in the summer of 1977. None of us were the outdoorsy type. I don't think we even owned a tent. Maybe we did but it was probably used once. Camp? Really? I went along, but very begrudgingly. I was homesick immediately after Dad left; I had it in my mind that I wasn't going to enjoy camp and I didn't. I participated in the activities that were required. I kept to myself most of the week, as I counted down the days that I would leave this God forsaken place. Even though I don't remember every moment of my week at camp, I do remember making friends with a girl named, Debbie. I believe Debbie was three or four years older than I, and she seemed very wise. In our last hours before leaving camp, I spent with Debbie, chatting. I felt ashamed that I spent the week pouting, instead of being more outgoing as she was. I also knew I probably wouldn't see Debbie again, and I never did.

One afternoon in late August, I came home from school and said I told Mom I didn't want to go back. She said okay. I was expecting more of an interrogation, or at least a question of why. Her response was simply, "Okay." It was already planned I was changing schools in the Fall. It is my assumption today that Mom and Dad wanted to spend some extra time with me before I headed to my new school up north.

Dad and I visited the school months earlier before my actual enrollment date, September 26, 1977. I don't recall what my initial thoughts were about the place, but I think I had a relatively open mind about it. Instead of going to school every morning and coming home every afternoon, I would be going to school on Sunday afternoons, and returning home Friday afternoons. This was a monumental change. It was very fortunate that I was used to different people taking care of me during the day at the school in Rhode Island. I also had that Sunshine Camp experience under my belt, even if I didn't enjoy singing "Kumbaya" around the campfire every evening while shooing away all the campground bugs.

Whether it was the strength of my Mom, or something else, I don't recall the actual moment when Dad put me in the car for that drive up north that late September morning. Martha came along. Dad and Martha spent the day settling me into my new surroundings. I shared a room with a girl named Laurie from Chicago. She liked John Denver; the fact that I wasn't a big John Denver fan was an understatement. All day I knew the time would come that Dad and Martha would have to head home without me. They left around 4 o'clock. It was the second time I saw my father cry. Recently, Dad told me that he cried all the way home. I think it was more difficult for them to leave me there than it was for me not to go home with them. I cried, they cried, we all cried. Soon, Dad and Martha left. I was on the children's nursing unit, which was slated for nursing care for children and young teens. Please forgive me, I forgot the name of the young aide that took care of me that night. I remember she was very kind and patient with me. I had my first success that night when I communicated to my aide and the nurse in charge that I felt more comfortable sitting up in the bathtub, rather than lying down. It was after the fact, but I got my message across.

It was up and Adam at 6 o'clock the following morning. I believe I slept relatively well after briefly crying before falling asleep. I was assigned to a veteran aide, Mary Beth. Her Grade A personality overshadowed her average looks. She had long auburn hair and eyeglasses. She interacted with me beautifully and even made me laugh. On that morning, it was my first time eating in the dining room with all the other children. There were about 25 children on the ward.

Even though I was homesick, the daily routine of getting up, going to school and all the other activities kept my mind occupied. School really geared my attention away from being homesick to totally focusing on the schoolwork. I wanted to prove to my teacher that I indeed was smart. Every day the students in the class had to complete a fixed number of pages in their individual workbooks. For the first month, the teacher, Lucille, worked with me for many hours on an individual basis to gauge my education level. I kept a very close eye on the clock every single, damn day to make sure I finished all of my work. I did this with precision. Soon, I became the "wiz kid". I became the kid adored by many. Lucille endearingly began calling me, Moo Moo. It fit—we were in cow country.

On my 30-day review, I was asked if I wanted to attend; I did not. I was extremely uncomfortable listening to people of authority talk about me and was my biggest weaknesses. I didn't want to do anything wrong even at the age ten. I had high expectations for myself and could be intimidated very easily. As I stated before, I was what the professionals call, a "compliant client". In hindsight, I probably should have "manned up" and sat in on all of my annual IEP meetings. I don't know if I would have made any difference in the course of my education. One can only wonder. I didn't attend my annual meeting until my last year in 1988.

At home, on that particular evening, I recall watching television with Mom and Paul. Paul was reading the report from my 30-day review. At one moment, Paul wanted Mom's confirmation that the report stated that I would never be able to walk. Mom tried to answer Paul without alerting me. I have lived with this body for ten years—I didn't have any grand illusions of my body being able to walk.

It took me about four to six months to really settle into leaving home Sunday afternoons to go back to school. I didn't want to leave my peeps. I didn't throw any temper tantrums, I just pouted for about a half hour before the bus arrived. Temper tantrums are also useless and too, all together exhausting. It helped when my Aunt Anne and Uncle Tom dropped by on some Sunday mornings to give me some distractions. Uncle Tom, always the comedian, would make me laugh in whatever he said or did. He brought levity. The event that gave me the belief and fortitude that my world wasn't going to fold up and swallow me whole if I couldn't make it home one weekend was the Blizzard of '78. New England was paralyzed and I wasn't going anywhere. The advantage was that the school never lost power or heat, but my peeps in Rhode Island were in the dark and the cold for five days.

Somewhere along the lines in these early days at my new

school, I developed a brief, but profound, illogical fear that Mom and Dad would not allow me to come home on weekends anymore. Sometimes I would see the nurse in charge and one of the aides chat quietly. I always assumed they were talking about me. Mom was a two-pack a day smoker back then and I worried about her health. This was the time when health officials didn't know the harmful effects of secondhand smoke were to non-smokers. My irrational fear finally broke when Dad picked me up at the designated bus stop in Pawtucket one Friday. In Dad's car, instead of 95 South, he took 95 North. *He's taking me back to school*, I concluded to myself. For my stomach seized up and logic went out the window. Nervous, my body jerked and swayed. One or two exits later, Dad got off 95 North, for what reason, I do not recall—possibly to run an errand. Indeed, we did go home to Warwick. It didn't occur to me that if they didn't want me to come home, they could have requested the bus not take me home. It was the last time I had an illogic thought that my parents didn't want me to come home on weekends.

Given the fact that I require physical assistance taking care of my daily needs such as taking a shower, dressing, going to the bathroom, eating, etc. has lead me to meet many, many people over the years. I would like to believe I am a master of seeing people for who they really are. I have met people from many walks of life, including an ex hooker from Provincetown. She was a trip! Some people present themselves at face value, and some do not. A few people have surprised me that gave me reason to doubt my perceptions. One or two people have given me pause to protect my own safety the best I could. Other people just grab onto your heart because they are so good and know you so well. I had to say goodbye to people, which I had a close relationship, and I have been very fortunate to kept in contact with many of those special people.

There were many people who had some kind of influence on me. She was about 20 years old, and had the maturity that most of the other young girls were slightly lacking. It didn't take long for Leslie to catch onto her job. If anyone was a natural at caring for children with developmental disabilities, it was Leslie. She was blonde and had very pretty features. I think her strong personality made her more inviting to nearly everyone she met. She had a knack for making every child she worked with feel special. It wasn't her knack, it was her nature. Her personality was a ray of sunshine; I don't think she was ever in a foul mood in my presence even during very difficult times. Other than my parents and siblings, I consider Leslie to be the most influential person during my eleven years in northern New England. She might not have realized it when I graduated. I hope someday she will read this book and know how special she had been in molding the person I am today.

If you are a nurse looking into working with children with disabilities, you have to a very exceptional personality. You cannot have an iron-fist and expect children to have the courage to come to you if they have an issue, especially if it is a serious issue. On the other hand, you cannot be too malleable because you will lose control if you're not truly careful. Kids, all kids, disability or not, respond better to people who listen to them. They don't want to be disregarded. Kids want to feel safe and know their needs will get met. It is your job to protect these children and look after them almost the same way as their parents would. You might even do a better job of it in some cases. Kids love to laugh, and if you have the ability to make a child laugh after they had a particularly bad day in school or physical therapy was arduous and painful, you have the golden touch.

Nurses ruled the roost when it came to the day-to-day care of individuals with developmental disabilities. The first nurse I encountered was an older woman, probably close to 70 years old. She had a very authoritative personality; I definitely didn't want to get on her bad side, even though I got to see her very caring side on one occasion during her very short time she continued to work. She did not like rock music playing during meals. It was classical music or nothing. When we groaned too much, it was nothing. There was another second shift nurse who was much younger but had the personality a gnat. Soon, we had a few more nurses that swung in and out. Some were extremely nice, and some were completely overpowering. In 1981, a young nurse came onto the ward and she was a breath of fresh air and one of the funniest people I have ever met. We welcomed, Debi.

Our first shift nurse was a lifer on the children's ward, and clearly enjoyed her job. Marilyn was small in stature, but she too, was incredibly down-to-earth and had a very good sense of humor. She had to have good sense of humor because some of us kids used to adoringly referred her as, "Old Bat". I called her this name a handful of times, but it didn't fit her personality. What I loved most about Marilyn was she talked to all of her kids with the utmost respect. She never once condescended anyone. On the mornings the ward was short-staffed, she rolled up her sleeves and helped get kids up and ready for school. She often tended to me on such mornings, and I loved it.

Modesty is one of those things that some take seriously while others do not. I have always taken my modesty very seriously. I even was complimented for my high standards to protect my modesty in the way that others didn't. You might ask yourself how can I, a person who needs so much physical care, be modest. Even though many people have seen me naked, which is not by choice, I have figured out ways to increase my privacy. I have known individuals who just let it all hang out. I'm not an exhibitionist, although when I and another person are training a new to become a PCA, I don't have any choice to be somewhat of an exhibitionist. I believe very strongly that only one person should be trained at once. It's altogether humiliating to have two, new sets of eyes looking at you simultaneously. This has only happened a handful of times. It won't happen again.

Retaining your modesty and privacy takes a lot of work and patience when you are in an environment when you could have one to three roommates at a time. My need to retain my modesty and privacy increased with age. I have never been the kind of person who can go to the bathroom in the presence of anyone within fifty feet. That is quite of an understatement, unless you have food poisoning of epic proportions and feel like you have gotten run over by a Mack truck. It's more of a mind game with me. If I don't feel safe on the toilet, if I'm not comfortable on the toilet, if I can't keep my legs and feet still, if the bathroom is the only one around, if someone else needs to use the bathroom, along with several other things with my mind, it's very difficult for me to do what I have to do. A mindset such as mine doesn't particularly fit well when you have athetoid cerebral palsy. I have adapted reasonably well throughout the years. I have been fortunate to receive the knowledge and resources to come up with a solution for my overwhelming shyness that I'll present later.

While I talk about the staff and the nurses who have influenced me a great deal, fellow students have also influenced me. As a whole, being surrounded by children who have significant developmental disabilities humbles you quite a bit. I have been humbled many times. There are also those individuals that have more capabilities than you do. Maybe they have the ability to walk. They might be able to talk with few or no deficits. I couldn't be jealous of them because I didn't have their abilities. Having lesser abilities than some of my fellow students didn't make me angry, but it rather made me appreciate what I did have. Having greater abilities does not guarantee your life easier and/or happier. I have known many children and teens who came from broken homes, where one or two parents were out of the picture. I have known children and teens whose home life was in great turmoil. Nobody's life is perfect but I soon realized I had it pretty good. I also came to the realization that there are limits you are faced with, especially at a young age, to help such individuals out of their situations.

One such individual that latched onto my heart was April

Green. She came from Rochester, New York. She came to our residential school towards the latter part of 1979. Oddly, she hardly talked about her life before transferring to our school. She had severe spastic quadriplegia cerebral palsy, although she talked fairly well and she only had mild learning disabilities. She had a quick wit that would bring you to your knees, and a loveable heart that could raise you up if you were feeling down. April embraced being at this new school from the start; it was my assumption she had a very difficult home life due to her overwhelming physical limitations.

We were exactly two months apart in age, with April being born first. She enjoyed that very fact. She was a girlie-girl who relished having her nails painted, makeup and her hair dolled up. I was the typical tomboy. I only need one hand to count how many dresses I have worn through my entire life. April loved dresses, especially sundresses. I loved rock and roll; April loved hip-hop and Motown; she loved Michael Jackson. Thankfully I didn't hate Motown or disco. How could we ever become best friends? Well—we did.

I am also the type of person who often gets frustrated when I see a person, disabled or non-disabled, not live up their fullest potential. You might be saying to yourself, "What gives you to right to judge what someone's potential is?" Maybe I don't have the right to judge anyone, especially when I feel I haven't lived up to my potential. When I see someone who clearly has, or has the opportunities set out before them and they don't capitalize on them, that makes me angry. People who don't try at all makes me angry. Like I mentioned before, my friends who did not have a chance to live out their lives, I strive to do my best in their honor.

Going to this new school, I brought with me my Bliss Symbol board that was actually a word board. It was big, bulky and a pain in the ass to carry around. The better solution was to put an alphabet board on my wheelchair tray. I pounded on the letters with my right hand to communicate with all of the new people until they got used to my speech. I was very proficient at pounding out words left and right. I had speed and accuracy. This alphabet worked extremely well for that first year.

My next speech therapist who stands out amongst any other is Sally Pore. Sally was very relatable because, she too, had cerebral palsy. She had a pronounced gait and a slur to her words, although easily understood. You bet your ass I admired Sally; she held a full time position, she drove a car, and of course she lived independently. We had a real connection.

Sally put me through the rigors of speech therapy that no speech therapist had prior. Of course I continued to practice my technics to pronounce my sounds as effectively as I possible. Sally put a lot of emphasis on my posture. She did not want my arms flailing around outside the confines of my chair. She wanted my arms down, by my side, inside of my armrests. My right arm cooperated, while my left arm did not. The more stabilized my body was, the more energy I had to put into pronouncing sounds accurately. It worked for the most part. Sally conditioned me so much that I usually try to put my arms down presently, especially when I'm not being understood so easily at times.

Her goal for me was verbalize every sound and syllable to the 'T' (pardon the pun), no matter how long the word was stretched out. She wanted me to talk like Jimmy. Jimmy was another student at the residential school who also had athetoid cerebral palsy, but at a tiny less degree than mine. He was about eight or nine years older and had a Grade A personality. Everyone found him very engaging. What was cool about this place was that almost everybody intermingled. This allowed me to 'idolize' some of the older students, like Jimmy, so I could envision what my future might be. He went onto college to study hotel management.

Unfortunately, I didn't have the control over my mouth, jaw and tongue muscles to accurately pronounce every sound.

Sally and I did do speech sessions with the aid of singing to lyrics, most notably, lyrics to Billy Joel's *Glass Houses*. I demonstrated for Sally that I had better control of my accuracy when I was singing rather than talking.

To my disadvantage, in my teens through mid twenties, I was very opposed to using any kind of augmentative speech device. I thought the speech output sounded like a robotic voice. Given that I already stood out in a crowd, I didn't want to seem more freakish, especially to people who were unfamiliar with people with disabilities. This subject has brought me to many tears, but ever since I graduated from Roger Williams University, I have embraced using an augmentative communication device on those occasions I present myself to the greater public. Technology has given us much better sounding voices, which don't sound like robots.

Thinking about how I got passed being so self-conscious about using augmentative communication, I had an opportunity to make a presentation to Rotary Club on the Cape in the mid 1990's. My motivation stemmed from the prospects of earning money with desktop publishing. I tend to wonder if I was given incentives to use augmentative communication when I was younger, I would like to think I may have been more receptive and might have learned that good things might have come of it. I wonder if there was an offer of basic music theory lessons in exchange of me using an augmentative communication device would have spurred me on. I believe it probably would have.

Through the years since, I have given a handful of speeches, to a number of large crowds. I have given a graduation commencement speech, a Civil Rights Day speech, I have given speeches and/or presentations on my architecture design concepts, and I have given presentations on the methods, which I compose music. I never pass up an opportunity to speak at an event using my AAC device.

Physical therapy began promptly once I arrived at the residential school. Previously, I was seen by a number of orthopedic doctors and neurologists. I think I was the few who hadn't been sliced open by a scalpel at my previous school. There was talk about cutting this tendon or that tendon. Today, it boggles my mind why any doctor would suggest cutting any tendon because every part of me is flexible. I have very little hypertonia. Of course there are times when my muscles tense up and extremities or joints don't bend. When I relax, my range of motion is good. I'm glad my parents were knowledgeable about all these different surgeries. My parents' belief was that if the surgery wasn't guaranteed to have benefits, they shut the discussions down. I would have been devastated if one of these tendons surgeries had taken place, resulting in the lost in my ability to "W" sit and crawl. There was even chatter about implanting a pacemaker into my brain. Mom said, "No guarantees: you are not cutting into my kid's brain."

What the collective heads did agree upon was that something had to be done about my turned-in ankles. I was born with dislocated ankles bones, where the fibula bone was detached to the talus bone, making my ankles turn inward. In my days in Rhode Island, there had been many discussions whether to surgically fuse my anklebones together to correct the issues. The orthopedic surgeons could not give guarantees the fusion would hold due to my powerful muscle contractures that inverted my ankles. Therefore, this surgery was also abandoned.

The therapists at the residential school main concern was supporting my unruly, dislocated ankles. A handful of times, I was chosen to appear in a bathing suit or in my underwear in front of a panel of physical therapists and orthopedic surgeons. They would study my flailing body in different positions and discuss the best course of action. Sometimes they would videotape these sessions. First and foremost, they wanted to fit me with AFOs (Ankle-Foot Orthotics).

The first step in fitting me with AFOs was observing my tolerance wearing them. The first attempt was putting fiberglass casts that stretched from below my knee to my toes. While the therapists applied the casting, the first thing I thought of was that bloody, blasting cast saw had to be used to cut off these things from my legs. Their standard practice is to put thick, rubber tubing under the casting for the saw to cut upon.

It was the hope of the therapists that I would tolerate the casts for two or three days straight. By the next morning, my ankles were fighting the casts, causing pain on the outside of my ankles. The therapists wanted me to go through the day with the casts, and they would reassess my tolerance before day's end. At the end of the day, I was still not tolerating the casts and they were removed at last. The saw was a little scary but I knew the relief would be Heavenly. It was Heavenly.

After a short time, the therapists did successfully fit me with AFOs that I could tolerate very well. They made transferring and pivoting much easier for all parties involved.

The next goal the physical therapists wanted me to be able to achieve was being able to sit up and transfer myself into my wheelchair independently. I believed it was a very lofty goal given my poor balance. I stayed with the mindset the PTs had that I would be able to transfer myself.

I got my first electric wheelchair in August of 1978. I was so excited! It brought me independence, but it also taught me responsibility. Sometimes I refer to 'motorized wheelchairs' as either the 'electric' wheelchair or the 'power' wheelchair. It will all depend on which decade I'm referring to. Before going to the residential school in northern New England, none of my classmates had an electric wheelchair. It was probably a very wise idea because the majority of the children hung out on the floor, and putting a child with an electric wheelchair into that mix would have been dangerous. It was also very uncommon for many families to have the ability, mainly the financial means, to accommodate a heavy, electric wheelchair into their homes.

Before I got my electric wheelchair in 1978, I had a manual wheelchair with projection hand rims, which allowed me to propel the wheelchair. I didn't have the ability to grasp a regular wheelchair rim, so these rubber-coated, two-inch projections gave me the ability to move. I did well on flat surfaces, but I didn't dare to maneuver up or down inclines without assistance. This chair was particularly bothersome because it had two, straight steel poles that the back upholstery was attached. The only problem with these menacing poles was when somebody cradled me to put me in the wheelchair, very often a pole would scrape my back if somebody wasn't cautious. And when a pole hit my spine, ouch!

One of the most important thing you do for your child, or for yourself, if a wheelchair is necessity, is to have a proper wheelchair assessment by certified Assistive Technology Professional (ATP) or a certified Seating and Mobility Specialist (SMS). I have seen too many people in wheelchairs not positioned properly, resulting in poor posture. These are the people who have the knowledge to create seating systems that can maximize a person's ability to be their most efficient with body movements. From experience, if I'm not positioned properly in my wheelchair, or in my shower chair, my body just goes haywire, as it tries to compensate for any support that is lacking. If this lack of support with regards to mobility equipment continues for an extended amount of time, it can have negative impact on certain muscles and/or joints.

Case in point: recently I obtained a new shower chair. It has tilting features, it has a headrest, it has footrests, but the standard seat cushion was horrible for me, personally. The standard seat cushion was a "horseshoe" type commode seat. Every time I tried to sit on any horseshoe seat, one of my legs fell into the front opening of the seat, causing my body to lean to one side. Without shoes on my feet, I am unless at getting myself repositioned in a seat. I have extremely sensitive feet

94

without shoes. Even getting my bare feet to rest on any hard surface is nearly impossible.

I asked my wheelchair technician if the seat cushion could be rotated 180°. It was possible. It was rotated. With the seat opening reversed, I eliminated one of my legs falling into the opening, but the cushion remained uncomfortable and I felt very unsafe, even with the seatbelt secured. Every time I sat in my new shower chair, my body fought to get comfortable; my legs were extended most of the time because the seat, in its reversed position, didn't provide enough support in the correct places. After each shower, my thigh muscles, hips and knees were achy; sometimes my neck muscles ached due to leaning awkwardly. I knew if the seat cushion wasn't modified, I ran the risk of have chronic pain in the future.

This particular mobility equipment company has its own website. Most do. I jotted off a little message to this company to see if there might be an answer for my specific issue. The company responded a few days later. It seemed like I was the only person who had made a request for a better seat cushion. Of course—there's always one in the crowd. I seem to be it. It was the owner/designer who had responded to my inquiry. He mentioned that he was able to manufacture a custom seat cushion. *Fabulous! Now I just have to convince Medicaid that I really need a custom cushion.* I imagined it would take months for Medicaid to process it; I was prepared to wait. In the meantime, I spent a Saturday designing my own seat cushion from a layout of an elongated, standard toilet seat. What I needed most in this seat design was the uninterrupted seat opening to be larger so I could sink into the seat to feel secure. I also added one inch of surface to the front of the cushion to provide more support under my legs.

I was very pleased when the powers-that-be made a great push to get this custom cushion approved by Medicaid swiftly. I believe I received the cushion within six weeks. The end result paid off immensely—the custom cushion is PERFECTION! I sunk into this cushion, resulting in a relaxed lower body. I felt

100% safer. A seating modification can mean the difference of a piece of equipment not working efficiently to that same piece of equipment working very efficiently, ultimately saving money in the long run.

Correct seating positions are very critical for the activity of eating, especially with individuals with moderate to severe cerebral palsy. In my case, I always eat with my seat in an upright position. I find it extremely difficult to swallow solids and liquids if my seat is tilted back. Due to my Dysarthria, I don't have the muscle coordination to protect the contents of my mouth from leaking into my throat if I am tilted back. Seating positions are very important to all activities of daily living and beyond.

It was determined that I would be a good candidate for a motorized wheelchair at age eleven. The rehabilitation engineers mounted the joystick/control box on a platform at my chest level. I believe it was the consensus that I would have more control controlling the chair with my chin. Within one or two months of having my electric chair, the engineers relocated the joystick to my seat, level on my right side. The position of the joystick was very reminiscent of a stick shift position in a car. I had better posture and a better visual view of controlling my chair with my right hand. My level of precision increased. Having four years of experience driving two types of electric wheelchairs, driving up and down long ramps, driving through the woods and on unpaved roads, I learned a very important lesson—to actually look where I was going. Ah yes, I remember it well: I was driving through the gymnasium. With my full attention on what was going on in gym class to my left, it is my own conclusion that I rode up on a small, front wheel of an empty wheelchair with my back wheel, and tipped my entire wheelchair onto its side. My head hit the wooden floor and was out…cold. As luck would have it, I dressed as my favorite character of the day, "Ralph Hinkley" of *The Greatest American Hero* for Halloween

1982. When someone asked me how I got my black eye, I said I flew into a brick wall.

In the goals my physical therapists lined up for me, there was a bigger picture to consider, seat heights with wheelchairs and toilets. With every new power wheelchair I have gotten, the floor to seat height changes, sometimes dramatically. Twenty years ago, I had a power wheelchair where my feet could touch the floor. With my power wheelchair I have today, my feet are five inches off the ground. If I was capable of transferring myself, I would never have been able to get myself back into such a high wheelchair. I had trouble getting myself back in the wheelchair in 1985. In 1986, it was deemed I didn't need physical therapy anymore, and I would always need assistance transferring in and out of my wheelchair.

Occupational therapy, for me, was very sporadic. The main things I do recall were trying my patience with an automatic feeding machine and a sandwich holder. Now, these devices are well thought out and might be practical in some instances, but when you are living by yourself, and need help in all aspects of eating, these devices are unnecessary. I would need someone to put a sandwich in the sandwich holder. Sandwiches tend to fall over while positioned in the sandwich holder, creating great frustration. Even if the sandwich did miraculously stay together and stand up, one-third of the sandwich would in a position where I couldn't reach the rest of it. I would need someone to reposition it. By this time, the sandwich is all mangled and soggy. I say let's cut out the middleman, which would be the sandwich holder, and allow human hands hold the sandwich!

The same holds true for the automatic feeding machine. Using this machine is sort of like going fishing at a pond. Sometimes you get a bite, and sometimes you don't. It's a crapshoot. You activate the switch that brings the spoon down on the plate; the plate rotates. Will anything be on the spoon once it comes back up? One never knows. If you are lucky enough to have anything on the spoon on its return up, now you have to be so careful not to knock the food off the spoon before you get it into your mouth. This is where having athetoid cerebral palsy plays with your mind a bit, because you know if you hit the food off the spoon, it's back to square one. Your stomach rumbles with hunger. Forget the $5,000 diet machine, and allow humans feed me!

Luckily the occupational therapists saw that these devices were not appropriate for me and this pretty much ended my participation in occupational therapy.

In the autumn of 1978, I was reassigned to upper school, out of Lucille's classroom. Oddly enough, lower school was on the top floor, and upper school was on the middle and bottom floors. Instead of being in one classroom all day long, I changed classes and teachers throughout the day. I would have science, art and gym classes throughout different times of the week, along with physical and speech therapy. I believe I was the youngest student in upper school. For three periods a day, I was in my main classroom, where we studied reading, writing and arithmetic. Out of the five students in that class, two of were twelve and eleven.

Before I delve into this particular education phase, I would like to share with you my incredible friend, Paul James. He came to the residential school in March of 1978 from Bellows Falls, Vermont. He had Duchene's muscular dystrophy. I never really knew anyone with muscular dystrophy. Although he never really talked about it, he came to our school because he was being teased in his hometown school. Today, we refer to it as bullying. He also required physical therapy, and later on, respiratory care. Like myself, he was intelligent, and unlike me, he had perfect speech. Paul had a pear-shaped body. His trunk, head, neck, and arms all moved as one unit, almost like a Weeble-Wobble. His arms were locked in front of him as if he was a maître d' carrying cloth napkins over his forearms. His hands hung downward but given their lack of range of motion, he could use them very effectively. Paul had a little more range of motion in his hefty legs and had the ability to propel his wheelchair backwards and forwards when needed.

Paul had a round face but a good-looking kid with jet-black hair and frequently rosy cheeks. He had a heart of gold and a charm about him everybody loved. He was just 15 months older than I was but he seemed to have more wisdom than I. We became fast friends.

In this second year, my primary teacher was Ellen Grantiz. I think of all my primary teachers I had, I enjoyed Ellen the most because she challenged us to do our best. She also allowed us to learn as a class instead of separately. Ellen was in her mid 30's and was a pretty woman with long, dark, frizzy hair. Ellen was very Earthy; she would have been the type of person who would have built her house into the side of a hill. I was the only student in this group who had a speech impairment. Paul could understand me rather well by this point.

I was also enrolled in science class with Mike. Mike, with his average stature, wire-rimmed glasses and sparse hair atop of his head fit the profile of a science teacher. For as long as I have known Mike, he has had a heart of gold with a twinge of a silly, devilishness. He taught science and computer science for four years before he took a radically different promotion of being head coordinator of the dormitories. Like Ellen, Mike taught his students as a whole, rather than individually. The science room was controlled chaos, as I have witnessed other science rooms to be. A number of small aquarium tanks held fish, mice, baby chicks and rabbits. There was a small greenhouse attached on the side of the classroom for growing plants. Thankfully there weren't any rigor mortise cats staring back at you. We had regular science books we had to read along in class, as Mike explained the Earth's core, astronomy, anatomy and botany to us by drawing on the chalkboard.

Recalling one particular day, it might have been after school hours, I dropped by the science room. Mike was concerned over sick, white mouse he cradled in his hands. He asked me what he should do with it: should he euthanize it? I don't think I knew what that term meant but figured it out. I answered no. Mike explained that sometimes medicine couldn't heal all things. Sometimes the best thing to do for a sick animal is to stop its suffering. I watched Mike hold the mouse by its tail as he let it drown in a clear cylinder of water. It hardly fought. Mike asked if I was angry at his actions. I said no, I wasn't angry. A peacefulness settled in my heart.

I never was an avid reader as a child. I always I was bored with reading, but I believe it was the difficulties I had with trying to hold my head still and trying to get the book to lie flat. Books never lied flat; pages flipped where they wanted to flip. For this, I hated reading. The school had one electronic page turner that worked just about as well as the automatic feeding machine. Pages would get folded underneath the rollers very frequently. The machine was often in need of repair. We had those special tape players that played audiobooks. Ordering audiobooks was a long and arduous process. We weren't allowed to take tape players out of school. Finding time to listen to audiobooks during school hours was difficult. Given all that, I didn't read many books.

It would have been very different circumstances if we had today's technology back then. Today, we have tablets and e-readers. We have audiobooks available on CDs or on digital media that you can fit in your pocket. People can go on the Internet to do research. We can pull up YouTube and visually obtain knowledge on almost any subject. I'm wicked jealous! I had Texas Instruments Speak 'n Spell, Dataman, Little Professor and Spelling Bee.

The school obtained their first Apple II computers around

the beginning of 1979. I think the teachers were just as baffled by these crazy machines as I was. If we didn't have any of those 5.25" floppy disks around, these machines were essentially useless. Floppy disks were everything. Mike became our main computer instructor. We learned some of the basics of the programming language, BASIC. We learned the programming language of LOGO. We thought it was pretty cool how we could have the Apple ask us, "Shall we play a game?" totally *WarGames* style. "Thermonuclear War?" Oh yeah, Baby! It was the coolest thing to recreate that particular scene from the movie.

The other thing we did a lot on the Apples was to play games, especially when the entire school went through a 6-month asbestos removal period. Some of our favorite games were golf and another game where you have to go through different rooms, looking for items that will eventually let you leave the house...maybe. Who knew that playing that golf game would have tremendous value to me years later when I learned CAD (Computer-Aided Drafting). When I had to direct the golf ball in a certain direction, I had to judge what angle to hit the ball. Choosing angles were extremely beneficial even if it was just a game.

As time went on, I embraced using the Apple in all types of applications, from learning fractions to learning the elements on the periodic table, from writing to doing algebra. Some people might argue with this opinion but by the mid 80's, I was often placed in front of the computer for most of the class period. Teachers were confident that I would be able to learn by going through problems on the computer instead of instruction from them. It was unfortunate, and very sad that the majority of my classmates that were with me two years prior either left the residential school or succumbed to their disabilities. Teachers were busy tending to the students who needed more attention and assistance. All students had IEPs that teachers had to adhere to throughout the school year. I was that individual who made people struggle to determine where I exactly I fit it. I was that individual who was bound for college. I wasn't challenged

101

during my last three years until I was partially mainstreamed into the local high school.

Today we hear a lot about school budgets and how shortcomings of budgets are eroding the sports, music and art programs within schools. I must admit, I loved art class. I had the same art teacher for all of my eleven years, Mr. Bill Corwin. I am a very creative person. I might not have known it way back in 1977, but I know it today. Bill was a gentle-hearted person, but very humorous person. He liked to tell us funny stories about his mother-in-law.

It was 1981 when he stepped out of the box and experimented with some right brain exercises. Bill told us to choose specific area of the classroom and just draw what you see. Of course Paul already had drawing talents far beyond any of us. Here I was, with a blue marker taped to my headpointer. It was WYSIWYG for the brain. What you see is what you see on the paper. The results were extremely impressive for everyone. I had to fight to keep my lines as straight and accurate as possible. I was even surprised on how well I interpreted what my eyes saw. I loved this era of art class.

Through my art classes, I did paint many pictures. I loved to paint landscapes and cityscapes. I had to have at least one building in a painting. Unfortunately, painting or drawing straight lines wasn't my strong suit. Bill, the generous teacher he was, used to use masking tape to help me achieve that straight line I desired. I ask myself today, "Was that cheating?" Maybe it was cheating. The art bug never really bit me, but I have been visually creative over the past 30 years.

Bill introduced the first Mac computer into art class around 1985. Even before this time, I was very adept with writing BASIC code to draw graphics on the Apple II computers. If I looked at similar code today, I might not recognize it. I could not use the Mac to draw anything simply because the first

Macs were strictly operated with a mouse. I didn't have the fine motor skills to work a mouse with accuracy. I stuck with drawing with code. With the skills I learned from right brain art class, I recreated, using code, the Bruce pose from his *Born In The USA* and Journey's *Frontiers* album covers. Thanks Bill.

Besides Mr. Bill Corwin, Ms. Jean Polovchik has dedicated her career to teaching kids with special needs. Even if I wasn't in her science class every year, I saw her almost on a daily basis. She inherited the science room of chaos, and its chaos remained unchanged. She loved teaching back then, and still does. Jean is a very Earthy kind of woman with straight, light brown hair and wire-rimmed glasses. During my school days, she was soft-spoken but had a great laugh. Even though she was soft-spoken, she was determined to get every student to do his or her best. She never sugarcoated anything, but she had the heart of hearts. She tried to get me to embrace chemistry and the periodic table. I probably would have embraced it a little bit more if I knew that I had to take chemistry in college. Who knew?!

In 1984, Jean embarked on a slide show project with some of her science classes. The film's theme was to highlight the abundant strengths that women possessed, especially young women with disabilities. Jean's classes conceive different circumstances where we showed our independence. For example, April displayed her independence by using her mouthstick to press the elevator call button. My contribution to this very fun project was to put together the soundtrack to it. I had over 30 cassettes, ranging from Billy Joel, Quarterflash, Journey, Foreigner and so on. Everybody had their favorite cassettes and it was fun to pin down a specific person for a specific song I needed for the soundtrack. I cannot recall the entire soundtrack but one of the memorable songs we used was Cyndi Lauper's, "Girls Just Want To Have Fun". We dressed up a CPR doll as Cyndi Lauper as our stunt girl. Us girls had a whole bunch of fun. Everybody loved our slide show.

As I mentioned before, physical education was a constant in my curriculum, except for the last three years, when I was partially mainstreamed. Gym wasn't high on my list of favorite classes but it wasn't the worst either. In those years with Paul and Ken in the mix was the most fun of all. We always had the knack of convincing our very agreeable gym teacher, Mr. Shiavoni, we had to play football. Ken and Schiavoni, both ambulatory, used manual wheelchairs to level the playing field. Ken always chose Paul and me as his receivers. Since the receivers didn't have the ability to catch the Nerf football, the rule was the football had to hit the receivers in the front, above the knees to count as a completed pass. Receivers could also reach out their hand and touch the ball to count as a completion. To stop a run, the person with the ball had to be tagged with a hand or with any part of a wheelchair. Quarterbacks had to be seated at all times during play.

On occasion, we used to take on the teachers with exhibition football games. The games were always fun, especially when the teachers used to get a leg up by breaking a rule or two. Teachers would always try to stand up a little bit. Students would frequently win these scrimmages.

Before these football years, gym class consisted of tetherball, whiffle ball and getting on the trampoline. I never dared "W" sit on the trampoline because I would catapult off it. I stayed horizontal. I must say the trampoline was good cardio workout, for me at least.

I had to take health class around the age of 15. By this age, I had a pretty strong knowledge what was going on with my body and other bodies. I learned gradually about sex at relatively young age. I don't recall any "Wow" factor that rocked my world, just like I don't recall or wasn't surprised that Santa Claus didn't really exist. I just knew.

Paul was a good source of sex education when he arrived in 1978. While I watched him play Pong, he filled me in on a lot of things. He was a wealth of information. And then came Billy Joel's "My Life". People really sleep with each other, really? Who was I kidding? I knew people slept with other. In our young lives, Paul and I took on dating for a week. Since we possessed maturity and intuitiveness, rules, or so-called rules, were slackened, usually without letting the in-charge nurse know. I was allowed to go in his room, and he in mine, especially after school. Since he had more electronic gadgets, I usually went to his room. Paul only had one roommate; I had three, which would bring about gawking and envy. We had our weeklong courtship, both concluding we made better friends rather than a couple. We kissed better as friends; it felt more natural as friends, as crazy as that might sound.

One Friday afternoon, after getting home from school, Martha had me sat with her in one of the living room chairs. She started explaining about how girls start getting a period every month. *Uh oh, Martha was giving me "The Talk"*. I don't think Mom was prepared to give me this talk herself. I really didn't want to hear this, and all I wanted to do was get down and crawl away under the dining room table. Martha resisted my efforts to get away. She tried a new approach of asking me if I knew about this or that. I settled down and answered all of her inquiries, believing I answered yes to everything. She didn't expand the conversation with too much detail, and I didn't want too much detail. I didn't want to admit to knowing more detailed facts. Feeling I satisfactorily knew everything about the anticipated arrival of my so-called "friend", Martha let me go on my way to probably play Atari Pacman. On the morning of December 9, 1980, while everyone was mourning the tragic death of John Lennon, my "friend" had made its entrance. Of course I had to tell Paul.

"School's out for summer!" No it's not. Unfortunately the summer of 1978 was the only one we didn't have summer school. That was the summer I first slept in an actual tent in an actual sleeping bag. Camping is definitely overrated. That was the summer I saved my friend, Paul, from a giant ant sitting on his shoulder. Shoo bug! That was the summer I went to see a production of *Godspell*. I loved it!

What else can I say about summer school? It was hot. It was buggy. It included classes that I didn't particularly like attending, such as Greenhouse and Workshop. Even today, I am as dumb as a stump as I try to name plants or trees. I definitely don't have a green thumb. Ninety percent of the time, George, the horticulture teacher, taped a metal spoon on my headpointer and had me spoon dirt into little green pots. When class ended, my neck muscles were tight and sore. Greenhouse was more of a lighter mood atmosphere, but George still expected your work to be done. George was a typical farmer-looking man who always wore jeans, a plaid shirt, and a blue jean jacket.

Workshop was a neck bender class. And yes, it replicated a sheltered workshop atmosphere. God only knows why anyone was subjected to such a class. Workshop class paid students for piecework. I despised workshop class because it was so monotonous and painfully dull. If I knew who Andy Warhol was then, I would have sworn John, the workshop teacher, was Warhol's twin brother. Workshop class was an exercise in patience and next, muscle strength, as I sorted plastic or metal parts into different boxes. Very often I would looked at the minute hand, wishing I could magically speed up time. When the school bell rang, releasing me from piecework, it was like breathing in fresh air from paradise. I surely wouldn't have minded an extra electricity class with Phil Towle. He often chucked televisions twenty feet onto the concrete basement floor to demonstrate how cathode-ray tubes exploded. Now that was entertainment!

The only summer class I didn't hate, apart from our regular classes, was woodshop. I have always enjoyed creating and putting together many objects. Even though the teacher operated most of the tools, I enjoyed watching the process. I used some elbow grease to sand and stain some of my own projects.

My days at the residential school were full of diversity, especially when it came to education. I had many teachers; many came and went. I don't know why their stint was so short, but it created this atmosphere for me, which I didn't know how new teachers were going to teach. Were they going to stick me away in a corner where I would essentially teach myself through reading books or doing exercises on the computer, or would they give me some one-on-one time? For the last three years, like I mentioned before, I worked by myself, except when I was partially mainstream. Before Paul passed away in August of 1983, he was supposed to be partially mainstreamed, the first in the residential school's history.

As I briefly mentioned before, September of 1983 was a turning point for me—a chance to take on more responsibility for myself. I didn't want it. Paul just passed away; Ken and I were struggling to even just get along. I didn't think I had it me to take on anymore change. I also worried about how my relationship with Ken would change since we would be living the same unit. Temptations were around where they weren't before. This was real stuff, real life, and I didn't think I was prepared for it.

Summer vacation was over. My Dad and I stopped at Burger King before he brought me back to school. I was already feeling very anxious about going into a new unit and having some new people taking care of me. I was very anxious to see Ken; it had been three weeks since Paul's death; the mourning and tension were still present. I met Robert and Anne, my new counselors. Robert had been promoted to lead staff manager. Anne was a newbie right out of high school. She was a beautiful girl, with long blonde hair and a magnificent personality to turn anybody's gaze. Robert wasn't all that bad looking himself. He had a very attractive face with striking black hair. They could have been on the cover of Glamour as the next hot Hollywood leading couple. Too bad I had to vomit my Burger King lunch all over my bed sheets and bedroom floor on poor Anne. It definitely wasn't the first impression I wanted to give.

By the next morning I was feeling a lot better. The morning brought some familiar faces directly over from the children's ward, Patty and Sue, which brought me a tremendous amount of comfort. I roomed with Laura, from the young adult ward, who I knew fairly well. Other than the change in my living quarters, the other notable change was eating with all of the dormitory residents. These residents were mostly ambulatory but had moderate to severe behavioral disabilities. It was a common occurrence to see a student being escorted out of the cafeteria. After a while, you could sense who was about to lose control. There was a time-out room on the opposite side of my bedroom wall, where these students used to get out their aggressions. The time-out rooms were padded inside.

After this first school day was finished, I went over to see Debi on the children's ward, and with great determination and fervor, I said, "I'll be back," meaning there was an injustice done, and I wanted to return there. I continued my ranting for a few more days until my team got together for a quick meeting. I wasn't allowed to attend, which was quite understandable given my piss poor attitude. I waited outside, near the rear entrance of the main building. Leslie soon met me. Like always, in her non-confrontational personality, she gave it to me straight: I could either remain in the Transitional Unit, or, I could reside in young adult ward, with another roommate; I would not be going back to the children's ward.

In a moment, I had to make a decision. The sky was gloriously blue and the sun shined like a star. I chose to remain in Transitional. Leslie was thrilled. She would be working weekends in Transitional. I don't quite remember how the subject came up, but I vividly recall my wish to "be a rock star" and to write music. I don't know where the hell that came from, but it came. It was a moment of clarity I would never forget.

God only knew how I was going to compose music. I was filled with the most divine happiness I ever felt before. It might have been divine intervention by our Paul in Heaven.

In the weeks that followed, I settled in Transitional well. I also decided to go home every other weekend rather than every weekend. That didn't stop my laundry from going home every weekend. My Mom was very protective of my clothes being washed correctly and not with others. I used to send home brief, but cute notes with my laundry to make my parents laugh.

After my puking episode on my first night in Transitional, Anne and I forged a true friendship that has lasted to this day. I considered Anne to be one of the smartest, and enlightened individuals I have ever met. Even at 18, she was brilliant. Some high school graduates take a year off before heading college and backpack across Europe; Anne chose to work with some interesting teenagers. She was good for answering questions about all things having to do with love and relationships. She set up a sex Q&A session with an outside professional. I asked nothing out of pure shyness.

The school year of 1984 had begun. Anne left and started college, majoring in English. Robert also left the residential school. Janet, who had worked the weekends with Leslie all through the previous year, had been promoted to lead staff. This was also the time that Seashell and Maura joined the Transitional staff. Seashell and Maura, although different personalities, became a very dynamic twosome. Maura, fresh out of college, majoring in psychology, was led by Seashell, who had been working on the young adult ward for three years. The next four years would be the most submissive and self-contradictory years I have ever lived.

When I talk about being submissive, I am referring to my belief that everything Seashell told me or believed herself, was Gospel. I kind of relinquished my thoughts and opinions to her.

She was very critical of people; critical in the way they thought, critical in the way they looked and presented themselves, and critical in the way they had different ideas than her. It was very difficult to see this for myself when I was in that atmosphere, and it took me years to recognize how damaging it was. Seashell was very critical of me, although she never stopped me to do anything I wanted. Sometimes she was encouraging, sometimes too encouraging.

Maura was my anchor; she was my cornerstone when I questioned myself. She was my sounding board when I needed one. We had more in common, and times, I agreed with more of Maura's ideas. Seashell would have picked me apart if I didn't agree with anything she did. It was self-preservation since I considered her a very good friend.

Sometime in the beginning of 1985, someone, either it was Leslie, Mike or Janet, broached the possibility of me being mainstreamed into the local high school. Immediately, I agreed. I wanted the challenge; I also wanted to carry on Paul's torch, which he was not able to fulfill. I didn't have any fear of being placed in a setting, which I would probably be the only one in a wheelchair. I would stand out like a sore thumb. Bring it on!

Who knew that arranging the logistics of what seemingly was a simple idea would be so cumbersome. I was never part of the Warwick School Department, my residential school, and the high school discussions. All parties were very supportive but liability was the main hurdle. Who would be financially responsible if I got injured. I wouldn't have a classroom assistant but only the first week of every semester or school year. How would this young woman with overwhelming physical and speech limitations tackle being left in a high school environment? Well, you are not going to find out unless you give it a try.

I have to applaud the very strong efforts of Mr. David

Jenkins, who represented the high school in the negotiations for getting me into the high school. He was a brilliant advocate. On a side note, Mr. Jenkins was the second in line in the state, behind Christa McAuliffe, to board the 1986 Space Shuttle mission. Tragically, one of Challenger's booster rockets exploded a minute and a half into the flight, killing the entire crew.

The first semester, I took computer programming and western civilization. To get all parties acclimated to the new situation at high school, Maura accompanied me during the first week. My computer-programming teacher was Mr. Jenkins. Maura didn't think she would find herself back in high school; she felt out of place. I felt a bit out of place too, but I was also very excited to be there. Maura chuckled many times under her breath, laughing at silly, little things. I was very focused.

Forgive me, I cannot recall who taught western civilization, but this was the class I became friends with Julie Bovin and Brown Eyes. Once I was on my own, Julie was the one who helped me get to my classes. The school had three levels. To make these floors wheelchair accessible, they previously installed two wheelchair lifts. The first lift was a simple vertical lift. I drove across a metal span to enter an open lift, enclosed on all sides. The vertical drop was about six feet. The next lift was almost as scary as a carnival ride. Like those people who are baffled over the physics that keep planes and helicopters flying, I wondered how this platform wasn't going to break off due to the weight of my wheelchair and my body. It was a leap of faith to get on this platform. Its function was to take a person in a wheelchair down two flights of stairs, while ambulatory people navigated the same flights of stairs. Soon, everybody became adept to the wheelchair stair lift, but I still had pause every time I drove on the platform. Going up was more settling than going down.

For my communication needs, I had a Canon Electronic Digital typewriter. It was great because it ran on batteries. It had a digital readout; I typed my line of text in, and when ready, I printed it on the single sheet of paper.

This was the first time in my entire life that I had homework; honest-to-God real life homework! Given the structure and overwhelming demands put on parents or caregivers of kids with disabilities, the responsibility of assisting with homework at the residential school, along the physical care in the evenings, would have been much too stressful. The other issue was, especially at the residential school, if one child had homework and another child didn't have homework, then circumstances with what was fair and what wasn't fair would be a constant issue. Homework was eliminated. I understood my own circumstances as being privileged to have this opportunity to be mainstreamed. I wasn't jealous that I was the only one at the residential school that had to do homework.

I had an opportunity to work at a very small store at the residential school. I applied for the job and was hired. Andy put his engineering cap on and constructed a customized ramp for me to remove and place the paper currency to the cash register draw. I easily slid the paper currency up and down the small ramp, which came in contact with the register draw when it was out. This device is illustrated in my companion book, *Design Projects and Concepts: Architectural and Specialty Design Works to Promote the Independence for People with Disabilities*.

Andy also attached a coin dispenser in an upright position. On the individual coin levers, Andy attached metal extensions so I could easily press them with my headpointer. The store sold candy and school apparel. Unfortunately, the store had to be closed do to lack of business. I loved my time being a cashier. It taught me more responsibility. I also loved having a job where I had a purpose. Following the cashier's position, I was hired to create forms on the computer.

"We are the champions, my friends
And we'll keep on fighting 'til the end We are the champions
We are the champions
No time for losers
'Cause we are the champions...
Of the world"

"We Are The Champions"
Queen
News Of The World

I will digress a bit and talk about my experiences in sport competitions between 1979 and 1987. If anyone told me at the age of ten that I would be competing in sports meets, competing in wheelchair obstacle courses and distance throwing events, I would have looked at them with a skeptical eye. Although I enjoyed watching the Olympics at very young age, imitating Mark Spitz, as I swam across the living room floor, I never imagined being a competitor; I certainly didn't imagine representing the United States in the International Games for the Disabled in 1984.

The residential school had a very comprehensive recreational program. It ranged from doing arts and crafts to competing in competitive sports, organized by the United Cerebral Palsy Athletic Association, a.k.a. the CP Games. Of course, Paul got involved with regional meets early on. It took me a little more convincing to become involved. Paul had been goading me to join our sports team. I resisted. Paul wanted a reason. I remarked I didn't want to miss a weekend at home. He thought that was the lamest excuse ever. I watched many practices, and I must admit, I felt a little envious. Many times I would catch Jimmy doing laps around the gym, pushing his wheelchair backwards with his legs and feet. He was fast. I admired him. One day, Paul asked me again to join the team, the Eagles. I acquiesced, answering, "Oh, okay!"

Bob, the recreational director, reminded me of Liberty DeVitto, Billy Joel's long time drummer. Bob appeared older than his actual years. Never known to talk lengthy about himself, Bob was a quiet man but well liked by everyone. What I knew about this man, I had learned from others. Walking through the halls, you always saw Bob with a smile. He had a tall and slender stature, which complemented his quick stride. He wore khaki shorts, solid colored short-sleeve shirts and Dockers loafers, only wearing a suit when it was absolutely necessary. Bob's swift pace didn't intimidate anybody to stop him to ask a question or simply to chat. Bob loved his job and he tried to do the best for his students. He loved his Eagles sports team. In going to these regional and national CP Games, he had the responsibility of organizing all aspects of our trips. Having his LPN license brought on more responsibilities administrating medications to many of the students. He expected the best of his staff and athletes. Most of the time he got it. When somebody didn't live up to his dignified standards, on or off the field, you were kicked off the team. On one or two occasions, he had to accompany staff members to the emergency room for intoxication. That was never how he wanted to spend not even one minute of his time. Being off the school's property gave few the assumption they could stretch the rules a bit. Some knew how to do it, responsibly, and some just let lose without thinking what the consequences would be.

Lee, Bob's recreational assistant, was always at team practices. Barely in his late 20's, Lee had a head full of untamed hair. His eyeglasses looked very naturally on his attractive face. His sense of humor was as dry as the Mojave Desert but it fit perfectly with his easygoing personality. He didn't waste his words in idle chatter, for his animated facial expressions communicated for him. He had a great poker face and all loved him.

It was decided quickly that my events would be wheelchair slalom, wheelchair sprint, and wooden pin distance throw. The wooden pin looked like a very slim and short bowling pin. I would be classified as a Class 1 athlete. The United States Cerebral Palsy Athletic Association established a classification distinction based on degree of disability. They ran from Class 1 to Class 8.

The classification of all 8 classes are as follows:

Class 1: Severe involvement in all four limbs; limited trunk control; unable to grasp a softball; poor functional strength in upper extremities; often uses a power wheelchair for independence.

Class 2: Severe to moderate quadriplegic, normally able to propel a wheelchair very slowly with arms or by pushing with feet; poor functional strength and severe control problems in the upper extremities.

Class 3: Moderate quadriplegic, fair functional strength and moderate control problems in upper extremities and torso; uses wheelchair.
Class 4: Lower limbs have moderate to severe involvement; good functional strength and minimal control problem in upper extremities and torso; uses wheelchair.

Class 5: Good functional strength and minimal control problems in upper extremities; may walk with or without assistive devices for ambulatory support.

Class 6: Moderate to severe quadriplegic; ambulates without walking aids; less coordination; balance problems when running or throwing; has greater upper extremity involvement.

Class 7: Moderate to minimal hemiplegic; good functional ability in non-affected side; walks/runs with noted limp.

Class 8: Minimally affected; may have minimal coordination problems; able to run and jump freely; has good balance.

        My first regional New England sports meet took place in Springfield, Massachusetts, if my memory serves me correctly. Finding any records of these New England sports meets has been very difficult. Usually meets were in Massachusetts or Connecticut. I was used to getting up at 6 am Monday through Friday, but getting up before 5 am on a Saturday was tough to take. The excitement of this new experience tempered the early morning hour.

        I don't recall having my own personal coach at this first meet, although I know I was with Sheila most of the weekend.

We stayed at the once, Holiday Inn, in Downtown Springfield. It was the first time I discovered revolving restaurants atop of buildings. We went up there just to see it turning, and it turned very slowly. I wondered if it had a speed control, like a dimmer for a light, because I wanted to see what would happen if it sped up a little. Obviously, I wasn't going to ask anyone if I could speed it up; the idea just amused me.

Although I have no memory of what transpired on the field with my events, other than the revolving restaurant, the only other memory I have was taking my first sip of rum and Coke. It burned my throat going down. "Well, that wasn't enjoyable," and I didn't take another sip.

In 1981, many of our teammates qualified for the National CP Games, which were conveniently at the University of Rhode Island. Since I was close to home, I chose to commute back and forth to Kingston. Looking back, I probably missed out on the shenanigans that might have taken place on campus; I might have missed out on a lot of laughs, but I can't change history.

I remember one particular day, Peter drove me down to Kingston. Since our family didn't have an accessible van, the residential school transported my electric wheelchair. In those days, if a family owned an accessible van, it was looked upon as a luxury rather than a necessity. When I arrived on the Kingston campus, a coach always met me. They transferred me into my wheelchair and we would go where we needed to go. It was always a hurry up and wait game.

April had qualified for these national games, and once she met Peter, she was quite smitten with him. What female wouldn't be smitten with him? He was a handsome, young and strong Marine. Who doesn't like a strapping man in a uniform? Actually he wasn't in uniform, but he oozed Marine. April kept given me that look: *Please set me up with your brother. Does he have a girlfriend?* I don't think it mattered to her that Peter was nine years older. I believe he did have a girlfriend at this time. April's facial expressions were priceless.

It was also at these games that I, along with some of the coaches, discovered the art of using arm and leg restraints during competition. These restraints gave me more control over my body. I recall before a heat of a race I noticed my wheelchair was in the low speed position. With my right arm duct taped to the pole that held my control box, I couldn't reach it to flip it up. *Shit!* I spotted Lee not too far away. I drove to him and tried to explain what I needed with a quickness. He finally understood and flipped my speed switch to high. With the help of the duct tape, I didn't false start and finished well. I was kind of surprised that no other coaches issued a protest over the duct tape wrapped around my wrist. For all future competitions and practices, the powers that be made very stylish arm straps. The leg strap was just a basic, black, webbing Velcro strap.

Paul was the only one who qualified for the International Games For the Disabled in Denmark in 1982.

Fast forward to July of 1983. About twelve Eagles athletes qualified to go to the National CP Games in Dallas on the Texas Christian University campus, including Paul and me. Paul's health was extremely compromised due to the progression of his muscular dystrophy, but he was determined to go. In the prior nine months, Paul often missed school. He was closely monitored, receiving regular breathing treatments, because he had difficulties coughing. Ken and I saw him at least every week; we noticed his steady decline. Even when Paul knew what was coming, he was always positive.

Bob wanted Ken to come to be the team's general assistant. If any of the coach's needed anything, he was the one to call on. Of course I was thrilled he was asked to come along for my 16-year-old's selfish reasons. It would be my first plane ride ever, which was kind of ironic because my Dad worked for Eastern Airlines. Dad and I met up with the team at Boston's Logan International. The flight was departing around one o'clock. Before the flight, we all gathered in the terminal. We were like one, big, happy family, conversing and laughing, excited about our upcoming trip. Over the three years competing in regional meets, our staff and athletes became friendly with the families who came to cheer us on. Ken and Paul were close by. Paul's were eyes closed. He was awake, but weak. I presume few knew how weak he really was. Knowing my father was near, Paul tried to push his voice over the airport chatter to say hello. Paul's voice failed. I tapped my father on his arm to get his attention for Paul. My Dad bent to hear him. He asked how Dad was doing. Paul opened his eyes. That memory will stick with me for as long as I live. Even in weakness, Paul managed to say hello to my father.

It was my first time flying. I was excited. I sat by the window; Ken sat beside me and Patty, my coach, sat in the aisle seat. I knew Patty for two years by this time. She worked on the children's ward and always has been an extraordinary woman and friend. We were two very, Irish girls who loved to laugh. Patty was extremely responsible and had her eyes set on becoming a special education teacher. She has succeeded.

Across the aisle, Bob and Ron, Paul's coach, situated Paul in his seat. A stethoscope was draped around Bob's neck: an unusual sight. Seeing the stethoscope, it registered the severity of Paul's condition, although not sinking in completely. Ken probably came to the same conclusion.

The speed of going down the runway at 150 miles per hour was exhilarating and nerve-racking. Leaving the ground was mind-blowing. I enjoyed staring out, watching Boston become smaller and smaller. My ears popped. I settled down and took everything in.

I was struck by the flat, green checkerboard pattern on the Texas landscape as we landed in Dallas. I have never seen an airport on that tremendous scale. I was awe-struck by these enormous things. Once we found our way through the maze of airport corridors, we loaded onto buses that took us to Texas Christian University. Who would have known it would have taken us another hour to get to the University, in Dallas. We were from New England; if we drove an hour in any direction, we would certainly find ourselves in another town, most likely, in another state, or possibility in another country. Apparently, driving an hour in Dallas didn't guarantee you would leave the city.

After several hours of travel, silliness broke through the exhaustion. Lee got things rolling with ideas for new events. Distance drool toss was amongst the staff's favorites. The strongest, the most self-composed individuals, took their ribbing well and laughed along. Maybe we didn't know any better. We laughed a lot during those first few days.

The boys and girls athletes stayed in separate dorms on the TCU campus. Temporary ramps were erected to make the dorms wheelchair accessible. Some ramps were extremely steep, and even at age 16, I recognized that they were built incorrectly. I shared a room with Laura. Some people thought Laura and I were sisters, but we weren't. We just looked somewhat similar and we nearly had the same degree of cerebral palsy. We weren't close friends but we got along throughout the years at the residential school. Laura's coach was Seashell.

The majority of our staff members were in their twenties, but that didn't make them any less responsible for looking after a bunch of teenagers. Every staff member had his or her own athlete to tend to through the week. Each staff member was allowed one day off, and Seashell took care of me on Patty's day off.

I rarely saw Paul during that week in Texas. After competing in his events, he was taken back to the dorm so he could rest. I did get to see him on that Wednesday afternoon.

We were lined up in a hall, waiting for God knows what. Paul was on my left side; his eyes were closed. I sat quietly and looked at him for the longest time. I might have asked him how he was doing. He struggled to answer, so I didn't ask him any more questions—he needed all his energy for his soccer game later that night. I kissed his arm. Paul had the softest skin; his scent will never leave me. I looked up and saw Patty looking on, smiling.

Patty and I attempted to get into the gymnasium where they were playing the soccer game. Literally, people were spilling over out into the outer corridors to watch this particular soccer game. The crowd sounded like they were at a rock concert. The energy was incredible! We knew we weren't getting into the gymnasium. We found a space between people that we could see Paul playing defense. His eyes were open. This was his last event that week. He made it.

Thursday, August 4th, 1983: nothing seemed out of the ordinary. After breakfast, Bob called for a team meeting. I remember the day perfectly. The sky was as blue as blue can be. There wasn't a cloud in the sky. We gathered in a nearby A/V room. The room was the perfect size for our Eagles. Everyone found a spot. The quietness of the room shot directly to my stomach. Something wasn't right. I held my breath until Bob spoke. Bob's voice cracked as he told us the devastating news. Paul had passed away in his sleep earlier that morning. Ken was in front of me. Time stood still, as I saw it on the VCR. My mind raced. I didn't want to lose it in front of everyone, especially Ken, who was trying to hold himself together. I felt hands on my shoulders, but I didn't look up. People talked, but I didn't hear anything they were saying. Paul was gone. Paul was gone. I couldn't believe it—my best friend was gone. My eyes were glued to that damn VCR clock. Ken and I sat three feet apart, but we were miles away. I wanted to go put my arms around him, but I couldn't. The fear of being vulnerable with Ken scared the hell out of me.

Not long after, some of us started leaving. In our state of shock, none of us knew where we were going. Ken was walking ahead of me, in obvious grief. I dared to catch up to him. My eyes were only focused on him. The next thing I hear was, "Stop!" I obeyed. I looked back and saw Debbie, a different staff member, glaring at me. It seemed as though a van was getting ready to pull out from a driveway. I looked at the man on the passenger seat. He smiled at me, but I didn't feel much like smiling back. I stayed put as they drove onto to the street. I looked back at Debbie. She was wearing that same smug grin on her face that declared she was better than I was. She had little respect for me, but I was shattering. I looked ahead; Ken was too far. I chose to not defy Debbie and walked along with her. Not going after Ken remains to be the biggest regret of my life.

For our last 24 hours in Texas, we all stayed under the same roof, as we mourned Paul's passing. The dormitory lounge was sunken below the main floor level. A makeshift ramp gave people in wheelchairs access to the lounge. The ramp looked like it was at a 45-degree angle, and I wasn't about to descend it, even if I did have all the hands to help me down. I stayed on the main level, holding up the adjacent wall. I spent the day looking down into the lounge, looking at the sad and confused faces. I suspect I was wearing the same, sorrowful expression. Ken joined the crowd down in the lounge. It seemed he remained there to punish me. I deserved it. I'm not sure if I would have taken the opportunity to console Ken if it presented itself. I had fumbled the day already, and I feared his rejection if I made a last-ditch effort.

Our friend, Sue, made the long drive from Fort Sill in Oklahoma to visit us. Sue worked at the residential school for several months before joining the Army. What a day to visit; grief flowed through everyone's veins. It was good to see Sue. She helped to pass the time on that excruciatingly long day.

The day had exhausted us all. While Patty finished changing me for bed, Ken was outside the door. Patty invited

122

him in. Wearing a T-shirt and underwear, I tried to act modest, but Patty didn't buy it. I gave up the act. Ken explained that he had been out walking the bleachers with Leslie. Ken narrated her story. Leslie stayed in Paul's room on the previous night. Unable to lie down in a regular bed, he had to sleep in his wheelchair so his lungs wouldn't fill with fluid. He had been sleeping in his chair for a period of time. Early that very morning, Paul awoke asking for drink. Leslie gave him some water. Then, I pictured her, in her great spirit and her great energy, giving him the water. Once he drank enough, she probably gave him a solid kiss on the forehead and offered anything that she could give him. Paul didn't ask for anything more. As Leslie drifted back to sleep, Paul's soul drifted up to Heaven. That was always how I understood and liked to imagine it. Bob visited Paul about a half hour later and discovered him slumped forward. Bob knew Paul was gone. He allowed Leslie to sleep a few minutes longer.

What turned out to be a long day, turned out to be an even longer night. Death happened a couple rooms down the hall—it could come again, in my mind, at least. That night, I truly believe I was the next to go. What 16-year-old's brain is rational after losing a best friend? Mine certainly wasn't. I feared death. I didn't want to die. Where would I go? At 16, I pushed away spirituality. It wasn't that I didn't believe in God. Religion was pushed in my face throughout my young life and I pushed it back. I wasn't angry with God for taking Paul. I knew he was sick. It was just that I wanted to see more of my life. Not many 16-year-old kids have the wisdom of adults. If I had that wisdom, I would have realized that nothing was wrong with me physically to cause me do die that night. I was as fit as I could be for a person in a wheelchair. If I looked past my nose, I would have noticed all the older people with cerebral palsy at the games. If there isn't some other underlying cause, cerebral palsy won't kill you. I wish that particular fact had hit me straight in the head that night. Instead, it waited until the next day. I don't know how much sleep I got that night but it wasn't enough.

Everyone was ready to leave Texas on Friday. It was my mother's birthday and home was the only place I wanted to be. In the airport, I watched Ken becoming too chummy with Bridget, another staff member I knew well. My last nerve was frayed. At the time, I didn't think I deserved his cold shoulder, but as the years past, I began to see the situation for what it was worth. I was being a selfish, little bitch who didn't deserve Ken. On the plane, my attitude didn't change; it only became worse as we got closer to Boston. We landed. Waiting at the terminal, my frustration still lingered. I surmised that moving myself over to the aisle seat would release some energy. Ken remained in the aisle seat as I tried to push him out of it. He pushed back. We were at the end of our proverbial ropes with each other.

As we entered the terminal, we weren't expecting the onslaught of news cameras and bright lights in our faces. Paul's death was one of the top stories of the day. Nobody had smiles on their faces or wanted to tell their stories. Once I saw my father, we got my bags and went home. Of course there was small talk, but we all wanted to leave this place.

Our ride home to Rhode Island was quiet. Nothing else could be said. I chose not to attend Paul's memorial service the next day in Bellows Falls; I knew I couldn't handle it. Voices in my head ridiculed me for being such a coward and for taking the easy road yet again. My mother was excited to have me home, although I continued to be solemn. I thought I would have a reprieve on Paul's death at home, but it became a national news story for Dan Rather and Tom Brokaw to report. I lied at the side of the couch wishing the nightmare would stop. I slept well that night in my exhaustion.

Later in the Fall of 1983, I learned I had qualified for the International Games for the Disabled. Paul had qualified also. I considered it to be a bittersweet achievement. I was proud but also humbled. The games would be on home soil, in Hempstead,

New York. It was an exciting opportunity, although I was going alone.

Practice began immediately. I had eight months to prepare. I settled in and everything became routine again. Leslie became my coach; she practiced with me twice a week. When we practiced, Leslie expected 110% from me. We talked about Paul. Leslie would look upward, always knowing that he was looking down on us. I continue to believe it to this day. An indisputable person was missing from our lives.

With the games getting closer, I felt apprehensive about the three weeks I would be alone. I kept this feeling of uncertainty to myself, especially away from my parents. They were already anxious about letting me go alone. Mom had several telephone conversations with Carol, the director of the United Cerebral Palsy National Team. I was totally dependent on others to shower, dress and to feed me in my daily existence. Going into a situation where the people didn't know you was a little daunting. Being speech impaired didn't help matters. In their conversations, Mom felt confident that I would be taken care of properly. I held that confidence watching my mother pack my bags for the trip.

Departure day: June tenth. Instead of catching a bus ride back to school this Sunday, my father drove me to Plainfield, Connecticut to meet Bob. I still carried apprehension in my gut. "Chill out," I told myself. Bob was driving one of the school's station wagons; in the rear of it, my electric wheelchair, in 1001 parts. I knew it would be silly to worry about Bob's ability to reassemble my wheelchair but a little part of me did worry. In reality, Bob had adequate knowledge about wheelchairs.

With the station wagon packed, Dad carried me to the station wagon's passenger seat. After he belted me in, my father kissed me goodbye more than once. He reiterated his plans to come see me in two weeks. Two weeks seemed like years away. With one more kiss, Bob and I were headed to New York.

We arrived at West Point Military Academy where the U.S. Team would practice for individual and team events. I didn't see much of the campus that night, but while Bob reassembled my wheelchair, I stared at this massive stone building and knew I was somewhere where I never expected to be. The building reminded me of buildings that surrounded the ACI in Cranston, Rhode Island. "All the bad, bad people are in there," my father always said. Looking up at this menacing building, one starts to speculate what you will encounter inside. This wasn't a Holiday Inn.

Bob fidgeted with my joystick control; my wheelchair moved back and forth—a sigh of relief. Our next task would be to find out where I was bunking. We found other team members outside of two different buildings. We were directed into the correct dormitory. Inside, the long corridor led to a number of rooms along either side. Voices could be heard. Bob made the announcement that I arrived—ready for duty. The rooms were plain and empty, except for beds and bureaus. This was definitely not a Holiday Inn—no televisions or radios in sight. Maybe I was enlisting in boot camp. Bob helped me become acquainted with Mary Ellen and Claudine, the two coaches who would be looking after me for the three weeks. With that done, Bob set off to find his own bunk. I was left to my own devices, if I ever did have my own devices.

On that first night, we settled in. The pale yellow paint on the walls did nothing for my colorless disposition. I missed my Rick Springfield and Duran Duran posters. I had no typewriter to occupy my spare time. Back then, writing was something I had to do for school. All that I had with me was my cassette Walkman knockoff and a few cassettes. Reality set in that my ordinary was far away.

Once everyone had a light dinner, athletes and coaches settled in for the night. Three or four athletes occupied each room. There were two other athletes in my room. I was the only individual who was unable to care for myself in any way; I was the only individual who could not verbalize clearly to be understood. My dependency surprised Mary Ellen and Claudine. As soon as they settled me into my bunk, my ears began burning from what they were saying about me behind closed doors.

The 6 AM bugle call surprised us all; I was definitely in boot camp. I suspected to find someone standing over my bed, holding a razor, ready to shave me bald. Thank God there was no one in sight carrying an electric razor. As I awoke from a very broken sleep, I watched my two bunkmates extract themselves out of bed. They weren't interested in talking to me; they formed an instant friendship. Soon, Claudine came to get me out of bed. Claudine was a mild-mannered woman who I came to respect and like. We got along admirably. Once I was washed and dressed, it was off to the mess hall for breakfast. The brilliant sunlight exposed all the massive stone buildings. I was struck by the tremendous strength of these buildings.

One felt two feet tall walking into the mess hall; the trusses reached up to Heaven. Inside was dark and immense. Lines of wooden tables went on into the shadows. Sunlight radiated through the tall and narrow stained-glass windows. *Now here is something to look at.* Once I tore my eyes away from the majestic interior, I noted our U.S. Team took up about one-fourth of the space.

I remained quiet, observing. If I did have something to say—a slim chance—who would understand me? My mind drifted elsewhere. If I was in northern New England, I would have been getting up for school. I looked at my watch— breakfast was being prepared. Being Monday, the kitchen staff cooked eggs. Talk around the breakfast table would have been harebrained—not a stretch for teenagers. I looked up from my cereal bowl and found I was face to face with a stranger; someone I met fourteen hours ago was feeding me. I remained the odd man out.

Carol, with her vibrant personality, spoke about the day's activities. I listened while I took in everything and everyone. I recognized Ted Judge, an athlete from Boston's North Shore. Teddy had a reputation for his turbocharged electric wheelchair. I hadn't realized Teddy qualified for the U.S. Team. I witnessed several of Bob's past protests on behalf our male wheelchair athletes who had to compete against Teddy's wheelchair. Protests were unsuccessful; judges were unable to prove that Teddy's wheelchair had been "tweaked". The fact that Teddy's wheelchair cruised at fifteen miles an hour and the rest of the power wheelchairs topped off at four miles an hour wasn't proof enough. Give me a break! Not even the most skillful could beat Teddy's turbo rocket. Knowing Teddy had qualified for the Internationals didn't warm my heart.

On this first day I spent following the crowd. How was I going to survive the next three weeks? Whenever I saw a clock, I would imagine what I'd be doing at school. I wondered if my friends missed me as much as I missed them. Concentrating on anything was futile; I wanted to return to my comfortable life.

Before turning in that night, I had a conversation with Mary Ellen. We learned that the other knew Paul. Mary Ellen came to know him during the Internationals in Denmark. The biggest smile appeared on my face. She told me her impressions of Paul. Everyone had the same impressions: smart, witty and a true friend. Needing to be somewhere else, she didn't sit and listen to my memories of Paul. I could have gone on for hours. Mary Ellen never discovered how much Paul meant to me.

That damn bugle—again it marked 0600. At school, I would have gotten another hour's sleep; at home—another four. Sleep, like my life, was two hundred miles away no matter how I cut it. Up and dressed, I found myself in the mess hall with the sunlight coming through the stained-glass windows at exactly the same angle. Everyone wore the same clothes as they sat in the same places. It was déjà vu. My silence continued. I looked around to see if anything changed, but nothing changed. When breakfast ended, a change hit me. Staring me down were four hours of unoccupied time. What the hell was I going to do for four hours? I cringed.

I followed the masses until they all dispersed into different directions, leaving me to do whatever I wanted. I turned in every direction under the brilliant sun. Going back into the barracks to stare at the walls was idiotic. I remained outside where I could watch different things. I found shade. I observed others in my solitude. Other athletes brought books, radios or portable televisions to pass the time. I would have killed for a book, although setting me up to read a book was like planning a tactical maneuver on the shores of Normandy. Watching television morning wasn't thrilling. Sitting and doing nothing was maddening. Thankfully there wasn't a clock in sight—I would have watched the seconds tick by.

Buildings were before me; I needed to go discover them. Would someone misunderstand my intentions and think I was trying to escape? I remained in sight as I wandered. If I landed in a ditch, someone would find me as they walked to lunch. Fearing to be reported AWOL, I returned to my shaded area for one. I felt worthless. The mind weakens when it doesn't have anything meaningful to do. I didn't belong here; I didn't deserve this extraordinary opportunity. I believed it to be true. Absurdly, I thought leaving was the solution. Paul entered my head, envisioned him before me, lecturing me to suck it up. If I went home, I would let myself down, and letting down all the people who got me here. I would be letting Paul down. Tears fell from my eyes. Brief as my tears were, they changed my attitude.

People started returning for lunch. I looked forward to practicing with the soccer team later. A woman caught me off guard. She was another U.S. Team coach. She insisted I follow her to lunch. Surprised by her insistence, I tried to explain that I was waiting for Claudine. She couldn't understand me. Her impatience and rudeness were weighing on my nerves. I wasn't going to follow her, especially when she didn't tell me her name or give a reason why. I might have considered going if she told me that Claudine or Mary Ellen requested it. I envisioned she would put my lunch in front of me and wonder why I wasn't eating; I needed to be fed. Finished with being civil, I refused to go. I disliked the crass woman. My refusal backed her away.

The unpleasant woman was gone. A trace of guilt seeped into my skin when I considered I might have handled the situation better. I had a tendency to second-guess myself. My guilt didn't run too deep given the woman's disrespect. Strangely, I felt vindicated, after the morning I endured. Claudine arrived and we walked to the mess hall. I suspected Claudine to ask me why I hadn't gone to lunch with the nameless woman, but Claudine didn't have an inkling of what transpired. I glanced the tables, making sure that we didn't sit eye-to-eye with Witchy Poo; I feared she would put a hex on me. We never crossed paths again.

Practice for the wheelchair soccer team was Tuesday afternoon and I was asked to attend. Whether fate or some other divine plan, I was selected to be Paul's replacement on the team. Big shoes to fill? Definitely. I hadn't played a game in a year and a half, so I was going in there with rusty wheels. Excited and humbled, I knew I could play the position well. Mary Ellen's husband, Jeff, was the soccer coach. Jeff, a no nonsense kind of guy, expected the best out of his players. It seemed evident that he knew some of the players well. Here I was, feeling like I came directly from the street to join the team. Being Paul's replacement was my only concern. Jeff worked his players into their positions. When it was my turn to scramble, I looked Jeff directly in the eyes so he would confirm that I understood his commands. I played my best. After practice I realized I hadn't looked the clock. My head was back in the game and I didn't want to leave.

My mindset dramatically changed within six hours—dark turning into light. Standing in for Paul finally set in. I could never substitute as Paul: I had to play my position well. The last time many of us saw Paul was on that Wednesday night in Dallas when he played soccer. This memory will remain with me for my entire life.

Day three at West Point—the bugle sounded again at six, but I chuckled. I looked forward to practicing for my beanbag distance throw event. Rather than looking at my wilted Corn Flakes wallowing in milk, I engaged my eyes to the people around me—a smile blasted through. My silence continued but my head wasn't a million of miles away. Carol conducted another meeting. Emphasizing that we were all here for a purpose, Carol spoke from the heart. She constantly received questions about curfews and drinking alcohol. I didn't come to the games to drink.

The beanbag distance throw may not sound like a serious event compared to events like running or swimming, but to a Class 1 competitor, it was a serious event.

Claudine and I went to beanbag throw practice. Very few athletes practiced for this event. I noticed the beanbag—leathery and empty. As Claudine positioned it correctly between my fingers, I stared at it, holding back my laughter. *You've got to be kidding?!* It wasn't leather—it was fake leather and didn't hold enough beans to feed a bean sprout. All the other beanbags were made from cloth and had weight to them. As I geared up to throw the faux-leathery bag, someone mentioned that this was the regulation beanbag. *Oh great.* Once the beanbag left my fingers, it traveled about four feet, thankfully in the right direction. I looked at the lonely, orange bean bag lying in the grass and raised my eyebrows over the short distance it had gone—far from the fifteen to twenty feet I usually pitched it. I let the other athletes take a shot. I continued to throw the farthest through the afternoon rounds. This fact didn't bring me comfort—I was unaware of what my competition would be from other countries.

The week of practice drew to a close. I still hadn't found any pals, but my spirits were high. It was planned for the U.S. Team to take a boat ride on the Hudson River. Being in New York and being such a fan of Billy Joel's, one might presume I would bring two or three Joel cassettes. I don't recall bringing any, for I was still infatuated with Duran Duran. In March, I saw them at the Worcester Centrum; four months passed and I was still pumped up by the concert. In those days, I lived and breathed Duran Duran. It had been days since I listened to one ounce of music; I needed it like flowers needed water. Music was my daily drug and I was in a severe drought.

On the boat, I saw Bob after not seeing him for days. Dinner consisted of boxed lunches, but what did we care—it was a beautiful night. After we ate, Bob offered to get my cassette player out. *Yes, music!* I was in my glory as I listened to Simon and the boys. It was more than glorious—it was mind-blowing how pumped I became being in my rock and roll world again. I was Simon Le Bon and I sang every song on two cassettes. I released so much energy; I lived to be on stage. I just wanted to sing. The hum of the motors drowned me out for the sake of others on the boat. I was euphoric.

Saturday, we left West Point on Coach Buses and trucks. I sat contentedly in an oversized passenger seat. My stay on the bus was extended because my power wheelchair needed to be loaded onto the truck. Overcast skies didn't hamper our views of the Manhattan skyline. My first trip to New York was about a year away, but I already fallen in love with the city. I never gave it much thought as to when or how New York City got into my blood. My lust for Duran Duran took a back seat to my love for Billy Joel. His music lives and breathes New York City—it is inescapable not to love the city as you love Joel's music. *52nd Street* is a New York album from the first note to the last. You can feel every inch of the city—the tastes of wines to the million of lights turning on at dusk—all of it is New York. *52nd Street* remains to be my favorite Joel album. I envisioned being dropped of at Grand Central and devouring the city. I only wanted an hour, an hour to soak in the people and the atmosphere. I never feared the city and knew someday I would get there.

We arrived at Hofstra University in the late afternoon. I waited on the bus until my wheelchair was extricated off the equipment truck. I liked the quietness. Back in my wheelchair, I followed others into Hofstra's Recreational Center where we spent a lifetime waiting to register. I tired quickly from sitting in one spot. Carol and the others walked between different rooms as they tried to speed up the process. I had a notion, true or not, that Carol kept a close eye on me. It was something that my mother would ask her to do during their telephone conversations.

The U.S. Team was housed in one of the high-rise residences: Constitution Hall. As luck would have it, I was assigned to the thirteenth floor. *How did I get so lucky?* In the Constitution elevator, "12B" technically was the thirteenth floor. Never being overly superstitious, I didn't fear the thirteenth floor. A single room! Yes! No more bugles at dawn. Oh sleep, glorious sleep!

Once everyone got settled, we headed to the cafeteria. Carol handed out ID tags to all the athletes and coaches. Without ID tags, you couldn't enter the cafeteria and a few other places around campus. Security was the utmost concern. I, being 17, never gave my safety a second or even a first thought. Terrorists were overseas. We were 17 years away from September 11th. To me, I had an ID tag so I could eat.

Claudine and I were in a new land. There were colors everywhere: red, green, yellow, blue, orange, white and gold to name several. They represented people of the world. 1,800 athletes represented 45 countries. Russia and other communist countries boycotted these games, as they did at the Olympics in Los Angeles. All I knew was that the Soviets wanted to bomb the United States the first chance they got. The 1980 U.S. Hockey Team's victory over Russia still resonated in all of us. I always imagined Reagan and Chernenko sleeping an arm's length away from that red button. The motion picture, *WarGames*, and the television show, *The Greatest American Hero* represented the touchy issues of nuclear war on a slightly askew level of fiction. I was entertained. I had no ill will towards Russians.

The few pins I collected in New York still adorn my 1984 Olympic cap. A kind man approached Claudine and me from Japan. He didn't speak any English; he wanted to trade pins. It is my favorite pin, depicting Mount Fuji—its summit covered by snow with the red, Japanese sun suspended beside it. We thanked each other for the exchange. As Claudine and I continued on, people talking in their native tongue surrounded us. It was wondrous to listen to even if we didn't understand a word.

I realized I made it through a week when I awoke Sunday. Two weeks left to go. Everyone needed to be ready by noon for Opening Ceremonies that afternoon. I knew this day was coming, the first day of two, which I had to wear a skirt. This was an excruciating thought; I had to grin and bite the proverbial bullet. Wearing a skirt was annoying; I couldn't remember the last time I wore a something girlish.

Opening Ceremonies were set to take place in Mitchell Park, north of Hofstra University. Organizers set up large, circus-like tents adjacent to the park to protect us from the elements. With the United States being the host country, we were the last in the procession and the first country under the tents. The day was partly sunny with temperatures in the seventies. Talk about people watching: I did plenty of that. My mind started to wander. I began scanning the crowd for cross-sections of the male persuasion. I couldn't help it—I was 17 and bored. Who was I kidding? I was as shy as a muskrat. Chances were that I wasn't going to talk to anyone. I speculated. I should have found a nice Italian boy. We could have shared a plate of ravioli and been happy with that. A nice, young Italian chap— just what I needed.

Playing matchmaker, matchmaker with myself soon got old. Patiently we sat. By this time, they kept telling us that it wouldn't be too much longer every fifteen minutes. I wanted to move. I felt a tap on my shoulder. It was strange—I didn't know anybody. Leslie and Lee arrived. My boredom turned into elation. Leslie, giving me a big bear hug, spoke about how my friends were rooting me on at school. I gave Lee a high-five. Both came to officiate some events. While Leslie caught me up on mountain news, Lee took everything in. Lee was our soccer coach for the short time our school had a team. His most endearing quality was how he spoke about his wife and ever-growing family. Whatever came his way, he appreciated to the nth degree.

Leslie and Lee set out to find a seat on the bleachers. The U.S. Team got into formation. I was positioned on the outer right side towards the rear. Cheers rang out—it was our time to shine. People in the stands wore gigantic smiles as they waved. We moved into position to complete the enormous rectangle of forty-five countries in the center of the track. Speeches were given in the true spirit of the games. Words emphasized ideals such as perseverance, determination and pride for one's own country. Marine One appeared in the sky, touching down in a secluded area. Ronald Reagan was campaigning for another four years; his visit to the International Games brought us national attention. I was too far out to get a good look at the man, but with interest and inspiration, I listened to the President speak in his captivating voice. Reagan spoke about determination. He was proud the United States was hosting such an important event. Reagan officially declared the beginning of the International Games open. The torch was lit. Reagan returned to Marine One and it disappeared in the sky.

After a night of mingling and celebrating, it was back to finding something to occupy my time. My first solo event wasn't until the following Saturday. Besides soccer practice and soccer games, I had a lot of down time. Jeff wanted us well tuned for our first game.

My little slice of Heaven on the thirteenth floor was sanctuary for sleeping. I tagged along with Claudine when it was convenient. Sometimes I would hang out in Constitution Hall's lobby. One afternoon, I must have seemed like wanderer having no direction because someone began talking to me. Unsure if this young man would understand me, I hesitated, only to realize that he was in the same situation. I welcomed the company. He played on the soccer team. His name was Tom. Tom talked slightly better than me. He asked where I lived. It was a simple question; I had two viable answers. Should I answer New Hampshire, which technically was the correct answer, or was I a true Rhode Islander? The prospect of explaining all this to Tom was tiring. I opted for New Hampshire; Tom had a better chance of understanding it. He was from Colorado. This was the first ten-minute conversation I had with anyone in eight days— thrilling to say the least. Tom had cerebral palsy also and looked close to thirty. He used his feet to propel his wheelchair; his arms were constricted. Tom's friend, René, joined us. He was a crucial offensive soccer player due to his upper body strength and coordination. Appearing to be a few years older than I, René had Latino blood and a charming personality. He was from Miami. René was the kind of guy to have all those pretty Miami Babes hanging over him. Even though we talked for a short time, it was Tom and René I most remember from New York.

With one win under our belt, our U.S. Soccer Team gained confidence that carried us through the next game. My playing time was limited to a few minutes every game, unless we had a big lead. I was classified a second stringer. I didn't care.

It was the eve of the last week of the games. Though I was enjoying my time, I missed my family and my friends. I was a few hours away from wheelchair slalom, deemed my best event. The pressure was great but I loved this event. Butterflies would be with me most of the day. My cheering squad would be arriving from Rhode Island. Ah—to see familiar faces again.

Claudine and I arrived at the site well before wheelchair slalom was set to begin. I saw Lee was running the show. Ah— another familiar face. I had no delusions that Lee was going to put in a good word in for me with the judges. Cheating wasn't my or Lee's style. He was as straight as they come. Other than a few friendly smiles, we kept it as business as usual.

I had time to study the course. The key element was the meter reverse box: a square meter box marked by tape on the floor. At each of the four corners sat a small orange cone with a small flag. The flag aided judges to view if competitors struck a cone. The wheelchair competitor had to enter the box in a forward motion, on the side designated the entrance. Once inside the box, the competitor was required to make an 180° turn without hitting a cone or crossing a line. With the 180° turn complete, the competitor was required to exit the box in reverse to continue onto the next obstacle. There were three-meter reverse boxes.

In slalom, it was a one-second penalty every time a competitor hit a cone or crossed a line. One approach was to painstakingly avoid committing any penalties. The other approach, which I referred to as the "Teddy Judge Approach", was to blast through the course like a rocket, committing numerous one-second penalties. All of those one-second penalties added up at the end. I took the middle-of-the-road approach, trying to limit penalties but using speed to pull myself out of a jam.

The figure eight was next. Arrows on the floor indicated which side of the figure eight to enter. A competitor had to make a complete figure eight before moving on. The third meter reverse box followed. The last obstacle was the 90°-angled wooden ramp. A competitor was required to ascend a short ramp leading to a meter square platform five inches in height. The competitor turned 90° and descended another short ramp. A fifteen-meter straight run led to the finish line. This was all the practical use I had with the metric system. A meter here, 39.37 inches there—it's all the same.

At last, my Rhode Island crew arrived. They included my Dad, Martha, Glenn, Paul and his girlfriend, Kris. Hugs and kisses for everyone! Knowing I was in good hands, Claudine left. We huddled on the bench. The most exciting news that I could offer my family was that I saw Reagan and my room was on the thirteenth floor. Glenn was the first person I knew who owned a videotape recorder. Back then, recorders were hefty in size. I guess bringing the recorder was worth it if I was to capture gold. What if I made a dreadful mistake on the slalom course? No retakes here, Honey! I had one shot at it.

We were a quiet group. They tried to keep me loose. We scrutinized the challengers. The size of the European wheelchairs struck me head on. Holy crap! European wheelchairs were compact. My Sherman tank could crush a European wheelchair like an ant. This difference between wheelchair sizes brought me down a notch. Surely I would buy a European wheelchair if they were available. No such luck, baby. Talk about being easy to transport: these chairs could fit into the front of a VW Beetle. I really wanted one. I had to do damage with my Sherman tank.

All the competitors were given a trial run through the course. Lee called out my name and I positioned myself at the starting line. I was anxious to get it over and done; it showed all over my body. Lee informed me I could start when ready. I breathed. I took off to my first meter reverse box. I got the feel of the course; I didn't worry so much about speed. I didn't want to make mistakes later. Coming down the wooden ramp, I sped to the finish line. The hours that I played Pac Man weren't all in vain.

We were totally engrossed in watching my opponents. I heard a familiar voice; Leslie arrived. She greeted my family with her gracious personality. Leslie and my father embarked in their own conversation. Australia and Ireland had the most talent. My gung ho attitude for conquering Australia differed from my attitude toward the Ireland woman. I couldn't allow myself to root against Ireland. This woman representing Ireland might have been a distant relative for all I knew. Secretly, I wished her luck.

Leslie knew how to pump me up with saying the right words. My cheering squad sang my praises. The butterflies in my stomach would be silenced in about four minutes. Lee announced my name first again. How did I get so lucky? All eyes would be upon me, judging my every turn. I had put all the pressure on my shoulders. I was squirming like a fish out of water. Inside the course, I would settle into a zone. It seemed like years before Lee declared I could begin. I started my attack. Penalty judges swarmed around me like mosquitoes on the hunt for blood; I closed my mind off to them. I headed for my second meter reverse box and completed it. The figure eight cones were ahead. I went in and out of the cones so tightly my tires squeaked on the floor. Coming around the last cone in the series, my sneaker grazed the top of the cone. It was a one-second penalty; it was a stupid one-second penalty that I almost never commit. I prided myself on the figure eights. The penalty continued to rattle me. It rattled me for too long; I had to let it go. I went on to the third meter reverse box and to the wooden ramp leaving the penalty behind. Crossing the finish line, the figure eight penalty bugged me again; I cringed. Everyone congratulated me. The butterflies were gone.

Without a stopwatch, I wasn't able to judge the speed and accuracy of my challengers. I sweated it out. This was my country, practically my own backyard—I wanted to win. Slalom was over and I was nervous again. Just tell me. Finally, Lee approached our Little Rhody group and informed us I captured first place. Relief, beautiful relief!

The men's competition was next. Okay, here we go! I gave Dad and Paul the lowdown about Teddy. Remaining to my

guns, I thought Teddy should be disqualified. If I competed
against him, I would have protested until I was blue in the face.

Teddy used speed to conquer the course rather than
strategy. His speed wasn't working for him; he had no control
over his wheelchair. Chills traveled down my spine. Speed
wouldn't seal a gold. Whoever tweaked his chair this time
tweaked it a little too much. G-forces paired with having
cerebral palsy were a terrible combination. As Teddy
approached the wooden ramp, I wanted to look away, but
suspecting to see a wreck on the highway, I watched. Teddy
nearly drove off the platform, unable to make the 90° turn. The
penalty judges prevented Teddy from rolling over. He crossed
the finish line at warp speed, nearly crashing into the concrete
block wall. "Please!" exclaiming in my head. "Somebody has to
issue a protest before he kills himself or another person." No
opposing country issued a protest because Teddy didn't place to
receive any medal. Speed wasn't all it was cracked up to be.

Time came for the winners to receive medals. Organizers
and volunteers set up a podium in the far corner of the
gymnasium. Looking at the podium, I couldn't believe my eyes:
the middle tier of the podium was a foot high. *Would I have to
drive up there? You bet. Dear God. All right, I can do this.
Our National Anthem is short—I can do this.* A young man
helped me drive up the 45° ramp and onto the podium that was
slightly larger than my Sherman tank. *Holy crap! This thing is
high.* Immediately I turned off my wheelchair so I wouldn't
accidentally drive off to my death. I didn't dare look up; if I did,
then vertigo would set in. My heart began to beat faster, as I sat
forward in my wheelchair, flapping my arms like a bird. If I fell
off, floating down to the floor would be out of the question—I
had a two hundred pound wheelchair strapped to my ass. All I
wanted to do was to receive my medal and to get back on solid
ground. Our medals were placed around our necks: bronze,
silver and gold. The elected man who handed out our medals
was beside himself with pride. The National Anthem played; our

respective flags, Ireland, United States and Australia, were raised. I searched the crowd; my family stood proud, and Lee wore a huge smile and gave me a thumbs up. I should have been more impassioned at that moment, but my nerves got to me. After the National Anthem finished, the same young man assisted me off the podium. I thanked him profusely. If I was able, I would have kissed the very ground I wheeled on.

The lateness of the day meant my Rhode Island crew would head home. A little voice inside my head suggested that I should hitch a ride. The idea was inviting, but I couldn't allow myself to leave. I won a gold medal—I had a shot at two more. No, I wasn't leaving. My Dad wanted to take home my laundry. Working on the assumption that my father would be able to park close to Constitution Hall, Claudine and I returned to retrieve my laundry bag. We waited at the fence for the longest time, but there wasn't any sign of my father. It was 1984 and cell phones weren't common. I learned later the guards wouldn't allow my father anywhere near the dorms; we didn't have a proper goodbye. Giving up our post at the fence, Claudine and I returned the laundry to my room and then headed to dinner.

Into my third week, I grew accustomed to spending my days observing people and their attitudes. *A time for self-revelation?* I wouldn't classify it as anything too deep—I was newly 17. My biggest concern was when Duran Duran planned to release their next album. With no great revelations about myself, my short time in New York, brought me to appreciate my life at home a little more. I didn't have the freedoms that I had at home; I didn't have the people that I loved. I looked forward to going home.

Tuesday afternoon I was set to compete in beanbag distance throw. Claudine accompanied me to the line. Claudine placed the fake leather beanbag between my fingers. I worked to throw it in the proper direction. My memories are vague. I won the event without setting any records. I acquired my second gold medal.

Now, my only concerns were for our soccer team to win games. What more could a 17-year-old want? A 17-year-old doesn't want to lose her teeth retainers. Three months out of braces and I lose my retainers. Boy, was I dead meat. We found the bottom retainer, but the top retainer was still missing. It wasn't until the next day that someone stopped us by the James M. Shuart Stadium. She was another U.S. Team coach. I was truly amazed when the young coach dug deep into her pocket and handed me my top retainer. *Holy Mother of God!* She found it in the grass in a football-sized field. Inspecting the retainer, a piece of the mold was missing but it was intact. If I was more spiritual like my Irish Catholic relatives, I would have thanked Saint Anthony, Patron of seekers of lost articles. I thanked the young woman who found it. After a five-minute vigorous scrubbing, the retainer was back in my mouth.

A crowd gathered outside of Constitution Hall one afternoon; their eyes were directed upward. Was it a bird? A plane? Superman? It was a pellet hole through a seventh floor window. Either someone got trigger-happy practicing for their shooting event, or someone else took pot shot at an American. Thank God I was on the thirteenth floor. I had watched my share of television crime stories; trajectory—my dear Watson. I looked up to draw my own conclusions—I didn't have any. Bob arrived on the scene to see if the rumors were true. I suspected he was slightly concerned that my room suffered the pellet shot. Given the humdrum days I spent twiddling my thumbs, this was pretty interesting. I never found out if police had come to a conclusion what happened.

There was a buzz around Hofstra University. Our soccer team was competing against Canada for the gold. Granted, this wasn't the U.S. Hockey Team in the 1980 Winter Olympics, but the high was palpable. Queen's "We Will Rock You" and "We Are The Champions" still had their place. In the corridor outside the gymnasium, our team was jacked up on adrenaline. Before emerging into the gymnasium, the sound system blasted "We

Will Rock You", a ceremonial song that the home team was about to kick some ass. It was the first time since the boat ride that I listened to rock music. I needed to tell myself that I wasn't going on stage with Freddie Mercury; I was going into the final game of the wheelchair soccer event. As "We Will Rock You" was still playing, we made our entrance. Everyone exploded in applause. We were stoked to deliver. Our hearts kept to the rhythm—Boom...Boom...Clap! We would keep fighting until the end.

Sidelined for most of the game, I watched with passion. The score was close until we broke it open near the end. Jeff put his second stringers in for the final two minutes. I played strong and hard, keeping Canada from scoring. Just playing in the game was enough for me. Paul would have been so proud. I celebrated with my teammates in receiving the gold medal. History will show I played on the 1984 U.S. Wheelchair Soccer Team who won gold. That is more than enough.

Completing in three events yielded me three gold medals. I was down to my last thirty-six hours in New York; sleep would take up a majority of them. The Closing Ceremonies would be later that afternoon. I had to face more excruciating hours in the navy skirt. *Help me, Lord!* Before I knew it, our U.S. Team was bringing up the rear in the parade of nations. Everyone's energy was drained. We had an experience of a lifetime that we wouldn't soon forget. It was time to go home.

At the end of Closing Ceremonies, Lisa and Seashell, two staff members from school, made a surprise visit. Knowing these two women well, I was excited to see them. I changed into jeans and a shirt. We were on our way to Beef Steak Charlie's for dinner. Lee joined us for a long, relaxing dinner; it felt wonderful. That night, I laughed, releasing all my pent up solitude energy with my friends. I was free.

It was one o'clock in the afternoon before I got up; I would be leaving for home in a few hours with Bob. Mary Ellen had the honors of taking care of me on this final day. I left my team without fanfare. I had my three gold medals and an experience I would have for a lifetime. Coming to the realization that day—it might have been later—I had done something that most people would never get to do. Getting to the International Games for the Disabled was an accomplishment, but it was the self-reliance of these three weeks that have remained with me. It was a tough being away from home, but I got through it extraordinary well. I was only 17.

The 1985 National CP Games were held on the campus of Michigan State University. The atmosphere of these games was dramatically different from Dallas. We didn't have to be cooped up in air conditioned buildings, we saw many more events at these games, and we had the opportunity to check out the little corners of Lansing that were within walking distance.

Instead worrying about a life being lost, I was excited about a life being born. Martha was close to her due date with her first child. I called home almost every day checking on things. Not yet! It was a very exciting time! The Gaynor family was getting ready to add another member!

This was also the trip I discovered Bruce Springsteen's *Born To Run*. With the success of Springsteen's *Born In The USA*, I wanted to hear more of him. Oh my God, what a work of music genius this was! Billy Joel had *The Stranger*, and Bruce Springsteen had *Born To Run*. There are several musicians who believe that God is the composer of all music, and He drops certain gems down to chosen people. I do believe some of that is true, but I also believe He blesses chosen people to have certain talents. Some people are blessed with gifts, extraordinary gifts. "Jungleland" is my favorite Springsteen song.

In Michigan, I also lusted after this very cute, young man who played table tennis. He was on the 1984 United States team. I remember smiling at him when we were at the Hofstra Campus. Although I imagined bearing his children, I didn't have the guts to ask him on a date. I thought surely he would reject me. I presumed he had a girlfriend. Seashell and Maura urged me to talk to the guy but I never gut up the nerve. I just smiled at him like I did in New York.

We met another gentleman. Actually he was a student at MSU. He was like me with athetoid cerebral palsy. He seemed to be at least five years older than me. He had the coolest, most ingenious, communication device I have seen and I have never seen since. The joystick that he used to drive his wheelchair could also be used for his communication system. There was a small screen that functioned as a readout with red, digital letters. As he moved his joystick around in different directions, red letters, and then words started to appear rather quickly across the screen. I wanted this communication system. In the age before e-mail and the Internet, it was very difficult to follow the leads to find this communication system. Twenty-eight years later, I still haven't discovered any communication system like the one I just explained. If such a communication system was available today, I would WANT IT!

Of course the girls thought this guy was perfect for me, barring the fact that he lived in Michigan and I lived in New England. Back then, I was considered to be shallow and unrealistic, especially by Seashell, with the young men I wanted to date, and maybe I was. It was a combination of feeling normal inside but rejecting that I was so different on the outside. I had all hopes that whoever got to know me would gradually not see my outside as much. I continued to believe that for a number of years.

We had a day off from competition and we walked into town again. This was when I picked up *Born To Run*. This was also the day I got a bump on my head from a Kahlua bottle.

Seashell had a lot of things piled up in her hands. She put the bottle, the glass bottle, of Kahlua on top of the pile. She moved awkwardly and it slid off and biffed me on the right side of my forehead. It smarted but only was sore for a few days. I had a few drinks on this trip; I usually drank just until I had a little buzz.

We flew home on August 14th, and I went home. August 15th arrived, and the temperature by noontime nudged 100 degrees. We received a call from Glenn that Martha was in active labor. I was home alone with Mom, and she was beside herself with anxiety. Thank God we had air conditioners blasting, because with all the pacing Mom did for nine hours, she would have reduced herself in a big puddle. She was having sympathy labor pains. She spent most of the day in the kitchen. I spent the day in the den with MTV on, but I mostly watched her. At times, I thought her head was going to pop off. We both agreed it was the longest day of lives. It was a Thursday and *Cheers* was on. Glenn called a little before 10pm. Our little Sarah Anne was born at 9:05! Cheers!

For whatever the reason was, the National CP Games of 1987 were transitioned into the Pan-Am Games, which were held at Hofstra University. It would be my last competition. Only myself and Tony, another classmate, qualified for these games. Lee and Seashell were our coaches. It was a quiet week at Hofstra, other than driving my wheelchair through a sprinkler after a few Sombreros, and eating at a New York franchise, White Castle Hamburgers. White Castle was an experience onto itself with us shooting a very short documentary about what goes into a White Castle hamburger. Hollywood, here we come.

I don't recall my results of the two events I competed in, but I believe I did well. One month later, I received notified I qualified for the International Games in Seoul, Korea the following year. Mom was not prepared to allow me to go to Korea; I didn't object. I didn't think about the fact that these were my last games. It didn't really bother me.

146

"No more turning away
From the coldness inside
Just a world that we all must
share
It's not enough just to stand and
stare
Is it only a dream that there'll
be
No more turning away?"

"On The Turning Away"
Pink Floyd
A Momentary Lapse Of Reason

Again, my parents attempted to send me to computer camp in upstate New York, but yet again, it was cancelled for the second year in a row. We had our suspicions that the administrators of the camp did not want me to attend, but there was no way to prove their intentions, unless we sent a spy. Mom and Dad felt I was slighted, so they offered funds for Leslie and I to spend four days seeing the sights in Montreal and Quebec City. We drove to Canada in her black Volkswagen Rabbit. Those were the days when you may have needed your birth certificate to cross over the border. Once you crossed into Canada from New Hampshire, there were farmlands as far as eyes could see. The land was strikingly flat. Miles per hour changed into kilometers per hour. What the hell was a kilometer? In years past, teachers touched upon the metric system but like a lot of kids, I didn't care too much about it.

We spent the first two days seeing the sights in Montreal. I remember being fascinated with the Olympic Stadium; it looked like a massive spaceship. The cool thing about it was that it was built into the ground. As you walked around the outside, you could see inside. I imagined what it would be like to be a rock star and selling out this huge stadium. It was never about having loads and loads of cash. It was about getting on a stage and giving all of your passion through your music to thousands of people. That was what I wanted to do even if I knew the reality of my limitations. I could still dream though, and dreamt I did. I don't think I ever told Leslie what I was imagining. I could have told her without fear of her telling me that it was stupid of me to imagine being on stage. It wasn't Leslie's style to cut anybody down. She would have lifted me up and probably joined me in my little daydream.

Driving north to Quebec City took a few hours. And what a beautiful city it is. In my mind, I refer to Quebec City as the Paris of North America. Only experiencing Paris, France through photographs and films, Quebec City felt like a scaled down Paris. I loved walking through all the brick sidewalks, and seeing all the quaint storefronts with the wrought iron streetlamps. Everything was so romantic. The Chateau Frontenac across the River St. Lawrence was a magnificent sight at dusk. I think I might have remarked to Leslie that if and possibly when I got married, I wanted to honeymoon in Quebec City.

The next day, before we headed back to the mountain, we stopped in the metropolitan section of Quebec and had lunch. Leslie always had a knack of telling us young adults what she thought our potentials were. No doubt, she thought I had a lot of potential. At that time I didn't have a clue what I wanted to do for a career. I don't even think college had entered my mind. Jimmy had come up in our conversation. She spoke about the way he presented himself and how he tried to pronounce every word so clearly. I admired Jim greatly, but I knew, again, I didn't quite have the speech capabilities he had. Leslie also knew my strong reluctance towards using a speech synthesizer. We also touched upon my drooling issues. She suggested when I leave any area after drinking, especially in restaurants, I should soak up my small, runoff puddles with a napkin or a towel. I have continuously have done that ever since that very day.

I successfully completed my first full year at the high school. It was time to consider what classes I wanted to take for the following September. Since I have done so well with my two classes the previous year, my team and I decided I could take on three classes per semester. If memory serves me correctly, my second year college preparatory classes included English, geometry, and psychology. I recall getting my only 'D' on one psychology test. My only 'D' I believe in entire academic career, and I was so embarrassed by it! The teacher left it on top of my typewriter cover and when I got out to the hall, I managed to turn it over. I had to find a trashcan. When I waited for my ride back to the residential school, there was a trashcan in the glass solarium. I fought so hard to get it in the trashcan and not drop it on the floor. That was that.

149

With all the reading I had for high school, myself, along with Maura and Seashell, had to come up with inventive ways for me to read comfortably. The best set up we did was to put two tack strips, horizontally, on the wall over the head over my bed. If I had paperback books or small books that wouldn't stay open, we photocopied these books, and whatever I couldn't finish reading, pages could be tacked up on the strips so I could read in bed.

Studying fractions, algebra and geometry brought another conundrum: doing complex math equations without having the ability to use a pencil. By this time, I was using pfs:Write for all of my writing assignments. It was extremely difficult to do any advanced math problems on a regular typewriter. So, I adopted using pfs:Write for doing math. I had a blank canvas I could work with. If a number was squared, I pressed the up arrow and typed '2'. I used dashed lines for fractions and define steps in each problem. Using pfs:Write worked beautifully because I could view all of my steps by scrolling up and down. I used to create different math symbols such as square root, with certain characters with the keyboard, which worked well. If I was doing advanced math today, most likely Microsoft Word would be my program of choice.

It was also during this second year of high school that I took Computer-Aided Drafting (CAD). Once I learned the basics, I excelled. Instead of writing BASIC code to draw line, circles and arcs, I was using simple commands to draw very quickly. When I wanted to draw a diagonal line, I typed "LINE", press enter. The computer awaited more information. Next, I typed, "@ 2" <(angle)45", press enter. I just drew a two-inch line at 45 degrees. In this CAD class, I also learned how to draw an object in different views, top view, and two different side views, also called sections. This was also the same time I developed the idea that I could be a building designer, especially for buildings that would be wheelchair accessible housing. The residential school had just built nine new wheelchair-friendly housing homes. Personally, I didn't think the houses were all that wheelchair-friendly.

In the Fall of 1987, I would embark on my final year at the residential school and in high school. I also took three classes at the high school, Oceanography, English, and Music Theory. Did I just say Music Theory? Oh, yes I did. I was finally taking Music Theory. It might also astonish you that I passed up on the chance to take my first music class in the very early 80's at the residential school. We had a new teacher who taught office skills. Our school never had an official music class, but this new teacher, Nancy Jones, began one, if it was only for a short time. I would pass by her classroom and see all the construction paper music notation above her door, and feel the strongest urge to learn what those notes were all about. The excitement was so palpable. Paul was taking the class, but I still resisted. Maybe it was the fact that I knew I couldn't play a musical instrument. Maybe I was afraid that I would like it too much and have no way to make music, but the urge was still present inside my spirit—an inextinguishable fire. Seven years later, I was ready.

Mr. Richard Sanders was absolutely the best music teacher any music student could ask for. He was patient, energetic and inspiring. His demeanor and looks would remind anyone of the late, great Tony Randall. Mr. Sanders had graying hair and wire-rimmed eyeglasses to had to his distinguished manner.

After taking a few classes with Mr. Sanders, I realized my portable typewriter wasn't going to cut it for music theory; I had to create an 8.5 by 11 inch, laminated music symbol sheet. I cannot recall what graphic program I used to make this music symbol board, but it had whole to 32nd notes, A to G, sharp and flat symbols, and minor 2nd to octave symbols to use during interval ear training drills. I didn't have perfect pitch then and I do not have it now.

I had to rely on Maura or Nancy Carney to help me complete my music theory homework. Nancy was employed in the recreation department. Fortunate for me, she had a degree in music, and had Mr. Sanders as her high school music teacher. Nancy had a seizure disorder that sometimes kept her from working in short periods of time. Getting my music theory homework completed was at times a feat. I had tremendous respect for Nancy.

Several months prior to starting Music Theory, conjunction with our school, Dartmouth College sent some engineering students to the school to meet some of our students. Their mission was to design products that would be beneficial to these particular students with developmental disabilities. I was fortunate enough to be chosen as one of their subjects.

I had six engineering students, Renee Foisy, David Lindahl, Christoph Mack, Corey Brinkema, Susan Smith, and Patrick Walsh, who all worked together as a team to create what my heart desired. The students interviewed me to see what they could help me do. As Seashell prepared to interpret, I answered, "I want to play chords". I had a small music keyboard that I used to fiddle around with. Using my headpointer, I could only play one note at a time. It was then the students decided to make me a piano.

Casio donated the keyboard to the Dartmouth students and they were off and running. They tested out different size squares and rectangles that would fit my fist size nicely. At Dartmouth, the constructed two separate cherry cases to build the piano in. They machined each key, black and white, and attached every one to a hinge. Every key was wired into the guts of the Casio keyboard. One case held the chord keys and the other case held the melody keys.

152

It was springtime of 1986 when the students brought the customized piano up to me. I played "Silent Night". My left hand would play the chords and my right handled the melody. Mozart—I wasn't, but I think I did okay. The students videotaped this performance and now it is forever on YouTube.

Although the customized keyboard was a wonderful achievement, I wanted to do so much more. The only way that I could hear what I had put on paper was if Mr. Sanders played it on the piano. In class we were studying first and second chord inversions. With my custom keyboard, I couldn't play chord inversions. If I hit the 'F' chord, it would play a root 'F' triad. This was very limiting.

I was the queen of making up excuses why I needed to go see Andy in rehab engineering. Rarely was anything ever broken, I just wanted to see what new things he was working on to bring more independence to the students. The other reason was that I was so completely, stick-a-toothpick-in-my-eye bored, reading that damn history book by myself in Dave's class. Crazy enough, he would always let me go.

One particular day Andy showed me the software program he had for music notation. I believe it was called Music Construction. My eyes lit up like the sun. He demonstrated it for me on his Apple. This was the first program I saw that actually had a grand stave that the user could put whole, half, quarter, eighth, and sixteenth notes on. It was beautiful! I had one other music program that I owned that used the piano roll technology. I did not like the piano roll technology; it was confusing and cumbersome. Give me a staff in which I can place musical notation on because that was what I knew! The only problem I had with the Music Construction was that it didn't allow the user to play two or more notes simultaneously, so harmonizing a melody was impossible. I needed to do harmonizing. *"Midnight masqueradersworkin' hard for wagesneed no vast arrangementto do their harmonizing.* " I had to wait a little longer.

High school was awesome! I loved every bit of it! It's not often you'll hear someone say they loved high school, but I did. I loved the challenge of doing all the work I had to do and being able to keep pace with the rest of my classmates. Luckily the high school didn't have many snow days. I hated snow days because the residential school education program was always in session no matter what weather brought. Not going to high school meant that I had to hang out at the other school and find something to do for four hours until the lunch bell rang. I believe I hung out in Jean or Dave's class. If I had homework from high school to finish, I would do that. Sometimes I would hang out in Cathy Carter's computer classroom and play "Where In The World Is Carmen San Diego?"

Also during this time, April was having more health issues, especially respiratory issues. Her scoliosis was progressing, resulting in breathing issues when she had congestion. Her coughing fits would scare the most confident of nurses. I would cringe when I watched her struggle to clear her throat of mucus. She would fight to get a breath. On a few occasions she was hospitalized for respiratory issues. Seashell explained to me that April would need surgery to correct her scoliosis so she could live a longer life. Seashell also told me April would probably not survive the surgery, so surgery was taken off the table. These are the times that you feel so helpless. Modern medicine could only go far. Luckily, April wasn't constantly sick. People did all they could do to keep April from catching colds and common illnesses. I tried to spend more time with April before we graduated and went our separate ways.

Our parents were big proponents about us having a good set of teeth. Unfortunately, when Paul was two, he accidently batted out Peter's two front teeth. Peter needed caps. Martha and I have small chips in our front teeth due to various dives in swimming pools, and splats when crawling as youngsters. Paul has the perfect set of teeth.

When I got to be six or seven, my parents were on the hunt for a dentist who could serve children with developmental disabilities. Here in Rhode Island, there is a dentistry office, which specializes in treating children and adults with developmental disabilities. I clearly recall my first and last visit to this particular dental office. The main issue they had with me was trying to keep my mouth open at a certain span and steady. There must have been six different technicians surrounding me. I believe my Dad was there also. The rubber dams came out. For a person with moderate Dysarthria, putting anything in my mouth while lying flat on their backs is very daunting. I feel like I have no control to protect what goes down my throat. As the technicians were trying different sizes of rubber dams in my mouth, my Dysarthria was in overdrive. It wasn't the fact that I couldn't keep my mouth open, it was the fact that I have such a tremendous gag reflex, that the rubber dams were triggering my gag reflexes, making my jaw open up to its maximum span. I didn't want to make their job anymore difficult, but I wasn't succeeding. It was time for the gas. For many years after, I still recalled the smell of that black rubber cup that was placed over my mouth and nose; total sedation was complete.

I recall playing in the living room after being gassed. I assured my Mom that I felt fine, and then I started talking to imaginary people. I was not fine; I was still feeling the side effects of being gassed. Soon, I was fast asleep on the living floor, as I slept for the next 18 hours.

During my eleven years at my residential school brought a significantly better dental experience. There were only the visiting dentist and his assistant. They did most of the physical transfers into the single dental chair, unless they required more assistance. The dentist and the assistant communicated with the students brilliantly. With total communication between student and dentist, trust blossomed. I made sure the dentist and the assistant knew about my adversity to using rubber dams. They understood. We discovered that if the assistant gently supported my jaw with her hand, keeping my mouth open to the limit where my gag reflexes wouldn't be triggered, the dentist could work very efficiently because I was comfortable. For the people who benefited from the use of straps and arm restraints, they were available. I was one who totally benefited from straps and arm restraints to make me feel secure in the dental chair. I was also one who benefited from the use of nitrous oxide. Nitrous oxide is a gas compound used as an anxiolytic effect, which relaxes the individual without complete sedation. Once removed from the individual's nose, the effects of the gas disappear within 3 to 5 minutes.

I think Mom and Dad had decided early on that orthodontics would be in my future, along with Martha and Paul. Poor Paul had it the worst because his mouth palette needed to be cracked apart by a palette expander. Every night Mom would need to use what looked like an Allen wrench to expand the bridge three clicks. I don't think it was painful, but it just looked Medieval.

I was a bucktooth beaver. Mom and Dad found the single orthodontist near the residential school. My first appointment, springtime of 1981, was on a Friday afternoon, convenient for Dad to come up and then bring me home. I didn't know how unpalatably difficult it would be to make molds of my teeth, especially my bottom teeth. This goopy, white paste put my gag reflexes into overdrive. It was a challenge to hold my jaw still for the two or three minutes the goop took to harden. I had hands all over my face and jaw to get good molds. I believe we got the top mold on the first attempt, but it took a few more attempts for the bottom. It made matters worse that I lied nearly prone on my back for this process. I was relieved when it was over.

156

About two weeks later, Dr. Khow put my braces on. The process was long but not too taxing because almost all the initial work was on the outside of my teeth, and not having to hold my mouth open was a cinch. What I was expecting to be some pain, turned out to be a whole lot pain for the next six days. The first evening at dinner, I hardly bit down on a spoon and I started bawling my eyes out. Debi offered me some aspirin, but I knew how nasty regular aspirin was, and I didn't think I could handle swallowing it. For the next three days, I drank milkshakes. On Thursday evening, a group of us went to the circus. I don't recall anything about the circus, but I do remember eating a McDonald's cheeseburger. I thought it was the greatest thing I ate that week.

Eating that cheeseburger didn't stop me from whining to Mom and Dad part of the weekend. On Saturday night, I was on one couch, and Mom, on the other. Still whining, Mom asked what she could do for me. I said I wanted my braces off. In a firm manner, Mom directly stated under no circumstances was I getting my braces off, and she didn't want to hear anymore about it. That was that: Mom spoke—I listened, like E.F. Hutton.

Barring the frequent stray wire making mince meat out of my cheek, my experience with orthodontics went rather well. I became accustom to the monthly wire-tightening. I had a workout every time I visited Dr. Khow's office; it wasn't accessible due to one step. The name of the game was the staff member whoever brought myself, and another student, to this small ranch had to hold each of us from the back, around our chests, and walk us into the office. Both of us had strong legs and leg braces, but I had a very short gait. I could move my legs fast to move quickly, making the entire trip tiring. I don't know why no one had the idea to bring a portable ramp, but I can't recall ever knowing portable ramps existed until many years later. Even if we could get our wheelchairs through the front sure, I'm unsure if we could have navigated the narrow halls of the orthodontic office.

Only recently, I learned that the orthodontic work Dr. Khow performed in those three years wasn't guaranteed to "last" over years due to my cerebral palsy, but it has. I continue to be able to close my lips over my front teeth. I am very grateful that my parents had the gumption to put me through the rigors of orthodontics.

In my adult years, I have found it difficult to find quality dental care that is covered by Medicaid. I have tried State Dental Clinics, but their quality is lacking, and on one examination, I was told I would have to return to the same dental office I was gassed when I was a child. The clinic staff stated I needed to be sedated to have a tooth filled. *Are you kidding me?!* As I attempted to explain to the clinic staff that I did not need to be sedated to get a tooth filled, the technician didn't care what I had to say. I was extremely frustrated, vowing to not return to another State Dental Clinic.

I returned to my private dentist, and he filled my tooth without any issues. Most private dentists stopped accepting Medicaid insurance because dentists only received about 60% of the cost from a Medicaid recipient. Also, filling for Medicaid payments can take several months. I can't blame private dentists for not accepting Medicaid insurance, but on the other side, Medicaid recipients deserve a higher quality of dental care. People with developmental disabilities who can demonstrate their ability to undergo typical dental procedures without sedation should not be forced into sedation.

Until people recognize that the Medicaid system, in regards to dentistry, needs to be overhauled, I choose to pay out-of-pocket for dental cleanings. Since I am a Medicaid recipient, I am not allowed to buy into any dental insurance plans. This doesn't make sense to me. I don't know what I would do if I needed more extensive dental work in the future. My choices are limited, and I don't want to be forced into complete sedation. I wish to work with state and government officials to attempt to improve dentistry for people with developmental disabilities.

Besides my buckteeth being a problem worth correcting, the other annoyance of my childhood and my teenage years was my excessive drooling due to my Dysarthria. The weird thing about it was that I never drooled a lot when sleeping. Mom always thought I had some ability to stop drooling. If I put all my concentration into it, sure, I could decrease my drooling. If my concentration moved to some other task, my drooling increased. I usually used my sleeve to wipe my chin. I always had a towel on my lap. When I was prescribed L-dopa for a short time around the age of seven, one pleasant side effect was dry mouth. I didn't drool for a week, but I didn't have any spine either.

Even though my drooling would leave wet spots on my pants, some children with disabilities drooled much worse. It was in the beginning of 1987 when it was brought to my attention that a doctor in Boston was performing a surgery that might decrease my drooling dramatically. The surgery is referred to a submandibular duct transposition. The easiest way to explain the surgery is that the two salvia ducts that are under the tongue are repositioned to the back of the throat. To this day, I can't figure out how the surgeon rerouted the saliva ducts to the back of my throat but he did. The results were better than anyone expected. Mom and Dad were ecstatic about how well the surgery dramatically reduced my drooling. Looking back on it, if the surgery was available earlier, I would have seriously considered it.

It was the mission of Seashell to prepare students in the Transitional Unit for life after leaving the residential school. Like all of us, most graduate high school and go down our each, individual path. Some students were destined to live independently in their own apartments, some would live in group homes and some go back home to live with family members. It was my decision to attend New Hampshire Technical College at Manchester. Seashell had a precise understanding of life for people with developmental disabilities living independently. Living independent meant you had to have a total grasp of how to hire and fire PCAs; you had to know how to manage your time, especially during your allotted PCA hours; you had to know how to manage and budget your money; you had to know how to shopping for groceries and other items of necessity; you had to know what to do in any kind of emergency. A program was developed that we had to stick to on a daily basis. Surely, we were kept on our toes.

One day I was given a mission to complete myself. I had to go buy a package of underwear in this one particular store. I was advised that it might be worthwhile to bring my typewriter for this particular mission. I had bought many things by myself before and I didn't feel I needed my typewriter. Like a bra, my wheelchair tray was a relief to get rid of every afternoon—I didn't want to ride around more than I needed to. So, with my wallet securely tucked between my side of the wheelchair and my right hip, I grabbed a package of underwear, the right size no less, and my athetoid hand dropped them on the counter. I pushed my wallet forward so the cashier would be able to see it, or I might have knocked it to the floor. The cashier probably asked me if I needed help. I might have needed to shifted my eyes between my wallet and the cashier's eyes a few times to relay I didn't have the finger dexterity to pull the money out. The transaction was complete. I went outside and find the van. The next part of my revealed: I had to return the underwear and get a refund. My eyes might have glazed over for a second, but I soldiered on. Now I understood the suggestion to bring my typewriter. I went back into the store. I felt a little like an idiot returning the underwear I just bought. I had to come up with a plan on how I was communicate to the cashier I wanted to return them. Thankfully, there weren't many people in the store. I circled the square customer counter and discovered a big sign, "Return Policy", on the side of the counter. My athetoid hand grabbed the bag and flipped it onto the counter. The cashier looked puzzled, as she walked closer. I hit the "Return Policy" sign with my hand. A few seconds later, she asked me if I wanted to return the underwear. I smiled and nodded excitingly. Mission accomplished!

Between 1984 and 1988 our Transitional Unit took End of the Year trips to destinations we could drive to within eight to ten hours, and that was only if our vehicles didn't breakdown. I'm not going to go in major details of every trip we took. The trip to Montreal was a trip where we had vehicle breakdowns, where we easily spent 20 hours driving. If someone wants details about the Montreal trip, it may cost you some big bucks.

In 1984, we camped in the rain in Tiverton, Rhode Island. In 1985, we broke free in New York City. Actually New York City remains my favorite trip. Thanks Nestor for your parents' Brooklyn house. In 1986, we drove to our Nation's capitol. Thanks to the Lacey's for their house on Gaynor Road (no lie). In 1987 was our infamous Montreal trip—please pay the mechanic. In 1988, we went to Portland, Maine, where I bought the best sunglasses at L.L. Bean.

We left on Thursday, May 20th, my 21st birthday. We stayed at another cheap motel so we could use more of the money to experience different tourist activities. The mission of the night: I had to roll down to the nearby 7-11, in evening darkness, and purchase whatever I wanted to drink. I waited for somebody to hold the door open so I could enter the store. I went over to the glass refrigerator and decided what I wanted. I wanted wine coolers. I waved to the young, male cashier. I pointed to the Bartles and Jaymes four-pack and the young man put it on the counter. I moved my wallet forward and I hit it with my fist to bring attention to it. He looked at my ID and took the cash needed. I was carded! He put the wine coolers in my back and held the door open. I drank two of the four wine coolers, legally.

My last, big undertaking that I wanted to do before I left the residential school was to travel down the mountain road in my electric wheelchair. I had that daredevil mindset at that particular time. Ever since one of my wheelchair clutches unlocked as I was riding down the double ramp in the main building once or twice, I made sure both clutches were constantly secure with a bungee cord.

Even though Maura was a smoker, she was up for the challenge. We picked one late spring evening to conquer the mountain road. Never having the experience of walking before, I had great empathy to feel what my legs would feel like if I was actually walking. Many people might think driving a power wheelchair is only moving a joystick, and for many people it is that simple. In many situations, like driving down hills and ramps, I had to be on my game. Due to my athetoid cerebral palsy, controlling my wheelchair became a multiple muscle process, especially with my thigh muscles. Constricting these muscles gave me more control over the joystick. Of course I didn't want to haphazardly drive off the mountain road, so my leg muscles kicked in.

I believe it took us about 45 minutes to walk to Route 31, and probably another 90 minutes to walk back up. It was a momentous occasion when we walked back into the house on Fox Meadow Lane. Maura flopped on the couch and I looked down on both sides of my wheelchair. Nope, I didn't see any smoke coming out from the motors.

Graduation was around the corner. The high school was having a student award ceremony but for some reason I didn't attend. I wasn't expecting to win any awards. The next day I found out that I won for the highest grade, an average grade of

93, in music theory. *I did what?!* I could hardly believe it. I have never played a musical instrument, I did not have perfect pitch, and I couldn't do my music theory homework on my own, but I had the highest grade. *I did what?!* When I received the 4 by 6 paper certificate, it was my proudest achievement. Wow!

Graduation at the high school was the day after the graduation at the residential school. The plan was that I would stay with Sue Smith and her young daughter, Mandy, who I had known a decade, at their apartment on the mountain for that night. I knew my parents, Paul, Martha, Glenn and little Sarah would be arriving later that afternoon.

Truthfully, I have little recollection what was spoken at the residential school graduation. All I remember was that April graduating also. We were both 21; we were aging out of the system. I didn't care that my family wasn't at this graduation; I considered the high school graduation the crème de la crème of my accomplishments. Not to say I didn't accomplish a lot at the residential school, but in specific regards to my education, high school challenged me.

Technically I was a free bird after lunch. The staff's end of the year party was starting in front of Hayden. I joined the party; what else was I going to do? This was the first time I experienced beer going up my nose. It wasn't a pleasant feeling. Carbonated anything isn't supposed to enter nasal passages. I believe I amused everyone, which I didn't mind. I think that was my last beer for a number of reasons, namely I didn't want to smell like a brewery when my family arrived.

This was the first time my Mom visited the residential school. She hated the black flies; we all hated the black flies. Mom wanted me to stay with them in town. Though I was a little disappointed I wasn't going to hang with Sue and Mandy for the night, I didn't put up much of a fuss. Many staff members who knew me for years and years greeted my Mom very kindly, as they spoke their admiration for me. I have never felt comfortable with people giving me praise for whatever the reason. I usually look down into my shyness until the admiration was finished.

Later, my family and a few of my closest staff members had dinner out. Not too far down Route 202 was the Jack Daniels Inn we stayed for the night. Jokes were flowing for a while over the inn's name, but I haven't found any evidence that it was named after the whiskey man. I don't think Mom liked its name, but I passed by it a lot throughout my nearly eleven years in southern New Hampshire.

Dad rented a Grand Caravan to transport my electric wheelchair here, there and then home to Rhode Island after graduation. We all got to the high school on time. I went on my merry way into the high school and got ready with all the others for the pomp and circumstance. I think I wore jeans and my class t-shirt under my jade green gown. Everyone was wearing the class t-shirt, in which all of our names formed the number "88". The graduation was held outdoors; it was a beautiful day. We got all of our diplomas and listened to all the speeches. Towards the end, Brown Eyes, Toby and another graduate performed Pink Floyd's "On The Turning Away." It was a beautiful rendition that I will never forget. Every time I hear the song, it brings me back to that very day.

I was happy Mom got to meet Mr. Sanders. I was extraordinary happy Anne was there; her brother, Teddy, was in the graduating class. Paul was struck by her personality and beauty. Charisma, Seashell and Maura all were there to cheer me on. I distinctively noticed Charisma had a hangover; I was not pleased but I didn't let it bother me. All of us hung out for a little while until we went our different directions. I didn't know when I would see Maura again; she was interested in changing jobs. I knew I would see her sometime.

My family and I stopped to have lunch at a restaurant down in town. I knew Leslie was waitressing there part-time.

She was about seven months pregnant with her son, Michael. Her once vibrant bright light in her eyes every day seemed a scant dimmer. I had known this woman for ten years and she was a rock. I was sure that newlywed life with her husband wasn't blissful but she was excited about becoming a mother. I wouldn't see Leslie for another three years.

*"For we are always what our situations hand us
It's either sadness or euphoria"*

"Summer, Highland Falls"
Billy Joel
Turnstiles

There was a quiet fight going on behind the scenes when I decided I wanted to go to college in Manchester, New Hampshire. The fight was between my parents and Rhode Island Vocational Rehabilitation Services. RIVR was hesitating to fund the residential portion that I required to going to college in Manchester. My vocational counselor, Andre, visited Mom and Dad, stating they were on the fence about funding residential services at Derry. Without these essential services, I would not be able to go to college in Manchester. Mom and Dad refused to take "no" as an answer. I hadn't come through all my schooling to be denied the opportunity to go to college. No, no, no! Mom was overwhelmed, as she stated, and she began to cry. Andre made the right decision: RIVR would fund my residential services.

Derry, classified as a group home, was the only adequate living arrangement available to me at that time. Seashell was hired to run the program. I believed it would be a good situation, but time would reveal all.

The summer of 1988 was chock full with activities. First, for graduation, my parents gave me concert tickets to two different shows: John Mellencamp and Steve Winwood at Great Woods in Mansfield, Massachusetts. Dad, the trooper he was, was my concert buddy through the 1990's. He has to love his daughter to accompany his daughter to a Van Hagar concert in 1995. Peter, and his fiancée were getting married at the end of August. I had another wedding to attend in New Hampshire in July. Lastly, I was moving to Derry in the middle of July. These were enough events to frazzle anyone. Mom was frazzled.

The role of maid of honor was given to me, and then, taken away by my future sister-in-law. Needless to say, this didn't sit well with Mom. Mom believed she changed her mind because of my disability. I don't really know what her reasons were but, like always, I gave Peter's fiancée the benefit of the doubt. Peter, a very proud Marine since 1977, was on assignment overseas. He left most of the plans to his fiancée, which led her to rely on assistance from Mom to decide on wedding details. Mom took the high road and gave Peter's fiancée the help. Mom always had that motherly instinct about all of her children and she didn't feel quite sure about this marriage.

My task for both of these 1988 weddings was to buy a dress. Okay, I have brought a dress before for a prom, and that black, satin, strapless dress was a knockout! How hard is it to get a dress for a wedding? Well, I bought this little, red dress that I really liked, but it didn't receive rave reviews in Rhode Island. A fashion diva—I'm not. Needless to say, I apparently don't pick out the just-right outfits for certain events. Since then, that kind of has been the crux in my life. When I have to buy something for a big event, I always fail. That what happens when your Mom or other family members have picked out 95% of your clothing for you. Mom spent countless of weekends washing, drying, ironing and organizing five sets of clothes for the week. All the girls would ooh and ahh over the magnificent color of pants, turtleneck and sweaters she would combine. You might call my style preppy. Mom's combinations are a lot to live up to. Today, I still wear turtlenecks with sweaters or sweatshirts. I cringe when I have to go shopping for clothes, other than jeans and leather jackets. Frankly, I would rather stick hedgehog quills in my eyebrows than go clothes shopping.

Peter's wedding took place at St. Timothy's Church in Warwick. Peter wore his Marine Corps finest uniform. As husband and wife walked out of church under a canopy of swords. The reception was held at the Wethersfield Commons Clubhouse. It was a typical, happy go lucky party. Whenever I saw a Michelob beer bottle, I was compelled to break into Winwood's lyrics: *"Don't you know what the night can do? Don't you know when it's touching you? Don't you know what the night can do?"* My singing became more liberated with more alcohol flowing through my bloodstream. Blondie, the girl my parents paid to be my PCA for the weekend, was enjoying the spirits too when she made a very embarrassing and slightly crude comment about my relationship with Charisma. I was floored, as I prayed that the clamor of the room would dull the comment. I tried to blow it off quickly so a few people would forget about it. I might have given Blondie a lightning fast look of disgust but I don't know if she caught it.

I was very excited about starting college. I had no idea what to expect but I was so ready to have something to do during the day besides listening to the mundaneness at the apartments. The students had an orientation day. Classes started the next day. All of my instructors had met me prior. My first class was with Quentin Walsh, who was a native Rhode Islander. He reminded me of David Letterman, and ironically had a similar sense of humor. Our class was made up of 25 males and 2 females. I was very grateful the building construction instructors chose to keep the females together, as there were two sections of building construction students.

I attempted to tape record all of my classes in the hopes that I would listen to them later. Listening to the recordings only put me to sleep. I had to come up with a better plan. Randi, the other female in my class, became my savior and my good friend through the two years. She was 27, married and had three children. I can't remember Randi missing more than two days of school. She was driven, as she wanted to change her circumstances. Her notes were meticulous and very easy to understand. She would photocopy all of them for me.

Quentin taught the basics of building construction, starting with the sills, floor joists and the studs. At first his drawings of all of these parts confused me. He drew a lot of rectangles with a big "X" inside every one. I have never seen a blueprint of a building before. After I realized the rectangles represented sections and elevations of sills, joists and studs, everything started clicking.

I took on a regular class load of five courses per semester. I was totally amazed how I excelled in my math skills. In the math areas I struggled during high school seem to all vanish. I loved every moment of this college. The majority of the instructors never made me feel any less capable, and they expected the most from me.

In my general math class I took in my first semester, I befriended, Kelly, a woman who had a son with cerebral palsy. From our conversations, me with my portable typewriter, it was evident that she was also striving to change her circumstances. There were a number of students who had overcome many obstacles to get to a place where they wanted to improve themselves. I admired them. They were good people.

In order to do my CAD work, RIVR purchased me an IBM computer with CAD software. It was the first personal computer with a hard drive. Wow, I didn't have to put floppy disks in to run programs because they were already loaded. The 5.25" disks were replaced with 3.5", more durable disks. I kind of liked this. I asked the college's administrator, Mr. McCann, if I could possibly set up my Apple IIE somewhere in the college. He didn't think that would be a problem. There was a small room in the college's library that served me well. There were two, very professional, men that served as the librarians. Hans was my favorite. Hans was a tall gent, with a sweet disposition. After a while, his nervousness seemed to dissipate when he set me up at my computer.

To conquer the reading aspects of college work, I drew up plans for a custom headboard. Since I was going to sleep on a futon on the floor, the special headboard would sit on the floor. In between two flat elevated surfaces for a touch lamp and a telephone, was a slanted surface for a book. At night, I would lie prone on my futon, with my headpointer on. With my chin supported by the futon, my reading comprehension and efficiency improved dramatically. When I needed to turn the page, I would get up on my elbows, and flipped the page with my headpointer tip.

I believe I mastered the art of book destruction around this time. Almost very college book I kept because I used to have to beat the shit of it to make it stay open. Sometimes I could crack the spines of the books myself, but I relied on other people to this task for me. Sometimes I had people open a book in the middle, place it face down the floor, and then I would skillfully drive over the spine of the book with my front wheel first, and my back wheel second. Depending on strong the binding was made, sometimes I had to do this two or three times to make sure the book was sufficiently flattened.

My life took on two separate arenas: the residential arena and the college arena. I never considered Derry a home because it was always chaotic in some fashion or another. College was tranquil, steady and fun. Not far from the apartments was a shopping center, which became an escape when I needed to get some "me" time. I became very adept at doing small shopping trips. I asked the staff if they wanted anything at the store. The usual items were soda, coffee and cigarettes. I would put a small shopping basket on my footrest to go about my shopping. Some items I could knock off the shelf and into the basket. Out-of-reach items were given to me by kind strangers. I treasured this time to myself because I could prove that I was somebody. The cashiers would put the bagged items in my backpack. I'd take my time going back to the group home just for the sake of my sanity. Granted, I did like most of the people who worked at Derry, although the total atmosphere had a very strange dynamic to it.

When I did see Seashell on some days after school, she was preoccupied; most understandably, she was running a group home. I must admit I missed our conversations. Those didn't happen too often. I noticed Seashell growing increasing frustrated, as she tried to put in place a similar personal care

171

assistant program that she had for our Transitional Unit. I was not working because most of the residents had moderate to severe intellectual impairments. It was a group home setting with very dependent people.

In the spring of 1989, Mom and Dad sold the condo in Warwick to head to Cape Cod. Mom always loved the Cape and wanted to live there permanently. By May of 1989, they had found a house in East Falmouth to rent for six months. This was where I spent my summer. Martha was expecting her second child in August, so she, Glenn and Sarah spent a number of weekends in East Falmouth. My Aunt Pat spent a lot of time there as well.

When we didn't have company, we took daily adventures out and about searching for that perfect house. The house in East Falmouth wasn't very wheelchair accessible, so Dad had to bounce me down and up five stairs. This was quite a daily workout for my 61-year-old Dad. Mom was still smoking two packs of cigarettes a day so I really enjoyed the car windows opened. We became very proficient in getting to know the roads from Bourne to Eastham. I was too young to remember going to the Cape when I was a toddler but I certainly understand its appeal. There are certain spots in Falmouth where looking out to the ocean would take your breath away. It wasn't hard to fall in love with it.

On August 9, 1989, Martha gave birth to a beautiful, baby boy she named Thomas John. He wasn't to be referred as Tom or Tommy, it was Thomas, T.J. or sometimes Teej. After all the name testing, Thomas stuck, unless he was around my Dad, and then his name was George. A few years down the road, I sometimes referred to him as Thomas Two-Tone just because I liked the song, "867-5309". Of course Thomas was a cute baby; all our Gaynor babies are cute babies. Am I a little biased? Of course, but the proof is in the photographs.

I relished going home on short and extended college breaks. I spent this time unwinding from Derry; I was never stressed over my studies. The love of college always made going back to the group home that much easier, but it wasn't easy at all. My unhappiness at Derry even spurred on the plan to move in with one of the employees at Derry until I finished college, but that plan never took shape because Ginger's apartment building was not wheelchair accessible. Ginger was a very nice girl from Texas with a new baby boy. I was sure I would handle living with a child better than I handled with my apartment mates. I liked my apartment mates, but they required a lot of guidance from me, guidance that Seashell put upon my shoulders.

Grocery shopping and meal preparation were the two activities that were the most stressful. On one shopping day, all four of us went to the market. Progress was slow, very slow, excruciatingly slow that after two hours, there were three items in the shopping cart. I told the staff, who was very young, that I was going back to the group home because I had to use the bathroom and I was hungry. I left the market and never returned that day. I wasn't allowed to assist them with shopping up to a certain point, per Seashell's rules. If I was allowed to shop solo, I would have it done in an hour. It took my apartment mates a total of seven hours to return from the market. My apartment mates had incontinent issues, and they were incontinent for most of those seven hours. I was very angered that no staff member stepped in and assisted my apartment mates to finish the shopping. Surely, the other shoppers were put off by their odor. It was grossly irresponsible for staff members to let them remain in public in their condition. I refused to go back for that very reason.

College was everything good. All of my instructors we, hands down, the best. Largely, our class of mostly men, didn't have an issue with women in the construction field. I never got any sexist comments from the "macho" men because I wasn't physically in the trenches swinging hammers side by side with them, but Randi was and she was sometimes a target of sexist remarks. All of our instructors, and some of our fellow classmates, were protective of us.

It was very cool that the instructors didn't preclude me from participating in construction lab. It was a big, steel building, filled with sawdust, tools, and most importantly, an actual house that had to be built. Rather than looking at blueprints day in and day out, I watched the all of the pieces of a house being assembled. It was an extraordinary opportunity I had. College made me feel like a whole person.

What didn't make feel like a whole person was when Seashell suggested I should find a new friend instead of her. I was devastated on the inside but I didn't let her see that. I was so wrong to believe we could be best friends for life. I felt worthless. There were a few afternoons I needed to collect my emotions before I entered the building. I needed to pass by the community room where she usually sat. We said a pleasant hi to one another and went on our way. One night, between having my period, watching *E.T.* and having my staff convinced that I could wash a sink full of dishes independently, I just lost it like I have never lost it before. I completely broke down in tears. She put me down on my futon as to say I was in time out. The following day, I didn't not want to pass by Seashell, fearing that she would interrogate me about my emotional breakdown. The subject was never brought up.

In mid December of 1989, Seashell was terminated from her supervisor's position at Derry. My first reaction was relief, although I felt a bit sorry for her. They hired a new supervisor who seemed very capable, but after I returned from college winter break, I learned the new supervisor had falsely represented herself on her resume. They promoted somebody from within. I got it in my head that Seashell still was my good friend and that she would be contacting me soon. I wasn't about to contact her; I wasn't about to show her my weakness.

With March upon us, I had a curious need to call April for her 23rd birthday. With Seashell not employed at Derry, old friends, Patty and Debi, came to visit. Debi continued to keep in touch with April after going back to Rochester, New York. She lived in a group home. I got her number from Debi, and I called her on or the day after her birthday. She was thrilled! One of April's housemates was a screamer, and screamed, she did. April would yell at her periodically to pipe down but it didn't help. We talked for about a half hour. After we said goodbye, I made a vow that if I was making a good living after my schooling, I would have April move in with me. I had this idea before, but this time I was determined as ever.

I got an unexpected visit from Debi about a month later. From her expression, I knew she had some bad news to share. She hesitated in her sadness. April passed away three days earlier, on April 16, 1990. She aspirated during the early hours of the morning and never awoke. I was heartbroken beyond my words could express. April 16 was Charisma's birthday, so he took this news hard. The world didn't seem quite right without April in it. *"See the stars that shine and give us light One less star is in the sky tonight Words alone won't keep our tears away But I know that star will shine again someday"*. These are lyrics from "Heaven Laughs" by the Hooters off of *Zig Zag*. I can't listen to this song without thinking of my good friend, April Green. When I wrote a letter to Army Sue, who April and me attended her wedding in the summer of 1988, Sue's written response was, "That's a bummer." Needless to say, Sue's 'bummer' comment didn't sit very well with me, and I never felt the need to contact Army Sue again.

Sitting on the floor, working at my final construction project, I was fully focused on drawing walls. I was distracted with the sudden rush of sirens across the street. I got up to my knees and looked outside my window, which had the best vantage point of the commotion. Red and blue lights lit up the clear May Day night sky. I had to take momentary breaks to rest my thighs so I can kneel up again to try to figure out what was going on across the street. Early reports were it was a robbery gone horribly tragic. I returned to my computer and finished my project.

The next day, reports confirmed a young man, 24, a husband, son and a brother, was shot fatally in the back of the head. Police were present for two or three days. One of the staff members and I attempted to get closer to the Misty Meadow condo, but we were asked to move back. I called Paul to wish him a Happy Birthday, and I also told him about the murder across the street, and not to tell Mom, for I didn't want her to worry. I hadn't realized the story would soon go national.

Pam, widow of Greg Smart, appeared on the local news a few days after his horrific murder. She pleaded with the public to come forward with any information that would break the case. I watched this newscast; to me, she seemed calm, too calm, too glued together. I chocked it up to being in shock. Four months later, Smart was arrested for murder. Yes, I was a neighborhood of one of the most infamous, conniving, women of our generation who orchestrated the brutal murder of her husband.

Mom bought me a flowery, black blouse to wear under my graduation gown. It wasn't my favorite blouse, old for my 23 years, but I believe I wore it anyhow. I don't recollect the graduation ceremony, but I did receive my degree, a General Associate's degree in Building Construction Technology. What I do remember was the almost impossible task of packing all my things into another minivan. Different from two years ago was that I had many more things: a shower chair, a futon, a computer, a television cabinet, and not to mention, my electric wheelchair. The plan was that I would sit in my wheelchair for the nearly three-hour trip to Cape Cod. Once Dad, Martha and Glenn situated me in my wheelchair in the minivan, I need about six more inches for my head. We needed a Plan B. Plan B had to consist of building up a seat of pillows, blankets and anything

176

soft in between the two front seats.

I finally was leaving the place I hated for the last two years. It was a relief even though the last four months had been more than tolerable. I wouldn't miss it. It was a warm, sunny day, but once we reached the Cape Cod Canal, the air cooled as if someone turned on a big fan. Also, my back was screaming as we crossed over the Sagamore Bridge. I had twenty more minutes to endure in this unnatural position. I was relieved once we hit our driveway in South Yarmouth. I could finally get out of my pillow and blanket, Jerry-rigged seat. Dad had to struggle to pull my stiff body onto the driver's seat. My body was finally in a different position.

"This frail reminder of its giant, dreaming self
While I, with human-hindered eyes
Unequal to the sweeping curve of life Stand on this single print of time"

"Human Wheels"
John Mellencamp
Human Wheels

I was accepted to Roger Williams College for the Fall of 1990. It was the first, entire summer I had off from school. I can't recall exactly what I did, but I'm positive it was relaxing. Six months earlier, Mom had quit smoking, cold turkey. My parents purchased a house in South Yarmouth. It was a ranch house with two bedrooms and bathrooms, with an attached garage: a very comfortable house, indeed. Mom quit smoking because she didn't want to yellow the newly painted white walls. Nobody argued with her logic.

Entering Roger Williams College brought on a whole new bunch of challenges. Due to all of my equipment, my electric wheelchair, my shower chair, my computer and futon that needed to be set up on the floor, there wasn't any chance that a second person could room with me.

Secondly, per RIVR, they gave me an ultimatum. Oh God, I hated ultimatums. Either I start using a voice synthesizer when I began classes, or they wouldn't fund my daily care services. Anytime anyone forces me to do something that I can't see myself doing, I get very exasperated. When Mom informed me of what Andre said, I became very upset. Mom became upset, and of course I didn't like to get Mom upset, ever. I pulled it together quickly, for her sake. She gave me some good advice that morning; she said get the voice synthesizer to appease RIVR. If you don't want to use it, don't, but if you do, it's there. I still believe that nobody should be forced to use a piece of equipment they are not comfortable in using. Devices such as augmentative and alternative communication should be introduced in a very positive and individualized way, and not jammed down somebody's throat.

RIVR sent me to Children's Hospital in Boston to acquire the AAC device. I was very open to learning to operate the software that would control the external voice synthesizer. Compared to today's augmentative and alternative communication devices, this communication setup was archaic. The Compaq laptop was Velcroed to the top of my wooden lap tray; the thick, metal box that was the voice synthesizer, was Velcroed to the underside of the tray. A short, gray cable flimsy connected both devices. Even though I had no current intentions of turning on the voice synthesizer, I found it frustrating that I wasn't able to turn on and adjust the volume myself. The synthesizer wasn't totally accessible.

It was also during this summer that Mom suggested that I should try to reconnect with Peter Falk, just to see if he remembered me from 1974. She also thought it would be great to inform him that I was a big time college student, studying building construction and how I dream up all of these ideas to make things more wheelchair user friendly. I wrote a letter and remarkably, Mr. Falk didn't take long to respond. His letter was full of pride, love and complete sincerity. This letter began our constant correspondence until he was unable to communicate due to Alzheimer's disease.

Mom, Dad and I would meet with the admissions director, and then have a meeting with several of the department heads, including instructors within the architecture program and the director of school housing. Looking back on this particular meeting and the rest of my time at Roger Williams, I did not have the knowledge I should have had about what I wanted out of my education and where it would take me. All I knew I wanted to design accessible buildings. I really wanted to showcase my inventive innovations to increase the independence for people with disabilities.

The director of school housing, a woman in her mid 40's, began questioning my ability to get out of my dorm room independently in case of fire drills or an actual fire. I said yes, I could get out myself. The woman looked skeptical. It was at that time that I felt the word, 'liability' being branded across my forehead. Whether it was coincidence or deliberate, I would live in the same building as the housing director and her family.

David Melchar, a Roger Williams student advisor, was assigned to be my advisor. He was also in his mid 40's, balding and in excellent physical shape. He was an ex Marine; I liked Marines. They always seemed to have an "anything is possible" mentality, and I needed a Marine in my corner. It helped he knew my brother was a Marine. Mr. Melchar communicated with me with kindness and respect. He saw me beyond my cerebral palsy. We had something in common. I got the feeling that nobody else wanted me there.

RIVR contracted my daily services with two different visiting nurse agencies in Bristol and Newport, and for the better part of the three years, I had the same people taking care of me, Mary and Debbie. I was allotted four and a half hours a day. The rest of the time, I depended on the kindness of mostly strangers to literally open the doors to places where I needed to go.

The campus of Roger Williams University, then Roger Williams College, sits on the southern most tip of Bristol, adjacent to the Mount Hope Bridge. Every morning when I emerge from my ground-level room, all I needed to do is turn around and see Mount Hope Bay 50 feet away. I was fortunate enough to attend two schools, which have tremendous vistas— breathtaking vistas! Since I have been so skilled at getting around the mountain for so long, this campus didn't scare me. I could make it from my dorm, Cedar Hall, to the student union in about seven minutes. The student union was in short walking distance to all the buildings I needed to be for all of my classes. I don't think I was ever late to a class; I was early because I didn't want to disrupt a class. I missed two days of class in my three years.

Before my arrival, Skip, the building and facilities manager, had the shower stall renovated for accessibility, and installed an automatic door opener so I was able to enter and exit my dorm room independently. I had a remote attached to the inside of my armrest panel. The second remote was always within arm length when I was out of my wheelchair in my room, which was every evening after dinner.

On my first full day at Roger Williams, during orientation, we had gaps of free time. It was a bright and beautiful early September day. I was just sitting in front of my dorm enjoying the weather. I have never been one to become too distraught when bees came buzzing around. I was always taught not to wave your arms like a banshee around if a bee is near. Unfortunately nobody ever told me what to do if I grabbed a bee out of thin air with your unruly left hand. Within my tight grip, the bee managed to sting me in the palm of my hand. The sting wasn't as painful as I always imagined it to be. As a kid, somehow I managed to grab the blade of a narrow, serrated knife. I didn't mean to but I did. Prying open an athetoid cerebral palsy hand under the influence of being nervous is nearly impossible, but Mom did it without a drop of blood being shed. I didn't even have a single scratch.

My left hand opened a little bit and the bee flew off. I was sure he went to die in a nearby bush after I squeezed the life out of him. The next thought that entered my head was the fact that a bee had never stung me, so I didn't know if I would be allergic. I went back in my room and debated whether to dial 911 or my mother if I started to go fuzzy. Two minutes had past without loosing the ability to breathe. I had the knowledge that anaphylactic shock would set in quickly if I was allergic. After three minutes, I was sure I would live to see another day. The first stop I made was to see Dave. I told him about my encounter with the bee. He was brave enough to open my left hand to have a look. There wasn't any stinger. Just to make sure, he called the infirmary to tell them I was on my way. The nurse looked at it and determined the stinger was gone. The pain was minimal, but after a few days, my palm itched like crazy. Bees don't scare me!

182

Again, I took on four or five classes per semester. The course load never intimidated me. I knew what I had to do; I knew how much time I had to complete a task; I knew my pace in which I worked. Other than getting tutoring in chemistry and calculus, I completed every college task independently.

Attending Roger Williams was much different than attending New Hampshire Technical College. Roger Williams was a vast campus where everybody went about their business themselves. I didn't have any classmates as friends like I did in New Hampshire. It was a very different atmosphere. I didn't mind it, and I probably didn't help my cause by not opening up to other students. There was one other student in a wheelchair. I believe he was a paraplegic and a little older. He was a nice guy and always said hello. I had it in my mind that everybody else was smarter than I was and I had no business being in this program.

I used to hang out in the architecture building quite frequently. It was there I discovered there was a lot more that went into becoming an architect, such as model building. I could never construct models with my very uncooperative hands I possessed. I supposed there was an argument to be made that I could substitute 3D CAD models with tactile models, but I wasn't ready to turn the architecture curriculum on its head. I was already seen as an inconvenience to a number of the architectural faculty.

It was nearly a year since I had any contact with Seashell. I often wondered how she was and wondered what she was doing. I often expected her and Maura to show up on campus to surprise me, but that never happened. Now, I believe they didn't keep in touch much after 1989. Before I went on Christmas break, I finally got brave enough to send her a Christmas card with a letter. I forget what I wrote in the letter said, but I guess it warranted a return Christmas card. She sent it to my parents' house. They were a bit surprised I received a Christmas card from her; they didn't think much of her over the past few years. Even though her Christmas card was only signed, I took it as a sign that maybe we could start communicating again. I believe I wrote her another letter when I returned to college. This letter went unanswered.

Days before my first year of college at Roger Williams was over, I received a call out of the blue from Debi. Oh gosh, it was so good to hear her voice, and she sounded very well. In the midst of our conversation, she told me she had brief contact with Seashell and knew I had written her. Debi explained Seashell had only sent me a Christmas card to be polite; she had no interest in keeping in touch with me. Instead of being upset by this news, I felt free, freer than I have felt in the previous three years. I figured that she was the one who was missing out. I felt strong; I felt powerful and I never looked back.

Sometime over that summer, I spent a few days in New Hampshire with Debi. Most of the time we hung out at her house in Milford. She was still working at the residential school and she drove me up for a short visit. This was the last time I saw Leslie. It was good to see her and her son, Michael, who was three at the time. Michael made her happy when I believed nothing much else did. Debi provided me an enjoyable few days of fun and relaxation.

In the Fall of 1991, RIVR urged me to hire my own personal care attendants. On paper, this idea looked good, but in reality, it was very challenging—extremely challenging. RIVR wanted to cut out the middleman, the agency, and allow me to do the hiring. I worked with a non-profit agency that provides a variety of services and information to individuals with disabilities. Their job was to give me the proper tools to hire my own PCAs. I put flyers up all over campus advertising the job. I had minimal hours for minimal pay. Nobody inquired about the job. I don't recall why but Debbie switched over to working with me privately.

184

With working more unpredictable circumstances, I wanted to devise a viable plan where I could relieve myself in case I ever needed to, especially during the night when nobody was present to assist me. Truthfully I had been contemplating a way I could use the bathroom without anyone present for a long time. I asked the people from the agency if they could help me build this padded, wooden box, which I designed, that would serve my needs very well. The agency required an evaluation be performed into the feasibility of such an object. *Are you kidding me?!* I just wanted to relieve myself freely if I had to during the night. To the agency, the evaluation was imperative; in my head, I knew this object could be built in less than four hours.

It was this time Dad was symptomatic for Type 2 diabetes. He was very fatigued plus all the classic signs of diabetes. When he finally got diagnosed, his blood sugar level was above 800. He should have been admitted to the hospital but I believe I was home on break. As he was feeling a little bit better, he was able to construct my wooden platform, my chamber pot. It would serve me well for many years. I was very appreciative. For someone who never has been able to relieve themselves without the assistance of another human, this achievement was very liberating.

Peter got stationed at Camp David for at least one year. He developed new security protocol for the president's retreat. We were extremely proud of him. As immediate relatives, parents and siblings were allowed to get a tour of the historic retreat. My parents drove down to the Catoctin Mountains in Frederick, Maryland. I believe they stayed three or four days.

Debbie was supposed to work the dinner and the night hours on this particular night. I returned to my room; my answering machine was blinking. Debbie called out sick for the night. "Shit!" Because she was working privately through the agency, I didn't have any substitutes to call. Mom and Dad weren't home, so they couldn't help me make any phone calls.

"Shit! Shit! Shit!" Mary would come right over, but I had trepidation about calling somebody who wouldn't be expecting my call. I feared throwing anybody into a panic thinking anything serious was wrong. The next best thing I could do was do have somebody else make that phone call.

I drove back up to the architecture library and typed out on my computer screen politely asking the desk clerk to call Mary. Mary was not home. "Shit! Shit! Shit! Shit!" I drove back to my dorm room, and phoned Pat at my parents'. Not home. I was striking out all over the place. My next call was to Martha. Oh boy, I didn't want to bother her. I phoned and Glenn answered. Of course since I never call, he assumed something was up. Martha was working. I was able to get across to Glenn that I didn't have staff. He called Martha at work. She left work and came to my rescue. Word got around the next day, and RIVR restored my funding with the visiting nursing agencies.

It was the siblings' turn to visit Camp David. It would be the first time I would travel anywhere with just Martha and Paul. We left on a morning that brought a couple inches of snow the night before. Martha was fighting some kind of lung illness although she wasn't contagious. To douse her sore throat, she always had a beverage close by. We had a white, rented sedan, which was packed to the hilt. I sat in the center of the back seat, with my braced legs straddling the central car bump. Stuff upon stuff, pillows and soft duffel bags, were piled up around me so I wouldn't get to that point where I couldn't sit myself back up again.

I enjoyed listening to Paul and Martha chat, and at sometimes, bicker about silly matters, like which fast food joint to stop at next. Paul had an obsession with Dunkin' Donuts coffee; Martha leaned towards McDonald's milkshakes to soothe her throat. I really didn't care; I had Colombo yogurts on ice in the car. Paul and Martha weren't accustomed of feeding me, so when they ate, I sort of had to remind them I had to be fed, nonchalantly.

186

We made it to Peter's place of residence in late afternoon. Expecting to be greeted by Peter's wife, we were greeted by Peter's neighborhood, who ironically, looked very similar to our sister-in-law, especially at a distance. Inside the two-story townhouse, we made ourselves at home after our road trip. We couldn't help to wonder about the peculiarity of her absence. Being there felt a little odd.

Peter arrived home about two hours later. He explained his wife had to go home to Rhode Island because her brother was ill. Three weeks later, Peter finally told my parents they have separated. Nobody was surprised.

On the next day, we were scheduled to go up to Camp David later that afternoon. We decided to drive an hour to Washington D.C. to see some of the sights. We had lunch at Union Station, visited the Air and Space Museum and the Museum of Modern Art. We were back in Frederick by 4pm. There was a delay in our visit to Camp David, but we did make it there. Driving up to Camp David was very reminiscent to going up to the roads in northern New England. The roads were longer and everywhere you looked, chain-linked fences wrapped around the woods like a ribbon. Sometimes you were able to see one or two sets of chain-linked fences. I had no doubt some of the fences were electrified. You knew this was something not everybody sees.

We reached the gated entrance in our rented sedan. Fifteen-foot high chain-linked fence stood before us. I assumed it might take a nuclear bomb to get through the fence. There was a small building at the gate where Marines kept watch. Two Marines emerged to search the sedan. I'm sure they knew of our arrival. The Marines searched our car, inside and out, backward and forward, and up and down. They used mirrors to search the under side of the car, much like a dentist uses mirrors to detect cavities. A few minutes later, the gates opened, allowing us to enter.

Shortly, we would come to another observation building. Peter exited and showed us where to park. Paul went to the trunk and pulled out my wheelchair, probably for the fifth time that day. He put the footrests on the wheelchair, and lifted me into it. Peter started the tour. Visitors not related or worked directly for the President were restricted from most of the buildings except for the Evergreen Chapel. The residences were small cabin-like buildings, much like the beaches of Truro. The only difference is these cabins were in dense woods.

The Evergreen Chapel matched the quaint architecture of the rest of the retreat. It was small inside, probably holding 50 to 100 people. It had light maple pews. It was an extremely peaceful space.

Leaving the retreat, we were lucky to see a helicopter land and takeoff from the helipad. It wasn't Marine One, but it was very impressive all the same.

With already visiting Washington D.C. and Camp David, there wasn't too much left to do in those mountains. We headed home. Just over the Pennsylvania state line, we found ourselves in Gettysburg. Paul was in search of a Dunkin' Donuts. During our drive around Gettysburg, I don't think we were prepared for the feeling that engulfed us, as we stared out on the lands that so many young men lost their lives. I believed the ground still held blood. I looked hard over the lands expecting ghosts walking the fields. These roads must be even more haunting at night.

It was my last year at Roger Williams. I think this was my most enjoyable year in Bristol. A few classes I took were Women's Study, Computers: Artificial Intelligence, and Frank Lloyd Wright: A Life's Work. Grattan Gill taught the Frank Lloyd Wright course understandably because he studied under Wright in Scotsdale, Arizona. At 61 years of age, a swatch of white hair horseshoed around his shiny and freckled baldhead. He was energetic as a child with every activity he pursued,

188

especially his teaching. He had a special passion for Frank Lloyd Wright.

Mr. Gill took an immediate liking to me, and he was never was put off by my limitations. He was a very patient soul with the kindness and the willingness to assist in any way he could.

During the semester in Mr. Gill's course, he organized a field trip for us to visit a Frank Lloyd Wright house in Manchester, New Hampshire, the Zimmerman House. Given the bus the college chartered wasn't wheelchair accessible, I had to drive in Mary's car. When we reached the Zimmerman House, as Mary removed my manual wheelchair from her trunk, we realized we had forgotten my footrests in Rhode Island. *Shit!* I knew how my legs acted when not supported by footrests—wild. I worried about my wild legs when I entered this historic house.

All who entered the house had to wear cloth booties. Unfortunately, my sneakers didn't reach the ground; if they had, my legs would have much more controlled. My feet were about three inches off the ground, and had nowhere to rest. As Mary pushed me around the Wright house, my feet often got in the way of the turning of the front wheels. I knew that if I leaned forward in my wheelchair, I could keep my feet back. Again, the front wheels turning caused me to lose control of my feet. There were a few occasions where my feet made contact with certain items in the house. Mary wasn't accustomed to pushing me in my wheelchair, and I couldn't predict where Mary was going to direct me next. The curator was shooting daggers at Mary and me. I grew very anxious, resulting in more exaggerated jerks. My heart started to pound, and my palms started to sweat. Even though I was awestruck being inside such a beautiful, and innovative home, I couldn't wait to exit the house.

I hope my presence in the house didn't cause the curator to ban the subsequent visitors in wheelchairs from entering this remarkable Wright home.

Somehow the subject came up that I wished to propose to the Providence Civic Center ways they could improve their wheelchair seating sections. After going to a number of concerts at the Providence Civic Center, people in wheelchairs had a distinct disadvantage of keeping their line of sight to the stage clear, especially when the majority of the crowd stood up during the show. I wanted to fix that. Of course I hadn't drafted my ideas on the computer, but I knew what I wanted to do in my head. I always have a plan in my head. Mr. Gill encouraged me to write to the Providence Civic Center to get copies of the blueprints. Lo and behold, Mr. Lombardi, the director of the facility, sent me a set. I looked them over very carefully, making sure I understood what I was reading. I consulted Mr. Gill from time to time. He showed me a different suggestion that could rectify the issue improving the sight lines for people in wheelchairs. My ideas were ambitious; Mr. Gill's ideas were practical and straightforward. As I kept up with my course work, I also did CAD mockups of two distinctive renovations.

Mr. Gill, Dad and I set up a meeting with Mr. Lombardi in his office at the Providence Civic Center. Mr. Gill presented most of the proposed renovations. Polite, Mr. Lombardi listened to our ideas, but I figured he already had his mind settled. A few weeks later, I received a letter from Mr. Lombardi stating that our renovations would result in the lost of a number of "regular" seating. I thought this was a lame excuse not to find a workable solution. I should have continued my pressure on Mr. Lombardi to address the issue.

I proved my ability to exit my dorm, fortunately only once, during an early evening fire drill during the spring. It was my routine every evening after eating dinner at the student union that Mary would gently drop me on my futon and remove my AFOs and sneakers. I can't crawl or "W" sit wearing AFOs. Of course it was always a relief to take those off every evening. With that, I was off to the races crawling around the light blue carpet Mom and Dad got for my dorm room. Like Derry, my computer was set up on floor level so I would have total access to it when I was on the floor. On this night, the fire alarm went off. I always had my automatic door remote within reaching distance. I pressed it to open the door. Since the exterior door was within five feet, I probably could have stayed in my doorway. I wanted to prove my self-preservation to all those people who doubted my abilities. Crawling on linoleum is one thing, but crawling on concrete and tar is quite another. I don't think I let myself feel anything on the way out because I was so determined to prove myself. While outside, I sat on the grass until we got the all clear. Somehow, my socks managed to stay on my feet. They gave the all clear, and looking back, the distance seemed to double. What soreness I didn't feel exiting the building, I definitely felt crawling back in.

When Mary saw my bruised and red knees and legs the next morning, she was very angry that I crawled out. She wasn't angry at me, she was angry that nobody stepped in and suggested I stay in my open doorway. I didn't want her to make a big deal out of it; I was tough and I have always been tough. Luckily, there weren't anymore fire drills between the hours of 6PM to 7AM.

If five classes weren't enough to handle during my last year at college, Dave arranged me to take a one-on-one music theory weekly study session with one of the music professors at Roger Williams. I hadn't thought or even looked at a quarter note in about four and an half years, so these sessions were like music theory refresher sessions. It was a great change of "scenery" compared to my routine studies for building. I also took a music appreciation course during one of my semesters. The music theory sessions were fun and relaxing. I enjoyed being in the moment.

It was about two weeks before graduation, and Paul Reiser was doing a show at Roger Williams. "Mad About You"

had been airing for a year, and I loved the show. Mary and I
went to the show, and he was great. The next morning I woke up
feeling like death. It wasn't quite as bad like when I had the flu
in 1979, but I wanted to curl up in a ball and not move.
Thankfully it wasn't a stomach bug; I just felt like a heaping pile
of crap. It might have been a sinus infection. Mary brought me
to the doctor and she prescribed me some antibiotics and told me
to take some Advil Cold & Sinus. It was Final week and I didn't
miss any finals.

The Providence Journal came to Roger Williams and
wrote an article about me, the third in 19 years. In this particular
article, I talked about how excited I was to have the prospects of
actually working for an income and not being dependent on
Social Security Income because I was disabled. I also mentioned
the letter I wrote to the newly elected President Clinton, urging
him to press for all buildings, new and old, to be fully wheelchair
accessible. I wanted to work and pay taxes, and in my mind,
making new and old buildings wheelchair accessible would keep
me employed.

With Paul's assistance, he showed me how to properly
write a cover letter and construct a resume. I collected about 200
architectural firms and addresses across Rhode Island and
southeastern Massachusetts in the hopes that at least one or two
of my letters would land me at least one job interview. The few
letters I did get back were all rejections: "at this time our firm is
not hiring an employee with your specific skills."

With one more week of college, a package arrived from
Los Angeles. It was a blue, Tiffany box, with their signature
matching blue ribbon. Mary helped me open the box. It was a
Sterling Silver picture frame. It was engraved with the words,
"Maureen, You're Something…Love, Peter Falk." Wow! He
was something.

Feeling almost back in good health from my mysterious

virus I had for the last twelve days, I came through all my final exams successfully. I was looking forward to graduation and moving onto bigger things. It was an all-day celebration with my family and Mary, who was always there to take care of me day in and day out during my time at Roger Williams University. We had a big celebration and lunch at the Old Grist Mill Tavern in Seekonk. Then the party moved to Aunt Anne and Uncle Tom's Warwick house and everybody just chilled there for a bit. We enjoyed having our kids run around like little monkeys, as they enjoyed playing outside. Evening came and some of us shot up to Shooter's at India Point and gave the day one last toast.

"Miss the beat, you lose the rhythm, And nothing falls into place
Only missed by a fraction
Slipped a little off your pace"

"Right Now"
Van Halen
For Unlawful Carnal
Knowledge

Out of school: what do I do now? That was the question that kept creeping into my mind for a long time. Cape Cod became my permanent home for the next eight years. It wasn't a bad place to live, especially if you are a laidback kind of person. I had already spent three summers and countless of weekends here studying during college. On the success of my college degree, RIVR kept up the pace with trying to assist me with finding me employment. In order for me to be employable, RIVR felt I needed my own vehicle to get to job site to job site. I couldn't argue with that. It was then RIVR introduced us to the PASS Plan.

The Plan to Achieve Self-Support (PASS) is a Social Security Administration program to assist people to achieve their employment goals by financial assistance. In my particular case, I was able to draw Social Security Disability Income under my Dad's work record, and still be able to collect my Social Security Income. The SSDI would be my monthly personal income, and SSI was strictly for loan payments for a vehicle. My new VR counselor, Bill, was flawless in setting up my PASS Plan, which gained approval by the Social Security Administration. Another advantage to being a Vocational Rehabilitation client is when you have a vehicle, VR is mandated to make that vehicle accessible for applicable clients.

RIVR required me to be evaluated for what type of vehicle I needed. Although it was very obvious that I needed an accessible wheelchair van, RIVR still required an evaluation, and for that evaluation, Dad and I had to travel to Wallingford, Connecticut—a three-hour drive from Cape Cod. The evaluation also was to determine if I had the ability to actually drive a vehicle. In the past, the driver's education teacher at the residential school, Paul St. Pierre, believed I may be able to drive, but I didn't think it was wise, given my athetoid cerebral palsy. I didn't want to take on that responsibility. I didn't want to injure or kill another person or an animal. The people in Wallingford also made that determination. Although I wouldn't attempt to drive on average city streets and highways, I always

195

thought it would be very cool to drive a car in one of those wide open Nevada deserts where nothing is around for miles and miles to just get the feel of what it's like to drive a car. In ten more years, vehicles will be driving themselves with advancements in technology.

The final report submitted to RIVR stated I required a full size van with a wheelchair lift or a minivan with a ramp. Given the amount of money I had to work with, a full size van was what we chose. Dad traded in his Grand Marquis in for my Ford F-150. The second process we had to complete was to obtain three quotes from different van conversion vendors. Dad and I hit all three within a day, which was another very long day.

During this process of applying for the PASS Plan and finally getting the van wheelchair-equipped took about eight to ten months. I received my first accessible van a few days into 1994. My cover letters and resumes didn't stop going out. I sent an inquiry to Adaptive Environments in Boston and landed a four-month internship with them. Unfortunately with the distance to Boston, and the fact that Dad was a full-time employee at Barnstable Airport, only allowed me to go to Boston once a week, with a rented minivan during the summer months of 1993. Some days were hot around South Station studying the sidewalks and curb cuts of that specific area. When I was home, I put this specific area into a 3D CAD drawing. My job was to pinpoint and to do my own modifications of spots that weren't wheelchair accessible to improve accessibility. I also studied, forwards and backwards, the Americans with Disabilities Act Accessibility Guidelines (ADAAG) and the Massachusetts equivalent to ADAAG.

Throughout this four-month internship was another period in my life that I felt very inadequate with regards to my education and experience. It always seemed that I wasn't up on all the architectural jargon I should know. I didn't really give myself any slack and realized that to learn all I needed to know would take time and working experience, and I didn't have that. Following my internship, I landed a job interview with an architecture firm in Boston, an architectural firm concentrating on accessibility. I didn't get the position; I wasn't prepared. If I did land a position off Cape, finding accessible housing and setting up PCA services would have been a logistical and timing gigantic hurdle that nobody considered.

After my internship in Boston, I continued to send out cover letters and resumes. I landed one interview with an architect in Barnstable, with an office that wasn't wheelchair accessible. I believe the entrance had one or two steps. Ironic. For all of these interviews I used my communication device. Unfortunately, I didn't get this position. I was striking out left and right. My well was running dry. What to do next? Maybe I'll write some music.

Somehow I learned about music software and gear through books and/or magazines. I learned that notation software had become highly sophisticated within the previous five years. Notation software played chords! Chords?! Chords?! Yes, chords, and so much more! First, I tried MusicPrinter Plus, which was a DOS based program. It was a good program for its time, but it lacked the ability to automatically line up notation on the grand staff. I used it for a very short time until I stumbled upon the rave reviews that the notation software, Finale, was receiving. Finale was a Windows based program, and frankly, switching to a Windows platform was very unnerving, mainly because I didn't know how I would control the mouse. I did a little more investigating and learned that Microsoft had contracted with a university to develop StickyKeys and MouseKeys. All I had to contact Microsoft and they mailed me this specific diskette at no cost. With the introduction of Windows 95, these Accessibility Options were programed directly into the operating system, which was extremely useful. The jump from working in a DOS environment into a Windows environment worked in my advantage, all because I wanted to use the Finale notation software.

The next thing I had to learn about were sound/tone generators. They were also referred to as sound modules. Sound generators produced sounds initialized by MIDI outputs. MIDI is an acronym for Musical Instrument Digital Interface. Whether you control a MIDI by a musical keyboard or software such as Finale, signals from both devices could produce sounds.

My first sound generator was the Yamaha TG100. It was a small, black box that connected to my PC through an additional, internal sound card. It needed two speakers for the sound to come out. The TG100 had 128 individual sounds, which sounded pretty damn good after just having individual tones in the past. The TG100 had an awesome piano, and the acoustic and electric guitars didn't sound half bad either. Remember, I only worked with internal computer sounds prior to getting the TG100, so anything sounded glorious at this point. Did I really know how to use it even when I read the manual? Not really. I was composing piano pieces with a single grand staff. I was using expressions to make specific sections of my piano piece louder or softer, which I thought was pretty, damn cool.

When I understood one element of a process, my curiosity acted up and I started experimenting with other aspects of Finale and the TG100. This is when I very happily discovered that I could play more than one instrument at once. I was ecstatic beyond my wildest dreams! Once I understood this concept, the concept of playing multiple instruments simultaneously, I composed my first, multi-track instrumental, "Live The Beat". It had piano, synth, bass, guitar and drums! *Holy shit! I just wrote my first song!* From this, another 18 instrumentals came rolling out over the next six months. Some songs are better than others but I'm still proud of all of them. It was a good first effort.

I didn't stop my pursuit in finding employment in the field of architecture, but it remained very difficult. Some old friends came calling from New Hampshire. The residential school foundation was getting prepared to build an accessible housing project in Portland, Maine. I was asked to consult. This was the first real work as a post-graduate. The architect on the Portland project sent me files on 3.5" floppies and I looked over the digital blueprints on my computer, before the age of the Internet, as we know it today. If I saw something that could be improved, I copied the file to make the change, which I deemed appropriate. I would mail my diskette back to the project architect. I clearly recall suggesting that the sidewalks around the complex be level with the road. It had been my experience that people with disabilities sometimes have visual impairments, and I have seen many people in wheelchairs, or ambulatory people misjudge the edge of a curb and become injured, sometimes severely. If we eliminate the elevation of curbs and sidewalks, we eliminate the danger of people injuring themselves. Completing this consulting project looked very good on my resume, and it padded my bank account just a little bit.

        In the following four years, I consulted on two more projects, but one never got off the ground, so to speak. This particular project was for my primary care physician who wanted to move her office to Route 28 in Harwich. The doctor had an open floor plan to renovation. Actually the space was huge. It was my job to design the interior floor plan to utilize all of the square footage available. I don't recall the exact details of the project, but I believe we had five or six exam rooms. I designed two of those exam rooms to wheelchair accessible. Of course these two rooms had wider doors and more square footage, which a traditional doctor's exam room doesn't necessarily have. If I have known barrier-free lifts existed at that time, I would have installed an appropriate barrier-free lift track in each of the accessible exam rooms. I earned a few hundred dollars for this project.

        The next, and last big project I consulted on was a Cape

Cod Community College in 1996. I enrolled in a small business course at the college and discovered their three separate lecture halls were only wheelchair accessible if people entered through the basement level of the building. Rightly so, the college believed entering the lecture halls from the basement, instead on the main level, was unsafe and discriminatory for their students in wheelchairs. Also, there wasn't a lot of space on the bottom area of the stadium lecture halls. It was very cramped.

Somehow I became involved in the renovations of these three lecture halls. What was so impressive with Cape Cod Community College was that they have a specific division to assist their students with disabilities with a range of services. The woman, Joyce Chasson, who ran this resource center, was visually impaired. She was just a great lady. The facility director, Robert Cleghorn, was also a very nice gentleman. We all worked seamlessly together to get this project completed. It was a pretty cool feeling that I was a part of this lecture hall project, which allowed all students, whether they had a disability or not, to enter the lecture halls through the same door, and on the main level. The renovations mostly consisted of leveling off sunken levels, building up levels and adding a ramp in the large lecture hall. It's not rocket science to create or renovate spaces to be wheelchair accessible. I like the term, Universal Design, myself.

Desktop publishing was big in the 1990's, and I taught myself CorelDRAW and then Adobe Illustrator. I'm not exactly sure what the main reason I got into graphic design, but I enjoyed it. It became another avenue, which I could earn a little income, and it was little income. By this time, the architectural opportunities had all but dried up, and getting into graphic design was sort of a natural progression from architecture, and part, music. I started designing just simple business cards, to flyers, to brochures, to postcards, and so on and so forth. I definitely learned a little bit more with every project, flying by the seat of my pants, if you will. My biggest order came from Los Angeles,

200

California. Oh yes, my buddy, Peter Falk, and his assistant, Shelby Rose, wanted business cards, stationery and envelopes. Peter supplied with his own rendering of his character, "Columbo" and that was my first test on trying to convert a hard copy into a digital format. I was extremely fortunate that I could visit a very nice man who owned a print shop a few miles away.

In 1995, Mom, Dad and I decided it would probably be to my benefit if I switched my resident status to Massachusetts. I would be able to get more services. Dad and I visited the Social Security Administration office in Hyannis. The representative we talked to initially became my representative for most of the time I lived in South Yarmouth. Jolly: she wasn't. She had a very abrasive personality and definitely got up on the wrong side of the bed each and every day. My PASS Plan was her target, and she essentially stopped my PASS Plan immediate once I transferred residency. She didn't think I was living up to my employment goals set forth in my PASS Plan. She felt if I didn't have fulltime employment, then my PASS Plan had to end. She didn't care that I had taken out a bank loan to pay for the vehicle. She didn't care that I had proof that I was still trying to find employment. She didn't much care that if I didn't have my van, I certainly couldn't look or hold down a job. My Dad, the very calm soul that he usually is, pictured going across her desk and putting his hands around her puny, little neck. He was livid.

This begun my two-year appeal with the Social Security Administration. We had to travel back and forth to New Bedford to meet with my appointed lawyer about every other month. During this two-year period, I lived off about $30 a month after I paid the monthly loan payment. We were not relinquishing my van, if at all possible. Mom and Dad kept a roof over my head and food in my belly. After almost two years with having the van, we have gotten used to the ease of going out without physical strain upon my Dad. We weren't relinquishing my van.

Ironically, at the final appeal hearing with a judge, who

travelled to Hyannis from the great state of Maine, with Dad at my side, I represented myself. Sometimes fools can represent themselves, successfully. With four years of using my AAC device, I had written what I wanted to say to the judge. With a few keystrokes, the voice, Uppity Ursula, spoke for me. It was decided upon, with the help of the lawyer in New Bedford, the main argument would be based on the fact that I had the responsibility to pay back the bank loan, and that I was still actively seeking employment. Following my argument, the judge immediately ruled in my favor. Two weeks later, I received a check from Social Security Administration for payments dating back two years.

"Can you find release
And will you ever change
When will you write your
masterpiece?"

"James"
Billy Joel
Turnstiles

Would I ever write that masterpiece? I would like to think this autobiography will be my masterpiece. For as long as I can remember, there has always been some little part of me that enjoyed making up stories. I hadn't really written anything substantial until I started conjuring up and outlining *Always A Place*. My Mom would always tell me I was a talented, humorous writer and I should actually write something. I didn't know what to write, or even if anybody else would be interested in reading anything that came out of this sometimes goofy brain of mine.

By the spring of 1994, a year out of college, feeling frustrated about my lack of employment opportunities, feeling a bit isolated, this story came to me like a bolt of lightning one late night. Bam! There it was! A lot of times I get my best ideas between 11 pm and 4 am. I must have a freaky, nocturnal brain of some sort that feeds off darkness and quietness. I believe it took me about six weeks to really cement the story down in my mind and another three months to write the outline of the story. In the process of writing the outline, I was still composing music left and right. The summer of 1994 was a very creative summer for me. I was listening and fallen in love with Counting Crows' *August And Everything After* and Live's *Throwing Copper*. These two albums fueled my blood; they fueled my energy. They inspired me where music hadn't really inspired me for a number of years.

I wrote this novel because I was bored. It was as simple as that. I also wrote this novel to live vicariously through my characters, as strange as that might sound. I had visions of what I should be doing with my life that I wasn't doing in reality. I wanted some kind of life beyond what I was living, and this book gave me that life even if it was purely fiction.

My protagonist, Kate, I modeled after myself. Surprise, surprise. Physically, Kate was a carbon copy of me; she had athetoid cerebral palsy; she had the same level of Dysarthria and speech impairments; she used a headpointer. Emotionally, I created Kate's character with much more strength I perceived I possessed. Kate was a go-getter. If Kate wanted to do something, or wanted something, she didn't let anything stop her. I also set up the scenario that Kate was happily married to a non-disabled man. This particular relationship certainly brought my personal perceptions of love and intimacy between a disabled woman and a non-disabled man. I had to explore all of my lifelong beliefs, fears and hopes and ring all those out in my first novel. It is true when other authors describe the writing process as cathartic for your personal soul. The writing process can also be very spiritual. You look at life so differently when you creating the plot, when you are creating characters and their unique personalities. Critical thinking must go into creating characters and their personalities because you must think how each character came to be, and what drives them and what doesn't. What was their childhood like? How were they raised? What influenced their character during their adolescence and young adulthood? Did they need to overcome some issues growing up?

The next aspect I needed to consider was how people without disabilities perceived people with disabilities. We all know different people have different conceptions about people with disabilities, and I really had fun creating all of these characters to demonstrate their views. Through the protagonist's own eyes, I had the opportunity to show Kate as a very smart, engaging, insightful, determined and loving person who had a physical disability that she had to contend with on a daily basis.

The most important objective I strove for was making this story believable. It was my purpose to show that what happens in the plot wasn't far-fetched. I don't do far-fetched fiction. I spent countless of nights combing through every aspect of my story in my mind, reworking minor or major parts of the story so they fit just right, like pieces of a puzzle. I didn't let any piece of the story not be filed without great care until it fit just perfectly. It had to be perfection.

One other facet of my story that was totally the opposite from my own life was the relationship the character, Kate, had with her parents. I used "poetic license" to make Kate's parents 180° different from my parents. In the back of my mind, I worried a little bit if some of my readers might think I had standoffish parents, which, obviously, wasn't the case at all. I had a little bit of fun with creating characters who I had to dig down deep to explore and give cause to their reasoning and actions.

It wasn't until I finished the second draft in December of 1999 that I let anyone read this 315-page manuscript I wrote. It had sex scenes in it, for Heaven sakes! How could I have my parents, siblings, aunts, uncles and cousins read such scenes I wrote? Well, I did, and it was one of the bravest things I had done in my life, and it felt very liberating.

This was also the period in which I settled on the novel's title, *Always A Place*. "Always A Place" is a terrific song written by Rob Hyman and Eric Bazilian of The Hooters, and this song fit my storyline extraordinarily well, so I used it. The "place" I used the novel was a real place. Leslie used to be a house sitter for a couple who lived in Jaffrey. They were rarely in Jaffrey during the colder months. A handful of times Leslie bought us to their property. Attached to the farmhouse was this awesome barn, which stood about two and an half stories tall. The barn consisted of only its four exterior walls, its roof, and its purlins that were its skeleton. At one end was a brick fireplace, surrounded by cozy chairs and couches. It was easy to imagine a romantic night in front of a roaring, warm fire with my Prince Charming. I used this very real barn as sort of my focal point in *Always A Place*.

I believe my Mom was the first family member to read it. Mom was an avid reader and she could polish off a book in one or two nights, lying comfortably in bed, or sitting with both bare feet up on the den couch. Sleep didn't come easily to her, so she read and read until her near-sighted eyes got weary. I felt

206

anxious, but not too anxious that I wanted to puke. She wasn't naïve, and I think she knew me better than what I wanted to imagine. She loved my 315-page torrent of words, sometimes incorrect grammar and many typos. Mom insisted that it was better than some of the books she had read and urged me to try to get it published. "It took Mary Higgins Clark 428 attempts to get her first book published," my Mom said repeatedly. I still didn't have any idea to get my book, let alone, an exercise in boredom, published.

Mom suggested I send my manuscript to Peter Falk. I might have looked at her with question marks all over my face. My thoughts were he's a Hollywood movie and television star—doesn't he have more important things he could be doing than reading my boredom? Mom assured me Peter would steer me in the right direction. Peter loved my novel and proceeded to find me an editor. The editor chopped off 100 pages from my novel. This insulted me. *How could anyone delete 100 pages from my book?* Once I read my edited manuscript, it worked perfectly. It is truly amazing how many words can be edited out while maintaining the integrity of a story. The editor asked me to rework one scene. I did as he requested. The editor sent it out to nine publishing houses and nine rejection letters returned. "428 attempts," Mom repeated.

"Now I need a moment that's mine
Oh my other world is
Just a half a mile away"

"Half A Mile Away"
Billy Joel
52nd Street

It had been two years since I graduated college. I changed residency to Massachusetts. Mom fractured her wrist on the ground in the backyard trying to tie her white, Keds. Yeah, maybe we should apply for PCA services.

I forget how we got in contact with United Cerebral Palsy of the South Shore, but they initiated and ran payroll for my PCA services. The first interview was with this gentleman, Keith, who had cerebral palsy, very similar to my degree of cerebral palsy. He was employed by United Cerebral Palsy of the South Shore. He had his PCA with him to assist him in what he could not do for himself. He was about 20 years older. Through our initial interview I realized that he didn't have the ability to read very well. After I discovered that he didn't have any formal education as a child because his mother didn't want him to send him to school, I must admit, I felt a little resentful that I busted my ass through school in the hopes I would find steady employment, and this man didn't have any formal education, but he had a part-time job. Maybe I was being petty but I was just a little annoyed.

He submitted my paperwork to United Cerebral Palsy of the South Shore and about three weeks later, two nurses came out to the house and conducted a comprehensive survey of the services I needed. Keith was also present, which felt a little awkward because the questions I had to answer were sometimes personal in nature. These nurses were wonderful because of their experience. This evaluation was very different from the Supports Intensity Scale (SIS) evaluation of today. No questions were asked about behavior, employment or education issues. The evaluation only concentrated on my physical needs: bathing, dressing, toileting, eating, etc.

I was approved for five hours a day for respite for my parents. This particular program was organized as similar to our self-directed programs. I would hire the people I thought were worthy to work with me, and United Cerebral Palsy of the South Shore would handle payroll. I hired, Debbie, Keith's PCA, as she needed more hours. Going through the tedious process of submitting employment ads to the newspaper, setting up interviews and doing the interview became an eye-opening experience. I performed almost every aspect of this process on my own. I still have the Teletype phone that I made countless of calls on, gave job prospects the directions to our house on, and called back the people I wanted to hire. It was never an easy process, not by a long shot. The biggest kick in the teeth was when I would spend at least 30 minutes on the Teletype machine, typing non-stop the directions to our house and they wouldn't show up for the interview. *What the fuck?!* This process was extremely frustrating and exhausting.

A good percentage of the women I did get through the front door for that golden interview were worthy candidates, but I went for the best. There was a time or two where Mom had some opinions of her own that I had to respect. The power of intuition speaks volumes when choosing a person for your PCA. Within five minutes of an interview, I always sensed that if I would "hit it off" with someone. A lot of times, personalities spoke louder than their experience. I hired a 21-year-old, Laura Sanders, just because she sat on the floor with me for over an hour as we talked about whatever we wanted. Those are the moments where you recognize that most of your efforts paid off.

I have treated the people who have taken care of me with the utmost respect, especially if they reciprocate that respect. You need to recognize that nobody is perfect, and you have to look past these little imperfections and look at the bigger picture. Tiny flaws you must accept, especially if one is totally devoted to their job caring for you. If you get the feeling that someone is not devoted to your daily care, your goals or expectations, they have to be addressed, sooner better than later.

I only had two situations where the women I hired were less than spectacular workers. I hired them out of timely necessity. Luckily, they left after a few months on their own volition, and with a little prodding. After getting home from a day trip to Rhode Island, one particular woman had the seatbelt so tangled around one of my wheelchair wheels that it took my Dad 20 minutes to extract the seatbelt. We sent her home for the night because she served no purpose just watching my Dad. She served no purpose and didn't care to lend a hand. I have never fired one individual yet. Whether I will have the backbone to fire anybody remains to be seen. I imagine if the situation called for it, I would.

For people who can organize their own lives, manage their own lives, hire and manage their own PCAs, or do this all with assistance of a family member or a guardian, self-directed programs gives the individual the most autonomy to go about their lives how they see fit. I think we all want autonomy over our own lives; I know I do.

Rhode Island has many, many resources for people with disabilities, but as with any system, improvements must be made. I dream of a community where people can go into a "one-stop" center and apply for services the require, whether they need PCA services, accessible or technology equipment, education services, job training, job placement services, and so on. It is rather exhausting to have to go from place, to place, to place searching out all of these specific services. If I had to decide on which two services I would have in the same building, hands down, it would be the Social Security Administration and the Office of Rehabilitation Services (formerly Vocational Rehabilitation) since they work so closely together. I would also put a job placement program in that same building.

While we are talking about integrating services and application processes in one cohesive center, I would like to see a division set up where people could go and pick from large pool of vetted PCAs to interview based on their availability. In our small state, chances are good that there could be a vetted PCA working five or ten minutes away who may be looking for extra hours. Of course in larger states, several of these informational "kiosks" would have to be established to serve appropriate areas. I truly believe that these informational kiosks are and will be available online in every state. A number of states have already set up these types of websites.

As I think about what potential these types of websites, websites that bring information about services for people with disabilities, the website could encompass job openings, PCA classifieds, and the like. Technology can bring independence to people with disabilities in many aspects of life. We just need to harness its full potential.

Feeling rather confident having this newfound independence with my PCAs, Mom, Dad and I decided it might be smart to get my name on the waiting list for an accessible apartment. In this case, the accessible apartment complex was in Orleans, Massachusetts, and a 20-minute ride from South Yarmouth. Frankly, it wasn't a town I could see myself living in for an extended period of time. Cape Cod was a tourist and vacation spot during the summers, and cold and lethargic during wintertime. I liked city life; I liked action. Orleans wasn't that.

About two years later, my name had reached the top of the list. I hadn't thought about actually moving there—I don't believe we even went inside to see an apartment. Mom wasn't crazy about the idea of me moving out, I didn't want to live in Orleans, and Mom and Dad offered to break through the garage and build me an office. I agreed to stay.

Staying under Mom and Dad's roof brought a good amount of funny, unforgettable moments, such as the tornado-warning incident. Sometimes I had to be the voice of reason when Mom and Dad were thinking on adrenaline. One summer night, I laid comfortably on my futon, waiting for the 11 o'clock news to begin. It was a typical, warm summer night. When the news broadcast began, the meteorologist reported there was a small tornado or a waterspout over the Cape Cod Canal. The

National Weather Service issued a tornado watch until 11:05 pm—just five more minutes. I was not worried.

The next thing I know, Mom and Dad were standing on either side of my futon, fully dressed. *Well, this is different*, I humorously thought, knowing full well what their intentions might be. They announced they wanted to bring me downstairs, to the basement. *Oh, this is not going to end well.* I strongly encouraged them to wait out the 5-minute watch. We were 20 minutes away from the Cape Cod Canal; chances were pretty good we were safe. *Just keep them talking for another four minutes.* I asked what the plan was how get me down in the basement. It wasn't like the stairs were padded with gold, shag carpeting, so I can slide down on my belly like I did when I was a kid. The idea of Dad trying to bump me down 15 steps was very frightening. *Three more minutes—keep them talking.* I asked Mom and Dad if they did manage to get me in the basement, how they would get me up? They didn't have a good plan for such a tactical and physical maneuver. If they would have suggested I come into the main part of the house and sit in the inside hall, I would have agreed to that. I wasn't about to put any of our physical well being in jeopardy for something I knew wasn't coming. By this time the tornado watch had ended and I had averted what could have been a very bad situation, all from the comfort from my futon. Mom and Dad returned to bed, no doubt watching the weather reports until the wee hours of the morning.

"Worlds are turning
And we're just hanging on
Facing our fear and standing
Out there alone
A yearning, and it's real to me
There must be someone who's
Feeling for me"

"Higher Love"
Steve Winwood
Back In The High Life

In March of 1998, I finished the first draft of what was to be *Always A Place*. I felt exhilaration, I felt that I might be deserving of the love that the character, Kate, had in the novel. It was a notion I didn't want to give up on.

By this time, the Internet was similar to what it is today, although without the many websites we have now. Myspace, Facebook, Twitter, social media websites were non-existent at this time. I searched for dating websites for disabled people. I thought it would be a lot easier to find that "special someone" on a website that catered to people with disabilities rather than a website that catered to the non-disabled. There was only one dating website for individuals with disabilities, and I paid $139 to join.

I caught the attention of some suitors. It's a funny thing, because I can't recall having the ability to peruse the profiles of the men. Matches were determined by the woman who ran the website. The owner would forward the contact information of the matches onto the interested parties. It was up to both parties whether or not they wanted to contact their chosen match.

The first suitor lived in Arizona. He had cerebral palsy and was very into music. The second suitor lived in Kentucky. He also had cerebral palsy and was a philosophy student at the University of Kentucky. I chatted with both of these guys for a while. I didn't let my parents know I was chatting with these guys until several months later. I didn't know how they would react. They might have thought I was off my proverbial rocker. I did tell my PCAs, and they were very supportive.

I really didn't know what to expect from all of this. Would it lead to a real, face-to-face relationship someday? Would it lead to marriage? Would is just be a relationship online? Where would it lead? The guy from Arizona seemed like a very nice, easygoing personality, but Arizona was on the other side of the country. Neither of us was willing to relocate. The guy from Kentucky was very strong-willed and wanted my undivided attention after I revealed I was in contact with a second suitor. He wanted me to choose him. Eventually, I did.

Kevin came from a very similar background, and very devoted family like I had. His father was a Methodist pastor, his mother helped with church affairs, and his younger brother was a resident at the University of Kentucky Medical Center. It often surprised me what services he didn't have growing up. In his younger years, they would have to travel over an hour to get to physical and speech appointments. Spending half of their week on the road wasn't working for their family, so Kevin stopped going to therapy. His father used to make handmade toys for Kevin when he was a child. They had a lovely family.

Kevin and I got closer and closer as time went on. I don't think there was anything we couldn't talk about. We e-mailed each other every day, a lot of times, handful of times of day. I don't recall the exact time when we knew our relationship was moving into the serious level, but I knew time was growing near that I had to reveal this relationship to my family. I finally spilled my guts; I think I had to spill my guts because Kevin and his parents wanted to travel to Cape Cod to meet me. Not remembering a whole hell of that conversation between Mom, Dad and me, I believed it was okay because we all lived through it.

It was something Mom and Dad did several times: meeting our girlfriends and boyfriends throughout those teenage and young adult years. By this time, Peter had married his true love, Sue, who ironically worked with Peter and Dad at T.F. Greene in the 80's. They were expecting their first child in a matter of months. Paul had married Karen in April of 1996 in St. Kitts. They resided in Singapore at that time. I knew how nerve-racking it was to meet these important people who might become a part of our family. We wanted to make a good, first, impression. They wanted to make good, first, impressions. For me, meeting my brother and my sister-in-laws, I worried about what they perceived how the future would look having a sister-in-law with a disability. I didn't want them to think that I was going to be needy as to require a major part of their attention. That wasn't who I was even though my future had a big, glowing question mark in front of it. After 15+ years since Martha married Glenn, we are stronger than ever.

On December 20, 1998, Sue gave birth to our sweet Grace Devlin in Detroit, Michigan! On that Sunday, Martha, Glenn, Sarah and Thomas were on the Cape. We went out for breakfast, and when we returned, the great message was on the answering machine that another, little Gaynor was born!

Murphy, in her cage for the night, was sporadically barking. It was a little unusual. I continued watching the U.S. Open Tennis night matches on my futon. Murph continued to be unsettled. I heard Mom tell her to settle down. A few minutes later, Mom walked into my office and opened the door, which lead into the remaining area of the attached garage. The far side of the garage was on fire! Mom closed the door and immediately yelled for me to get out of bed. I heard the urgency in her voice. I don't think I moved so fast in my entire life. Somehow I even hopped over the bottom-left corner of my futon that easily was a foot high off the floor. Murphy was already in the backyard when I crawled into the adjacent room. Smoke was everywhere and my throat and lungs were just burning. I tried to hold my breath while I debated whether to dive out the back door, where Murphy was, or just wait for my Dad to throw me in my manual wheelchair that was a foot away. The fire department arrived within two minutes, as they found my Dad trying to douse the fire with the garden hose. I knew he was coming, but I really wanted to dive out that back door onto the wide, wooden step. Getting out there might hurt a little, but fresh air waited my wanting lungs. Finally, Dad threw me in my wheelchair, and pushed me out the side, front door. I nearly slid out of the chair going down the ramp, but I could finally breathe.

The cause of the fire was that the electrical cord to the trash compactor was folded underneath a leg of the unit, causing the voltage to burn through the casing of the electrical cord. If the fire went unnoticed for another five minutes, the fire officials stated the fire probably would have spread across the roofline, engulfing the entire house, possibly resulting in tragic consequences. I was checked out at Cape Cod Hospital for minor smoke inhalation, and then swiftly released. Soon after, I recalled the smell of rubber burning coming from the garage the day before the fire occurred. I was drumming in my office and the door leading into the garage was open. Months before, Dad had constructed a big screen to put in front of the large garage door so we could get major airflow into the house. I remember bringing it to my parents' attention that I smelled a strong odor of burning rubber coming through the garage. They didn't seem concerned and presumed it was coming from the outside. These days, if I smell any hint of burning rubber, I seek it out like a cat on a mouse. I also periodically check all my electrical wires and cords making sure no wire is bent, curled, folded or under a heavy objects. I can be fanatical at times.

The house smelled like we had a big barbeque inside. When Laura arrived the next morning, she remarked the house smelled like "burnt hotdogs". It did. By noon, a representative from the homeowner's insurance arrived. Since my office took up three-quarters of the garage, when Mom initially opened the door the previous night, smoke billowed in my office and into my clothes closet. I had no idea that clothes exposed to smoke and soot have to go through several cycles of professional cleaning to remove the odors. The insurance gentleman wrote my parents a check for me go buy new clothes while my clothes went through the cleaning process, which could take several weeks. Along with my clothes, my computer had to be professional cleaned.

Besides the significance of the fire and nearly losing our lives (through the grace of God, we and the house were saved), Kevin and his parents were coming for the first visit in a week.

It took four, very long days for the cleaning crew, which consisted of a young man and a young woman, cleaning every inch inside of the house, every piece of furniture, every knickknack, every pan, every cup, everything that took up space. If there had been a pin lying on a table, they were obligated to clean that pin free from soot. Even if the soot wasn't visible to the naked eye, it was on everything. They did a fantastic job, working steadily, and sometimes for ten hours of day.

I spent most of that week in the den with Mom and Dad, watching endless amounts of television. I was thankful the U.S. Open Tennis matches were on because almost anything else was mind numbing to watch. Laura and I went to the movies once or twice. We went out many times that week only to have something new to look at besides the same four walls. I gather it was a vacation for my neck because I didn't have a computer. By this time, Mom and Dad, and Kevin's parents had talked on the phone at least a few times with regards to their upcoming visit. They were happy to know we were all fine following the fire. They were excited about the trip to Cape Cod to meet us all.

I wouldn't have been myself if I didn't feel some anxiety before meeting Kevin and his folks. On this trip, they flew into Greene and renting an accessible van for Kevin. I must say it is a daring task to trust the cargo handlers with a heavy, power wheelchair and have it come out on the side without damage. Kevin's wheelchair had minimal damage, although his father was keen on fixing wheelchair and computer issues for his son.

I must say I wasn't surprised about anything upon meeting Kevin and his parents. We had e-mailed almost daily for a year. We knew everything about our respective cerebral palsy and limitations. I knew he didn't have the ability to speak, lending him to depend on using his AAC device, or Morse code. Eventually I did learn Morse code. He also had a square alphabet board, where he would gaze at the letter, and the person who he was talking to, usually his mother, would need to guess what letter his gazed on. It was tricky for novices, but his mother was a pro. His father could do both methods.

For us, communication was trial and error in the beginning. I was pretty sure that he rarely heard others with cerebral palsy vocalize like myself. He wanted to understand me, but he had difficulty doing so. Either his mother or father translated for him on this visit.

It seemed like everyone got along fairly well. Being Methodists, they did not drink. Being Catholics, we drank. I saved my drinking for special occasions; Mom had a glass of wine or two in the evening; Dad might have had a beer or two on weekends. I believe we respected each other. Kevin and I went to see a movie—it might have been *The Sixth Sense*. Unfortunately, someone had told me the gist of the plot beforehand, but I enjoyed the movie anyhow. It might have been the first time Kevin and I had been truly alone for any length of time; most likely we probably kissed. He wasn't a bad kisser given his profound Dysarthria.

Our relationship would continue after this initial, and important visit. It deepened, so much so, marriage was a high probability. We loved each other; we were very passionate about how we wanted to live our lives. We wanted to make each other happy. I had all the confidence in the world that we would be a happy couple.

Kevin and I discussed the possibility of having children. Of course, as a young girl, most girls dream about becoming mothers. I wasn't any different. I recall writing a paper in college where I had to consider what I wanted my life to be 10 or 20 years in the future. Of course I speculated that I would be working in the field of architecture. I would be happily married with one or two sons. In this paper, I wrote that the boys were school age. I made sure I spent all my free time with my boys, much like Mom did with us.

Over the prior few years, especially when I was writing *Always A Place*, I really had to dig deep to explore the many issues that a person like myself, with athetoid cerebral palsy, would need to consider before having a child. Once, I saw a segment on a news program about a husband and wife, who both had cerebral palsy very similar to mine, and the wife just gave birth to a healthy baby girl. The big question on several people's minds was how was this couple going to care for this child when this couple needed daily assistance taking care of themselves. There was no question that they would need additional services to care for their child. The other aspect of this equation was that when this child reached her teenage years, would she be responsible to "pitch in" with providing some physical care for her parents. Personally, I would never have a child if I was in similar circumstances. If only one parent had a severe disability, then having a baby might be easier. Kevin and I both agreed that having a child would not be appropriate in our circumstance.

The next thing we needed to consider was where to live. Kevin's parents put an offer on the table that they would happily renovate their large porch into a suite for us. I didn't want to move to Kentucky because I knew the difficulties Kevin and his parents had in obtaining one hour of respite/PCA services per day just to shower him. I refused to have my future mother-in-law being responsible for the major part of our physical care. It wouldn't be fair to Kevin's mother, and it wouldn't be fair to us. I'm a very private person, and I thought it would be extremely awkward to have my mother-in-law greet us every morning, and see us to bed every night. Cape Cod is beautiful, but I didn't want to settle there. I have always been a realist: I knew Mom and Dad wouldn't live forever. I wanted to live in Rhode Island, close to Martha, Glenn the kids, and where many of my extended family members lived. Everyone supported this decision, including Kevin and his family. As luck would have it, Peter got stationed at the Naval War College in Newport. He, Sue and Grace would live in Sue's late mother's childhood home in Jamestown.

221

Soon, Martha and Glenn would be doing major legwork in trying to find the appropriate services for us. As much experience I had hiring and managing my own PCAs, I didn't feel that I could do it for both of us. Martha and Glenn visited an agency, and found their services would be very accommodating. They would hire the appropriate PCAs for us. They would have coverage to care for us if one of our PCAs called out sick. It would be their job to make sure all of our ADLs were met daily. I must admit not having the responsibility to hire PCAs was very welcoming, extremely welcoming. We would have the authority to turn down any PCA we deemed inappropriate for our care.

The next giant hurdle we had to jump over was deciding where to live. People with disabilities wait the average of two years or more for accessible housing to become available. Kevin and I required accessible housing for a couple, which is even harder to come by. There was some discussion about the possibility of adding an addition onto Martha and Glenn's house. The fact that we would receive more services, mainly PCA hours if we lived in our own residence tipped that scale.

One day, Martha saw a listing for a single ranch house just around the corner from her and Glenn's home. She went to the open house and judged the house very suited for our needs. Phone calls were made, funds were pooled and our families bought the house. We closed on the house on May 26, 2000. Kevin's father flew up for the closing.

It was my time to visit Kentucky. It was April vacation of 2000. Martha, Sarah, Thomas, Debbie, her daughter, Samantha, and myself took a 6-day road trip to Kentucky. We all piled in my van and drove. Like all road trips, there were some aspects we will never forget, like losing Samantha every time we stopped. She, at age 10, had a curious tendency that propelled her to explore. If we had a quarter for every time said, "Where's Sam?" we could have paid for the entire trip. This was also the trip that Thomas had finally gotten an appetite. The boy was as thin as a rail up until age ten. We tried endlessly to get him to eat more than five bites a meal. Finally, he was eating! We also discovered Krispy Kreme Doughnuts on this trip.

We took two days to drive to Kentucky, stopping in Hagerstown, Maryland. We stayed at an EconoLodge that was rather creepy. This was my second attempt using a blow up mattress. The year before, my parents, Martha, Glenn and the kids spent a few days in Nantucket at Paul and Karen's vacation house. I slept on a blow up mattress in the living room. By morning, I was under the coffee table. In Hagerstown, I slid off the air mattress. Would there ever be a third attempt?

"Where's Sam?" We left Hagerstown, with Sam of course, by 10 am. By 7 pm, we arrived at Kevin parents' house. It was a ranch house with a brick exterior. I looked to the cloudy sky and reminded myself we were in an area vulnerable to tornado activity. They were all pleased we had arrived safely, despite that one tire that was down to the rim. We traveled up and down the majestic Virginia hills with one, very bald tire that went unnoticed until Kevin's father pointed it out to us.

Kevin and I were happy to see each other after seven months since our initial visit. I had a quick tour of the house. It was nice. I gazed at all the family photographs on the walls and tables; there were plenty. I wanted to take everything in. They had a Sheltie and a cat, which was technically Kevin's. I hadn't been too keen on cats since Aunt Pat gave Martha a Siamese kitten when I was about eight. It broke free of its basement containment, and like a heat-seeking missile, searched me out, as I was lying on the couch and started attacking me. That same afternoon, Dad gave it to the cesspool man. Bye kitty-kitty. Kevin's cat and I didn't have much interaction.

I believe Kevin's mother cooked dinner that evening. She wasn't a great cook, but she tried, hard. Before dinner, Kevin and I had some alone time in his bedroom. He had a long line of Disney movies, practically the entire collection on VHS tapes, on one of his shelves. Even if this did give me the tiniest bit of pause, I didn't let it bother me too much. There weren't any *Rocky*, *Terminator* or action movies that men typically owned. I would understand if he had young nieces and nephews who wanted to watch these movies with their Uncle Kevin, but he didn't have any. I didn't want to be judgmental, so I let it go.

"Where's Sam?" We stayed at a Comfort Inn in Downtown Lexington. On this day, Kevin and his mother bought us to the Keeneland Horse Racing facility, which is only open in April and October. Kentucky is the thoroughbred capital of America, which is very evident once you cross over the border into Kentucky. Sprawling acres of open land went on for as far as the eye could see. Green pastures engulfed you.

Keeneland was a few miles north of the Blue Grass Airport. Driving into the facility, we saw this gargantuan, chrome underside of a jumbo jet coming in our immediate direction. "Holy…Sh…Cow!" (because we had kids in the van). This plane few over our head as if it was only 50 feet high. It wasn't like Martha and I hadn't seen low-flying jets all the time, living close to T.F. Greene, but this view of a jumbo jet was something entirely different.

I can't recall if any of us Yankees made wagers on of the races we watched. I didn't know anything about horseracing and I wasn't about to lose any money. It was the first horse race I ever saw that wasn't on television. I just prayed that I didn't have to witness any horse accidents that might require the horse to be put down on the spot. Now I realize the veterinary medical staff would take the horse off the field to do such a thing. Even though the tradition of horseracing goes back hundreds of years, I don't believe to race any kind of animal for the financial gain of people, especially if there is a great chance the animal will get injured. With that said, I love watching Equestrian competitions. Horses are majestic, and beautiful creatures.

That night, we had a delightful dinner at one of Kevin friend's beautiful home. Here I discovered the advantage of portable, wheelchair ramps. Was I that out of touch not to realize the possibility of them? I guess so. Kevin's friend was a sweet woman, with a husband with two children. Southern hospitality: it really does exist, and we felt it everywhere we went. We grew accustom to partaking of a prayer before every meal, for these were religious people. I never heard anyone swear.

Kevin and his friend were classmates, from what I could gather, from a very young age. He was very excited to show me off. I enjoyed this night, but I remained reserved. I'm always reserved meeting new people, as I hope to make a good impression. Of course I didn't have to get passed the cerebral palsy thing because Kevin had cerebral palsy. I guess I had to prove my self-worth in respects to Kevin.

I don't think I would change anything about our trip to Kentucky. We discussed how we wanted to be set up and changes we wanted to make inside of our house. Since I had more mobility, I would set the course of what would work out the best for both of us.

We all had a good time. We experienced another part of the country. It also deepened my understanding where Kevin grew up, who the people were that surrounded him. I got the chance to see his home, the church where his father gave his sermons every Sunday, and I got the chance to meet his brother between shifts at the hospital. I appreciated all that I saw in Kentucky.

Before I go onto Kevin and his parents' next trip to Cape Cod, I would like to acquaint you all to Linda J. Dewey. After returning from Kentucky, I had a need to hire another PCA. With this particular interview, Mom and I sat at the table and met this 44-year-old woman. Instead of Mom and/or I asking the questions, Linda told her life's story in about 45 minutes. Not being overpowering or fake, her honesty shined like a lamp at the top of a lighthouse that called people to her. This woman was genuine; she was funny. She explained a man who cheated on her with her best friend had just jilted her. She was in this relationship for ten years. Linda had two grown children, Jeremiah and Jennilyn, who were the lights of her existence. She had been talking care of this older gentleman for a number of years. We soon learned that she had a never-ending capacity to take care for anyone who reached out a hand for help. She told us she had an uncle who had cerebral palsy. Mom and I hired Linda on the spot.

The one-year anniversary of the garage fire, September 1, 2000, was met was very sad news. Mom's oldest living sister, Helen McDermott, had suddenly passed away from a massive stroke. Aunt Helen was 82. Mom was very distraught, understandably. The wake and funeral would take place in Charlestown, Rhode Island, where she lived with her husband, Joe. They were the very proud parents of two sons, Michael and Paul, and the grandparents of five. Aunt Helen's nickname for me was Agnes. I'm not sure where how that nickname originated, but I liked it; I thought it was a classy name.

I was unable to join Mom and Dad in Charlestown for Aunt Helen's wake and funeral because Kevin and his parents were coming to Cape Cod for a two-week visit. Linda stayed with me while my parents were in Charlestown. Like Mom, Linda liked to clean and do laundry. What chores Mom couldn't finish before leaving, Linda completed, and well. Linda worked in a Laundromat for a time and mastered the art of folding clothing and towels. Before Kevin and his parents arrived, Linda and I became accustomed to grabbing lunch at her favorite hangouts with her friends, and she had many. A cocktail in the afternoon wasn't uncommon for us to have, at Rum Runners, with our big lunch. I soon became one of the Dennis crowd.
Soon, Kevin and his parents arrived from their long drive.

I wasn't too sure how they would take to Linda's exuberant personality. She had the energy of a hummingbird. Once you met Linda, she was hard to forget. It wasn't long before Mom and Dad returned from Aunt Helen's funeral. Mom didn't have a moment's time to rest and mourn her loving sister. She was the perfect, tired, host who kept appearances very well. Over the next 12 days, Mom cooked about seven lunches and dinners. The other nights we ate out at restaurants.

Kevin's father wanted to lend a hand to the work that Martha, Glenn, Peter and Dad were doing practically every weekend on the house for at least six months. I don't recall Kevin and I travelling to Rhode Island to see the house. I had visited the house a few other times with Dad and Linda to see its progress. Everyone was doing an incredible job painting and constructing various items in the house. I was certainly humbled at, what seemed like an endless amount of work, that my family was accomplishing. I often wondered how would I ever repay them.

Both families hired a contractor who specialized in building for people with disabilities. This is where my skills as an accessible housing design specialist came into play. I specifically wanted to design a bedroom, and a small bathroom to fit my needs since I have the ability to crawl. There was no doubt that our bedroom would be carpeted, so I could crawl to any place in the bedroom. The next question I had to answer was how I would get in and out of bed independently. Futons on the floor weren't going to work out for Kevin, since someone had to physically cradle him in and out of his wheelchair.

My thought process started much too complicated. I thought the bed could be raised and lowered by a hydraulic system. Other than manual hospital beds, I had never seen a bed with the capabilities of rising and lowering. I knew a custom hydraulic system would be expensive to maintain. I had to think simpler. Then a childhood memory flashed into my mind. Visiting my Aunt Anne and Uncle Tom's house many times, they had a living room sunken down by one, 4-inch step. I was still very adept at crawling up and down that one step that was between my bedroom closet and my office. That step was about six inches high. The answer to my independence was steps! Simple, simple steps!

With steps exciting my mind, my thought processes went even further. If I could have steps leading up to my bed, why couldn't I have these same steps leading to a small lavatory? There was no reason why, unless the new plumbing runs became an issue.

Let me give you some background of this concept of putting a toilet at floor level. One day, when I was five or six, my Aunt Florence drops in, which she did on occasion. While she was there, I guess I had to use the bathroom, like most humans do. Aunt Florence made a comment within the context of, "She hasn't learned to go to the bathroom on her own yet?" This comment didn't sit very well with Mom. It wasn't that I didn't know how to use a toilet, it was the fact I didn't have the muscle balance and coordination to lift myself up to the toilet and sit on it without falling off. Aunt Florence seemed not to understand the related difficulties associated with athetoid cerebral palsy. I felt bad that I wasn't able to toilet myself. This began my long time project to figure out how to toilet myself.

Details and illustrations of this small lavatory are included in my companion book, *Design Projects and Concepts: Architectural and Specialty Design Works to Promote the Independence for People with Disabilities.*

I knew it was coming: the ring, and the proposal. I was excited, although I couldn't help being a tad nervous. Kevin and I, along with Kevin's parents, Debbie, Samantha, Martha, Glenn, Sarah and Thomas went the Cape Cod Mall. The kids and some adults took in a movie, while the rest of us went ring shopping. Due to my athetoid cerebral palsy, I wasn't a jewelry maven. I wore small, looped earrings, but I didn't wear necklaces or bracelets because they are easily broken. My left hand has a tendency to grab onto necklaces around my own neck and yank. I have broken many necklaces over the years. I have worn rings on occasion, although they need to be very plain and have a low profile. I needed low profile rings, both engagement and wedding.

Of course this was a new experience for both of us. We entered a very reputable jewelry store and began our quest. I tried on a few different low profile diamond rings. I wasn't the type to become obsessed with getting that perfect diamond ring, it just had to fit my personality, and I had to love it. Luckily, I achieved both. It was a symbol of our love and I was very proud of that. I admired it often, bringing to mind that someone loved me. I was caught a little off guard when Kevin officially proposed to me in the jewelry store, in front of our entire gang and everyone in the store. The spotlight was on me. My heart was racing. I said yes. Down deep, I was disappointed that Kevin didn't wait to propose when we got back to my parents'. They would have enjoyed sharing in this moment.

Onward and upward: there was a wedding to plan, along with everything else we had to accomplish. Personally, I would have been ecstatic if Kevin agreed to elope. I can't recall having those young girl dreams of having that big, elegant wedding, full of glitter, lace and flowers. I didn't want that spotlight. I wanted to take after Martha, who eloped with Glenn. Since Kevin and his family, especially his father being a pastor in the Methodist Church, I respected Kevin's wishes. Kevin's father would marry us.

Oh the dress—I had to pick out a wedding dress. Martha, Sarah, Debbie and I went to David's Bridal one Saturday afternoon. Never been a big fan, which is quite an understatement, trying on numerous articles of clothing during one, long stretch, I tried on about four wedding dresses. The big obstacle we had was getting the correct size. All were very pretty although none fit just right. We struck out. A few days later, Mom saw a classified ad in the Cape Cod Times for a seamstress for hire. Mom called her to inquire her experiences with making wedding dresses, and she had done a few. She was a lovely woman and hired her to make my wedding dress. It was elegantly plain and I loved it.

On March 24, 2001, Paul and Karen proudly welcomed their first son, Samuel Thomas, into the world in Singapore. There was another Gaynor to love!

"Oh don't sorrow, no don't weep
For tonight, at last I am coming home
I am coming home"

"A Sort Of Homecoming"
U2
The Unforgettable Fire

Moving day had arrived: April 24, 2001. Sam was exactly a month old, and Nana would have celebrated turning 102. No doubt, she was looking down from Heaven celebrating my new home. Somehow, over two days, Dad had packed up an U-Haul truck and my van with my things. I didn't have much furniture to take, probably just my parents' wicker bureaus, a table and some chairs. Our king size mattress was already set up on the custom mattress platform base Peter had constructed. I had my usual things that always traveled with me back and forth to college: clothes, computer, television, stereo, etc. I was taking Murphy also.

For a late day in April in the Northeast, it was hot—like 88° of scorching sunshine hot! Before heading to the house, Linda and I met Martha at the Social Security Administration Office in Downtown Providence to switch my residency back to Rhode Island. It is always quite intriguing to observe the cast of characters sitting in the waiting area, waiting for their number to be called. The security guard at his post, with his gun in his holster, keeps an eye out, looking over the patrons, judging everyone's demeanor. The agitated receives more of the security guard's attention. Sometimes the Social Security Administration Office can be an unsettling place to linger.

We waited for about an hour before my number was called. I was thankful I didn't have to face "Ms. Jolly" at the Social Security Administration Office in Hyannis ever again. It took us about 30 minutes to have the representative switch my residency. No, I don't have any assets. No, I don't own my home. Yes, I do own my own vehicle. No, I don't work, although I was very willing to do so if I could find steady employment. With that, my SSDI would be direct deposited in my Rhode Island financial institution on June 1, 2001. It was too late to get May's check switched to Rhode Island.

Back at the house, it was all hands on deck, as the rented U-Haul sat in the driveway. Even though everyone made an effort to pace themselves for a long day, everyone was truly

232

upbeat. Of course, my parents, especially my Mom was apprehensive about letting her little girl leave the 'nest' once again, I think she believed it would be okay—I would be okay. She had total faith in Martha. We all would be safe.

With everything moved in and in their proper places, it was 5 o'clock somewhere—it was 5 o'clock in Rhode Island. There were a few, little chores that still needed to be done, but no rush. We ordered pizza for dinner and celebrated my big move. Relatives began to drop by. By 8 o'clock, the kitchen and dining area were full of people, and a dog. Knowing my parents had to drive back to the Cape, and knowing how exhausted they were, made me worry. They got on the road by 9, and they got home by 10:30pm for my Dad to get up five hours later to go to work.

For the next six weeks, Linda very graciously agreed to take care of me from Sunday through Friday afternoons, while Mom and Dad came on Fridays days and went home Sundays. Since Dad worked for Nantucket and Cape Air Airlines, he was able to fly Linda back and forth at little or no cost. On Mom and Dad's first weekend, Martha, Mom and I went to La-Z-Boy furniture to pick out a recliner and a sleeper sofa that Paul and Karen wanted to buy us for a wedding present. We succeeded. Mom and Dad had a place to sleep.

During the renovations, we added a full bath in the basement. It was decided upon to have someone living in the basement if ever there was an emergency during the nighttime hours. One of Thomas' classmate's mother, Karla, happened to mentioned to Martha that she would be interested in taking the position, and live in our basement. Martha agreed. Karla and her son, J.J., would move in the week prior to our wedding on June 9, 2001. Linda would make the basement her own until Karla and J.J. moved in.

These next six weeks seem to fly by like lightning. I don't think there was ever a day we didn't need to do something, especially for the wedding, or the house. Linda and I kept very busy. Sometimes we attempted to take Murphy for walks because Linda wanted to keep her girlish figure. This was before I realized that with a short lead, I could hook Murphy up to my chair to walk her. Before that bright idea, Murphy walked Linda around the neighborhood. She certainly got her workout. There was neighbor who warned us that if Murphy pooped on his lawn and we didn't pick it up, he would make sure to find us to make us pick it up. He protruded arrogance without Murphy putting a paw on his lawn. After we turned the corner, Linda voiced her opinion of the gruff man, and I had the same opinion. We often saw things in the same perspective.

I found it decidedly difficult to deal with the idea that I wasn't going to see my newly found friend all the time after I married Kevin. I had been through this many times before, saying goodbye to people who had taking care of me throughout my life, some people who had taken care of me for several years, and I just recall just a few times I have been moved to tears over goodbyes. Maybe I was growing more sentimental. Some people just grab onto your heart and never want to let go. There are just people who take care of me so well, they do the littlest things such as picking an eyelash out of the corner of my eye, washing between your toes, washing behind your ears, washing your hands, clearing the dry skin from ear, wiping a toothpaste spot off your shirt, and many more tiny acts of caring, just as your mother would do, these are the folks you want to treasure. Linda took care of me very similar to the way Mom did. Linda and I got along simply, like two peas in a pod.

I also felt incredibly guilty about keeping Linda away from her life routine, family and friends on the Cape. She had a relationship with her boyfriend, Paul. He missed her so much. They would talk daily on their mutual cellphones. Sometimes when he had particular bad days working construction. Linda was his anchor when he was feeling adrift. Linda was seven years older than Paul. They lived together in Dennis. He missed her. Besides Paul, Linda had her two kids, her mother, sister, brother, nephew, and her 94-year-old maternal grandmother, who was a spitfire in her own right. I was keeping her away from her loved ones and I felt incredibly guilty.

Karla began coming around more since she would be my primary caregiver until I gained state approval for daily services. This process could take three to four months. The idea was extremely daunting, but I had no other choice. I would handle the situation the best I possibly could.

Kevin and his parents arrived to Rhode Island on Thursday, May 31, 2001, ten days before our wedding. The collective we, in Rhode Island, spruced up the house in the previous six weeks. It was very homey. Kevin was excited to finally be where he wanted to be: here with me. I was excited too, but a spot of cautiousness remained in my gut. I knew it was pass once we got settled into a routine.

Kevin's father spent the week doing various jobs around the house. For a wedding present, Kevin bought me two Pottery Barn, wall mounted lamps for our bedroom. Kevin's father put the lamps on the wall, and he adapted a box with a rocker light switch so that we both were able to turn the lamp on and off ourselves. He also changed most of the smoke detectors in the house, remarking that the batteries had a 10-year life span and we shouldn't need to change them until our ten-year wedding anniversary. He continued doing odd jobs around the house.

Before leaving Kentucky, Kevin's parents had his van outfitted with a standard wheelchair tie-down system behind Kevin's EZ Lock Wheelchair Docking System. Here again, before I met Kevin, I never knew docking systems existed. Kevin's Permobil wheelchair had a bolt attached to the bottom of it. He would drive his wheelchair onto his lift backwards. As he backed into his van, he turned, as he would face the front, and then drove backwards until the bolt slid into the groove to the EZ Lock Docking mechanism bolted to the van floor. Once the bolt on the wheelchair was locked in, his wheelchair was securely locked down. To release the wheelchair from the docking mechanism, Kevin just need to press a button, positioned within his reach, to disengage the lock on the docking mechanism. I was very impressed with this docking system. It was impossible to put an additional EZ Lock Docking System simply because if I had a bolt installed on the bottom of my wheelchair, I would never get past the first docking system, unless my wheelchair developed magical powers of levitating over his docking mechanism. Boy, did I miss the lowered floor of my one wheelchair capacity van. You never realize what six inches of height affects your view. In Kevin's van, my view, and his view, was severely hindered just because the floor of the van wasn't dropped six, lonely inches. Sometimes six inches makes all the difference in the world.

With Linda back for her last week in Rhode Island, sleeping arrangements were like playing musical chairs. It was very unorganized most nights. During this week, Kevin tried out sleeping in three different beds, including our king size bed, but I didn't sleep with him, choosing to sleep on a twin mattress on the floor. You see, I had a very emotional night on Tuesday, June 5, 2001. It was one of those nights you might want to scrub from your memory and history, but in hindsight, it is a night I can't deny. I had a bridal shower a month earlier. Linda, Karla and I decided we would go out for a few drinks while Kevin's parents assisted him with going to the bathroom, his routine every three nights. The three of us landed at Sticks Bar and Tavern in Chepachet, probably ten minutes away. The tiny bar was empty on a Tuesday evening. It was never my intention to drink as much as I did, although I did not drink enough to make myself physically ill. My emotions were all over the place that night; I was excited about marrying Kevin in five short days, but I was also very melancholy that Linda would be returning home to Cape Cod in five short days. Alcohol was the truth serum for me that night. I had five Kahlua Sombreros within the span of two and a half hours. We were the only three in the bar besides the bartender. After about four Sombreros, I really needed to pee.

236

There was only one tiny bathroom in this very tiny bar. I was only able to fit half of my wheelchair in the bathroom. Karla stood outside, blocking the bartender's view while Linda helped me on and off the toilet. What was so awesome about this very tiny bathroom was that if you did happen to lean, you couldn't fall because you were boxed in on all sides. Linda said I practically transferred myself on and off. The thing about alcohol and cerebral palsy is that alcohol relaxes muscles, so much so that I have more control. People who don't have cerebral palsy, but have a good buzz on, lose a bit of control. And with the bathroom being so confined, I knew I wasn't going to fall. Linda classified it as a tiny miracle for my actions in the bar's bathroom.

After the girls played one game of pool, we decided to go home before Kevin and his parents sent out the Calvary. Kevin's father had already gently chastised Linda for her fondness for wine. Let's just say Linda and my future father-in-law didn't see eye-to-eye on many issues. When Karla, Linda and I pulled into the driveway, I got a case of the giggles. I felt like the defiant teenager who was about to be scolded, and I couldn't stop giggling. The more Linda urged me to pull myself together, the more I giggled. It was a vicious, vicious cycle. What made it worse was I had to pee again, and usually when I really need to pee, I get the giggles.

We all entered the house and I tried to hold it together, but I failed. I acknowledged Kevin and his parents. I giggled a little. Thankfully I had the reason to go use the bathroom. I pulled up to my bottom stair in the bedroom and Linda guided me down to the bottom stair. I had to be still giggling after I got up to and into my bathroom because she bit me on my ass to divert my giggling, to surprise me. Of course she didn't bite hard, just enough to grab my attention. Actually, I had forgotten all about the "bite" until I reread a thank you letter I had written to her Paul only days later. While she was helping me in the bathroom, we discovered one of my knuckles bleeding. Linda was confident I had cut it on an exposed piece of plywood; I was

237

confident I had cut it in the bar's bathroom. She ran and fetched a Band-Aid and placed it over my mysterious wound.

I crawled back down the three steps and sat at the end of the bed, folded over. Like a light switch, my remaining few giggles suddenly turned into tears. The dormant volcano of pent up emotion just erupted. I cried like I have never cried before. I was acutely aware that the three pair of eyes were looking upon my sudden geyser with apprehension. I couldn't stop the emotion. I needed this—I needed to cry. Linda picked up my shoulders and sat in front on me. I just leaned on her and cried. Karla sat on the bottom stair and rubbed my back. By this time, Linda was crying too. She assured me that she'd always be there for me, and that we would always, always, be friends. There wasn't a dishonest bone in her body. She reminded me she was only a phone call away, and a short drive away. I continued to cry. I still feared I was scaring Kevin and my future in-laws. I just cried, cried, and cried. It took me about fifteen minutes to pull myself semi together.

Linda helped me dress for bed, which usually consisted of a t-shirt and sweatpants. I climbed on the twin mattress that lied beside our bed, which Kevin slept in that particular night. I had this very nagging feeling that I had to reassure Kevin that I would be all right, that we would be all right, but something held me back from doing so. I could have easily joined him in our bed; I think he would have disregarded the idea that we should wait for our wedding night to sleep together. I did not join him in our bed. My head was telling me that he needed my comfort to some degree, but my heart told me something altogether different. My heart was stronger than my thoughts.

The next three days were very happy and exciting days. Witnesses to my major Tuesday night meltdown didn't speak a word about it, not even Kevin. I was still very embarrassed by it, but history was what it was.

Rehearsal dinner was set for Friday evening, June 8, at the Hoof-Fin-Feathers Carriage Inn in North Kingstown. I wore a pantsuit, with a tank top and a short jacket. My parents were staying at Helen and Ray's condominium on Newport's Goat Island. Linda and I took my van to the restaurant. We arrived early. Linda's Paul was just about at the end of a thread missing her so very much. She continued to reassure him she would be home in a day's time. I felt so bad for both of them, so much so that my heart ached. *Just hang on for one more day, just one more day, Paul.* It was because of me that this man was waiting for Linda to come home. Matchbox 20's hit, "If You're Gone", spoke volumes for Paul.

I have vague memories of little details of our rehearsal dinner, but it was very nice indeed. Very moving speeches were given. I averted a situation before dinner. I began to feel a little flush and woozy. Under my tank top, I had on this strapless bra made of rayon that I had bought months earlier. Its material was making me sweat. It had to come off before I fainted. Mom was sitting was my left and Linda was on my right. As quietly as I could, I told Linda the bra needed to come off. She got up and whispered in Mom's ear the plan. Linda and I swiftly went to the bathroom and removed the bra. Oh yes, I could breathe again! I don't know how many brides in history had to dispose of their bra during their rehearsal dinner, but I did. Chock one up for this Babe!

With Karla and J.J. all but moved in downstairs, Linda bunked with me. We woke around 8 am. Kevin and his parents had left for the church before I started stirring. I was marrying Kevin at in four and a half hours. It was a gloriously beautiful day. I was on top of the world, quite the contrast from Tuesday night. I was truly happy and truly excited. Linda showered me and put me in some sweats until we got to the North Kingstown Methodist Church. After a quick breakfast, we went to the local beauty saloon to get our final beautification touch ups. A week earlier, I got a haircut, my first dye job and my eyebrows waxed.

I was handed over to Martha after the beautification was complete. She, Sarah, Thomas and I drove down to the church. I have never witnessed Martha extremely tense in my life, but on this day, she was very, very intense. I made sure I answered her questions, if she had any, with quickness and accuracy. She had a lot on her agenda, including making sure everything was set for the entire day. She was my wedding planner. There was a cassette sticking out of the player in the van. She pushed it in. It was one of my mix cassettes I had made years earlier. Van Halen's "Why Can't This Be Love?" started playing minutes later. When I am happy, I sing, and I sing loud. I was trying to bring Martha a little levity during our 40-minute drive to North Kingstown. This was my wedding day! I wanted everyone in high spirits like I was in.

We arrived at the church and people were gathering, especially our families and people within our wedding party. Martha was my bridesmaid and Sarah was my maid of honor. Kevin's best friend, Justin, was his best man. I was escorted to a large room where people were dressing and doing make up. Mom and Dad were there, and they now were set to get me ready with one or two others. We had ample time to do what we had to do. It was my first time I laid my eyes on two and a half-month-old Sam. I loved him at first sight. He was so beautiful, very content in Paul's arms. I could have kissed him all day long.

With 30 minutes to go until I would take my sacred vows, my usual anxiety started kicking up. The butterflies were unleashed in my stomach. I didn't have cold feet, I just feared being the center of attention. I didn't want to screw up anywhere in the process of the ceremony. I knew I would have a million eyes on me because I was the bride. *Holy shit—I was the bride!* I got a half of a Xanax to calm my nerves.

As several of us shuffled around the room trying to get dressed, either Kevin's mother or father would pop their heads in and told us how many minutes we had left until liftoff. Like clockwork, they announced the time every five minutes. There was a standard, classroom clock in the room; we knew what time it was. Fifteen minutes before, Dad put my AFOs on, and took me took me to the bathroom. Mom and Linda helped put my dress on and do the final touches. For months, Martha and some others urged me to where something, anything, on my head. I refused. I know my head; I know my neck. If I wore something on my head, there was a strong chance it would fall off halfway down the aisle. I wasn't having that. I was ready to wheel down the aisle with Dad.

I paced a little outside the entrance of the main church, as we waited for the wedding music to start. It began. Here we go.

My first order of business was driving down the aisle without going off course and walking my Dad into a pew. When 80 pairs of eyes are looking right at you, it was a challenge for this very skilled driver to keep her head screwed on straight. People, some who I hadn't seen in years, were smiling. Some were crying. I managed to get down the aisle without injuring Dad.

With a kiss from Dad, I pulled into position, as I smiled at my husband-to-be. Kevin managed to control his athetoid arm better than he ever did in my presence and positioned his power wheelchair beside mine. Immediately he reached for my hand. Kevin's father stood in front of us, as he commenced our wedding ceremony. It was a traditional ceremony with traditional vows. The only thing different about our ceremony was Martha and Justin had to place our wedding rings on our respective fingers. Martha and Justin also had to do the lighting of the single candle for Kevin and me. In lieu of reciting the vows, Kevin's father recited each part of the vow. We both verbalized, "I will" after every part. Soon, we were declared husband and wife. We kissed each other in the spirit of true love. We both turned around for everybody to view the new, happy married couple. People broke out in applause.

Kevin and I exited the church and found ourselves

surrounded family and friends. I loved seeing everyone. It was a beautiful day—a glorious day for a wedding. Many of our guests came from out of state, from Cape Cod to across the Mississippi River. It was a day for celebration.

Our next task was to get to our reception venue: the Officer's Club at the Naval War College in Newport, the same venue that Peter and Sue had their very post wedding reception in 1995. Unlike their reception, the weather wasn't brutally hot. I got in Kevin's van first, and he, next. Strangely, I had a wave of sadness come over me when I looked out to see my lonely silver van, sitting without me. It was my first personal and accessible vehicle I have ever had. It brought me independence. It brought me to the place where I found myself on June 9, 2001. *You served me well*, I thought.

Before all went into the Officer's Club, Kevin and I, along with many of our family and friends went down to the open grassy area for some photo shots. The bay was directly behind us. Our hired photographer was snapping pictures left and right. We definitely enjoyed our public displays of affection in front of the camera. We must have kissed each other about 30 or more times. We were very happy.

Our guests were waiting inside. It was a very simple reception. Kevin's father, my father-in-law, said a prayer, as he did before every meal, but this time, it was a special prayer. Justin and Kevin's brother gave moving toasts. Kevin and I sat at the same table, but directly across from each other. I was flanked on both sides by Linda, Laura and Mary, who cared for me when I attended Roger Williams University. I ate, they ate we all ate. We had a wedding cake, of course, but we never saw the cake before it was cut and eaten.

After I ate, I made a point to greet our guests, especially Helen and Ray Watson. About six months earlier, Ray was diagnosed with ALS, and unfortunately, it was very progressive. Ray had already lost the ability to talk. Before he lost that

242

ability, he vowed to make it to my wedding. I had known Ray and Helen all my life and it was particularly difficult to see him withering away from the awful disease. I could feel my heart sink because I knew his time was getting short. One of his last wishes was to see me get married. I touched his hand. I looked back and Mom was looking on over my shoulder. Surely she had a tear in her eye.

I changed out of my wedding dress and into a causal, beige suit I picked out with Martha. So many were in the bathroom, it was like a mini bachelorette party after the fact. About four women were trying to jam me into this suit. It was funny as hell!

Guests were gradually leaving. It was about 4 o'clock. Time came for Linda to get on the road and back to Cape Cod; it was Jeremiah's, 24th birthday. Linda, Mom and I had a few minutes where nobody wanted our attention. I could feel my chest grow heavy. You could always count on Linda to bring levity to almost any kind of situation. She informed Mom to what had transpired the previous Tuesday evening. Of course Mom grew upset. I was hanging on for dear life not to crumble in tears again. Linda said something outrageous and funny, and she saved me from what could have been another difficult scene. Like always, she promised to call, urged me to call and she would visit Mom and Dad. Knowing that she was ten minutes away from Mom and Dad brought me a lot of comfort. We hugged and said goodbye to Linda.

After all the festivities were through, and after we said our goodbyes, a large contingent of us went to Peter and Sue's house in Jamestown. With Kevin's portable ramps, it was easier to get inside to their small house and out to their back deck. By this time in the late afternoon, I was finally feeling more relaxed. I relished this down time, surrounded by family. The feverish pace of the day had come to a brilliant close.

Peter and Sue put hamburgers, hot dogs and chicken on

the grill. Macaroni, potato and a number of other kinds of salads were included in this incredible spread. Justin joined us. I witnessed Kevin and Justin's true lifelong friendship, as they reminisced about their shenanigans during their school days. I was glad to hear they had shenanigans, because I had plenty of my own.

Memories are fuzzy on who fed me my burger and fixings, but it was probably Mom. Kevin's mother and/or father fed him. It took a little bit of skill to fed Kevin, due to his severe Dysarthria. He coughed many times during each meal. It might have alarmed the average person but I had witnessed a number of kids with severe feeding difficulties, and Kevin had similar difficulties. He required food, which had to be chewed, to be placed between his teeth, on one side or the other. He didn't have the ability to position the food himself. Also, Kevin didn't have the ability to use a drinking straw.

By 8 o'clock, the mosquitos were coming out as the beautiful sun set in the west. As darkness fell, we knew we were leaving for home. Clearly, our wedding night had been on our minds for some time now, but we weren't raving lunatics scratching to get home. This surprised me a little bit, because I considered myself to be a very "eager" teen. Maybe it was my wisdom of age. Maybe it was the fact that everyone is aware what happens on wedding nights with newlyweds. I was a grown woman; I was a responsible, grown woman. It was still a little embarrassing realizing everybody knew I was going to share a bed with a man, for the first time, as far as anyone knew.

Home, for the first time as husband and wife, Karla got me ready to for bed. After brushing my teeth, she put me down on my first step, undressed me and put a baggy t-shirt on. I was set to take it from there. I crawled into my adapted bathroom and closed the door. Kevin might have had a quick bite to eat and something to drink before his father put him in our bed. Patiently I listened through the bathroom door to gauge their progress. I might have been the only bride that night waiting for her father-in-law to put her husband to bed. It seemed a bit surreal; he was a man of God. When I knew my father-in-law left our bedroom, I took a few more minutes before I opened the door and crawled out to a very dim lit bedroom. We wanted to leave something to the imagination and that was why I wore a t-shirt and he wore happy face boxers that I bought him. They were two articles of clothing we knew we could help each other take off easily.

My stereo controls where in reach, and I put on Sarah McLachlan for a little ambient music. Kevin's parents would sleep on the living room for the next week, and I wanted enough privacy that I absolutely could attain. I had to be the logistics manager since I had the ability to crawl. I had to figure out the orchestration of making love with two bodies that weren't that easy to control.

Even though things didn't work out perfectly as we imagined, it was still a very loving first night together. We had the rest of our lives to figure things out. Kevin had this incredible ability to wrap his arms around me and hold me tight to him. Sleep came quickly.

"Am I faithful, am I strong
Am I good enough to belong
In your reverie a perfect girl
Your vision of romance is cruel
and
All along I played the fool
All your expectations bury me"

"Perfect Girl"
Sarah McLachlan
Afterglow

I have never felt exhaustion like I have felt the day after our wedding. The emotions and endless activities for the last ten days just drained everything from me. My mother-in-law wanted to spend the afternoon opening wedding gifts. I just wanted to tilt back my wheelchair and shut my eyes for a few hours. Kevin's energy level didn't miss a beat. I was outnumbered—we were going to open presents. Martha joined us as well.

I made an attempt to unearth some kind of reserved energy, but I just was spent. The most I could do was to watch Martha and my mother-in-law open our wedding gifts. We got the usual wedding gifts: silverware, a blender, towels, bedding, and glassware. Peter Falk sent us a 9-piece CorningWare, French White Baking Set. Kevin's parents kept whatever money we received. During the following week we spent a majority of our money on a new dishwasher, two air conditioners and a few other small appliances. We were very grateful for all of the generosity our family and friends showed us.

My father-in-law went back to Kentucky a week later, after our wedding, while my mother-in-law remained in Rhode Island to tend to Kevin. The Department of Developmental Disabilities visited us the first week of June to determine our eligibility for services. There wasn't any doubt that we needed services, but the question remained how long the approval process would take. Also during this first week of marriage, we visited the Social Security Administration Office to change our status to a married couple. This instantly threw me off SSDI and back on SSI. For instance, as a married couple we would receive $953 per/month, compared to $1330 per/month if we lived "in sin". Kevin wanted marriage.

Long before our wedding, I was clear that I wouldn't be taking Kevin's name in marriage. In the '50s and '60s, my Uncle Matt and Dad changed their last name to Gaynor for a number of practical reasons. My cousin, Elin, kept her maiden name when she married. Martha kept her maiden name when she married. I wanted to do the same. Kevin didn't object.

Kevin had his mother to take care of him; I had Karla to take care of me, when she was home. Karla was caring, but she was not Dad and/or Mom, and she wasn't Linda. When around, Karla did pretty well, but on many days, I waited for her to come home to help me to the bathroom. When Karla definitely couldn't commit to feeding me lunch, or dinner, or helping me to the bathroom, Martha or Sarah would lend me a hand, for which I'm externally grateful to receive. Day-to-day existence was certainly a challenge due to Karla being so inconsistent. There was only one time I had to rely on my mother-in-law to help me to use the bathroom. Having her feed me was entirely different than having her help me to the bathroom, which was very awkward, as I always expected.

As time progressed, I began to see Kevin a little differently. With his father in Kentucky, I observed the way he was with his mother. For 33 years, he had been the center of his mother's life. She fed him, she bathed him, she helped him with his bowel care, she helped him get his laser light just right so he could operate his computer, among the rest of the household chores she had to complete every day. When Kevin called her to give him a drink of sweet iced tea every hour, she came into the office with his iced tea. Sometimes his mother had him wait a few minutes, but not too long. It was a delicate process to position his laser light perfectly, because he wanted it perfect. As I observed their relationship, firsthand, without the presence of his father, it was fraught with frustration and fatigue. She was at his beck and call 24/7.

Sam's baptism was set for June 23, 2001, on Nantucket. That day was also Mom and Dad's 45th wedding anniversary. I had to accept the fact that Kevin and I wouldn't be able to attend this family event due to logistical reasons. It would have been very difficult to set up everything we needed to get and stay on Nantucket. I could see my mother-in-law didn't have it in her to pull off such an adventurous trip. Martha and her family stayed in Rhode Island as well.

Another thing that sprang up was his temper outbursts. They ranged from quick and mild to lasting about a minute, to kicking the wall. When he kicked the wall in the office, I nearly lost my head. There, he was kicking a wall that my family spent weekends painting, weekends fixing up, and here he was kicking the wall that started our lives together. I was livid. His mother yelled at him like a four-year-old child, which I discovered she had a lot of practice doing. Showing my anger, I tried to reason with him as an adult, as he was, not to kick the walls of our home out of frustration. Soon after, he sent me an e-mail, because that was how we continued to communicate half of the time, telling me he wouldn't kick our walls again. He might not have kicked any more walls, but his varying outbursts continued.

I usually got down for the night at 9:30. I went to the bathroom and got comfortable in bed. It was Kevin's routine to have a snack at 10:30 at night. This boggled my mind. There was no medical need that he needed a snack at that precise time. Many newly married men would jump at the chance to join their wives in bed. I wanted to wear a sign around my neck saying, "Your wife is going to bed now. Feel free to join her." Kevin was not one of those men. He came to bed around 11pm. By 11 o'clock, I was tired. He had about six glasses of iced tea through the day; he wasn't ready for sleep.

Within weeks, I had made another revelation that I wasn't prepared to uncover. Kevin and I were still trying to have intercourse, but not with a lot of success. We were close a few times when he struggled to be on top, but for some reason he thought he was succeeding, when in fact, he wasn't. The first time I asked Kevin to touch me with his hand, he started to gag and make awful faces. When I asked him why he gagged, through Morse Code, he told me that he didn't know grown women had hair in different places on their body other than their head. I was blown away. I asked him if he had any sex education. Not much, he answered. I asked him if ever saw any movies or books with nude women in them. Still, he answered no. I was chuckling on the outside at the absurdity of it all, but completely devastated on the inside. With only a few more times I asked Kevin to touch me, he continued to gag. Soon, I didn't ask anymore.

This threw me into a state of deep depression that I hadn't experienced so profoundly before. I only recall slightly being depressed on two different occasions, which only lasted one week. It began when I tried to reason with myself that I could possibly hang out in my bathroom all day long. I reasoned that I didn't really have to eat or shower, I just could hang out in my quiet, little space. I did not do any of these things. I had to keep going. I had to believe that the days might get a little better. My depression continued and very gradually became worse. Almost on a daily basis I imagined going outside of the constantly air conditioned, darkened house, and go for a long walk in the summer heat to find an uninhabited spot just to bawl my ever-living eyes out. I wanted to do this at some point every day, but never really got the chance. This was not who I was and I felt I was losing a little part of myself every day.

Even though I completely hated the design of the new Providence Place Mall, Kevin, Karla, J.J., my mother-in-law, and I found ourselves there many times through the summer of 2001. It was a place to go to when we needed a change of scenery. I used to follow the others like a zombie, not really looking at anything. I just passed the time by wondering how I could bring back some happiness to my life.

Whether Kevin noticed my sadness remains to be seen. I don't believe he did because I tried to hide it so well. I began to sense that Kevin lacked empathy for others. For all the people who surrounded him, he seemed to not acknowledge people when they did something or just walked in our home for a visit, especially youngsters. I always was happy to see Sarah or Thomas. They have always meant the world to me. To Kevin, they were just two more people in our house. He perked up when Martha came to visit. Martha and Glenn were always very helpful to us, and Kevin appreciated them, which in turn, made me pleased. On the 4th of July, we all went to Deerfield Park to watch the fireworks. Martha's very pregnant friend, Nancy, came with her young daughter. I was watching Nancy like a hawk, making sure she was comfortable and stayed warm. There was a precious life in that belly and I sat directly behind Nancy, watchful there weren't any incoming Nerf footballs or drunks that mistakenly came in her direction. This was who I am and I don't think Kevin recognized any of my efforts that evening.

On July 14th, Ray passed away, succumbing to his ALS. I wanted to attend his funeral alone with my parents. I didn't want Kevin to accompany me. I just needed to get some time for myself; I also didn't want my mother-in-law to be under that time crunch to get Kevin up, dressed and fed before 9am. I rationalized with Kevin that he really didn't need to come. He finally agreed. Karla got me up and ready to go to Ray's funeral. We took our accessible van. I loved seeing my parents even though I had seen them a few times since our wedding. Ray's Mass was beautiful for the lovely man he was. His son, Billy, had already taken over the Watson Funeral Home business, and was well respected like his father. I accompanied Mom, Dad and the Watson family to the cemetery where Ray would be laid to rest. Karla and I joined Mom and Dad for the luncheon afterwards. I felt like I could be myself in this very short time. I think I even laughed once or twice. I didn't want Ray's funeral to be a way to feel some relief, but it was.

I tried to squeeze any happiness out of anything. We went to see *America's Sweethearts* in the theaters. What could be more uplifting than a romantic comedy? I tried to hold onto the joy I felt after this fantastic movie and turn it into something positive at home. The joy might have lasted a day or so, but than I was in the thick of my concealed depression again, looking desperately for my next jolt of being slightly happy. It was hard to find. I needed to take that walk every day, but I did not. Kevin told me he loved me several times a day. I didn't understand why he loved me so much, because he did not know me at all. I began to get the sense that he loved the idea of having a wife. He loved the idea of marriage. It was his idea of paradise.

When my parents came to visit us in Rhode Island, which was every other week, I always made up excuses why he and my mother-in-law should stay home. Once, my parents took me to get my first pair of eyeglasses; I was becoming nearsighted—I had my Mom's eyes but blue like Dad's. I knew my mother-in-law didn't want to sit and wait two hours for me to get eyeglasses. Due to Kevin's specific needs, it was difficult to take him places without his mother.

I wasn't that perfect wife that I always imagined I would be. I wasn't perfect because I was so unhappy. Once or twice, I hung out with Karla at her friend's house, which was within a short rolling distance. One time, I stayed a little longer than Kevin expected. He was a little bit upset, which I understood. He gently scolded me. I apologized. There was another time when Linda invited me to a pig roast on the Cape. I asked Kevin if he would mind if I went. He didn't mind. I needed anything to be able to get some life back into these lungs. Kevin didn't mind my overnight stay at Mom and Dad's.

My father-in-law came back for a week's visit at the beginning of August. I kept busy with doing some plans for a local veterinarian to make their office wheelchair accessible. Kevin was continuing his online course study in philosophy through the University of Kentucky. I just acquired a new shower chair. My father-in-law's task was how to construct a hole in the mesh so Kevin would finally be able to move his bowels while in a seated position. It was beyond my comprehension why Kevin's parents never tried getting him a proper commode chair. We all put our collective heads together and created a hole in the mesh using scissors, vinyl material, dental floss and a heavy-duty sewing needle. It worked perfectly. Instead of Kevin taken an hour to go to the bathroom lying horizontally on the bed, now, in the shower chair, the entire process took less than 30 minutes.

Plans were already in the works for a Maguire family reunion during the third week in August in Narragansett. It would be a one-night event. Of course I was psyched up for this because I loved all of my extended family. It would also give me another jolt of happiness that I desperately needed. The morning of the event was when I learned that my mother-in-law had prescription for Paxil, and she had run out. I didn't want to cause her anymore anxiety that day that she was already feeling. I was anxious that day, waiting to hear if she could get a refill here in Rhode Island. If she couldn't get her prescription refilled, I knew we weren't going to Narragansett. She was on the phone all day long to her physician in Kentucky. About two hours before we were scheduled to leave for Narragansett, her prescription came through to our local pharmacy.

Thomas, 12, the brave youngster, drove down with us to direct my mother-in-law to Narragansett. Martha planned to drive us home. I was so thrilled to see everyone even through I felt spineless. I refrained from drinking that night out of respect for Kevin and my mother-in-law. Almost everybody else was drinking. We are Irish and we enjoy a drink or two. We also enjoy showing off new additions to the family, and one-year-old Kaleigh Morgan was definitely the spotlight of the evening. In a large room filled with fifty people or more, she was the talk of the night.

I was very reserved and quiet that evening, remaining close to Kevin and my mother-in-law, not wanting them to feel abandoned. Mom, Dad, Martha and a few others sat at our table. Among the missing were Paul, Karen and Sam who returned to Singapore. Peter had recently got reassigned to The Pentagon. My mother-in-law looked tired. She definitely did not want to be there, which made me anxious. I had a chance to have a moment to go out onto the rear deck that faced the ocean. I will never forget the rolling, dark gray clouds that nearly touched the matching, dark gray ocean below. It was frightening and beautiful all at once. I hoped that all of the seamen were safe that night.

My Uncle Fran from Indianapolis almost loved his Irish music as much as he loved his Rhode Island. We had some Irish music happening that night. What Irishman doesn't like "Danny Boy"? Kaleigh joined in on the fun and began to dance. We just loved our babies.
Occasionally I would look over to Kevin and my mother-in-law. A glaze swept over them, as they didn't move from their original spots. My mother-in-law was ready to leave but Martha wasn't. She just needed to feel a fraction more alert before she drove home. This meant spending another hour in Narragansett. This, the stretch of time when the first guests start to leave and the last fifteen or so remain, I call the catch up hour. The hall is relatively quiet where you can have actual conversations with people. You can catch up with the little things in people's lives that you may have missed before. The catch up hour—try not to miss it.

Martha was set to leave. We said goodbye to Mom and Dad before they headed back to the Cape. I said goodbye to everybody. Heading north on Route 4, I listened to Martha and my mother-in-law in causal chat. My mother-in-law's voice was finally calm.

It was the thing we had been waiting for two and a half months to begin: our services were finally approved. Glorious, glorious services. I might have breathed a little easier knowing some type of security and routine would be coming soon. Our new social worker came for a visit. He told us he was new at the Department of Human Services, and it clearly showed. It was quite evident he wasn't used to interacting with people who didn't have any intellectual disabilities, although had substantial physical needs. During his visit, he explained how things would work with the Department of Developmental Disabilities and our chosen agency, the agency, which would provide our services. One surprising nugget of information he supplied us was that we were eligible to receive $17,000 in recreation funds. It was a jaw-dropping amount, but we had no reason to doubt him. I had always wanted to check out Vegas.

Three administrators, including a registered nurse from the agency, made the initial visit to our home. My mother-in-law represented Kevin's needs, while Karla represented mine. I was a bit unsettled because Karla had only known me for three months, where Kevin's mother had known him for 33 years. Would I be well represented? I had to be prepared to interject for myself. My mother-in-law explained, in great detail, what Kevin's needs involved. We sort of made comparisons between his needs and my needs, and what differed. Since Kevin needs exceeded mine to a certain degree, I knew someone would always be here. And that $17,000 for recreational activities was very misguided information from our newbie social worker. There wasn't any state funding for strictly recreational purposes.

This was the first time I had heard the term, consumer, placed on me. Kevin and I were now "consumers" of this agency. I didn't like this particular term from the start. We were consumers. What were we consuming that was any different from the rest of society? We all consume air from the atmosphere to breathe. Everybody consumes food, so it wasn't that. Were we considered consumers because we were consuming tax dollars from our state and federal governments? It sure felt like it was how that term was designed to be used. I hate this word: consumer. The word connotes something, or someone not giving back anything in return. It is an ugly word when it comes to referring to people with disabilities. A good percentage of us don't want to be consumers, but rather, contributors. We want to contribute to everything possible in life. It is my wish that agencies change this terminology to 'people supported' or 'people we support."

Kathy S., our team supervisor, was assigned to Kevin and me through the agency. Kathy was responsible for training other staff members who would eventually come on board, responsible for scheduling and running a tight ship when it came to staffing. She was a spunky 52-year-old woman who wasn't afraid to be hands-on. I must say, it was quite a refreshing sight to see her face on her first morning. I could just tell from her eyes that we would be well cared for.

To make caring for us ten times easier, the agency brought in three different barrier-free lift companies to provide quotes to install these lifts. I had never seen barrier-free lifts before this time, and it wasn't long before I saw the value in them. Barrier-free lifts are battery-operated hoists, as large as an average kitchen toaster, that attaches to a ceiling track. Once a body harness is placed around the person, the barrier-free can lift a person to Point A to Point B without physical exertion on the caregiver. The tracks can be simple to complex depending on the individual need.

Kevin and I didn't quite see eye-to-eye about the complexity the track should be. I wanted two, separate straight tracks; one would be over our bed, and one would be positioned over the toilet and extended straight into the shower area. Kevin wanted more of a complex track that started over our bed, S-curved down the hallway, and S-curved into our bathroom. I had many issues with the complex track, namely I didn't want to travel on what I perceived as an amusement ride, bare-assed, down my hallway. Kevin didn't have any issue with being exposed to whoever walked into our bedroom in the morning. Every time he threw off the covers from his naked body, I used to cover him back up with a sheet to maintain some kind of level of modesty.

The second issue I had with the complex track was they would need to cut grooves into the bedroom and bathroom headers that would leave a gap above both doors. I know how private I am about using the bathroom. Can you imagine

256

someone trying to use the bathroom with a big, gaping hole above the door. No, it was not happening. Kevin finally understood my reasoning and agreed to have two separate tracks. It would take another five months to get the approval for funding for the barrier-free lift.

My emotions were all over the place by the end of August 2001. Depression still had its stronghold on me but I wanted so badly to find a way to love Kevin as I once did. I didn't want to fail at my marriage, but I so desperately wanted to feel whole again. I had to have hope that things would get better between Kevin and me after his mother returned to Kentucky. People always said the first year of marriage is tough; for me, it was stifling. For some reason, 20 years popped into my head. I rationalized with my weak mind that if I could give our marriage 20 years worth of my effort, then it would prove I gave my marriage a fighting shot. I felt like I was in a very dark trench, craving any light I could capture. Twenty years seemed like an eternity in my fragile mind but I talked myself into it.

I had scheduled to return to the Cape for an appointment with the gynecologist I had been seeing ever since I started taking the birth control pill. In all actuality, I would rather get run over by a Mack truck than go to the gynecologist. But on this day, my appointment would be moved to a day later. Hearing this news, I just broke down in tears. *What the hell was wrong with me?!* This was not who I was. I don't suddenly go to pieces; I definitely don't fall to pieces when things change like a fucking doctor's appointment. This was not who I was.

The next day, Karla drove me to the Cape where we met up with Linda at the doctor's office in Hyannis. Inside, Linda prepared me for my exam, trying to decrease my anxiety any way she could. Linda was always good for a joke or two, or ten. Laughter was the best medicine. What I liked most about this doctor was that he had a low, and wide exam chair, which I didn't feel that I was going to fall off. For athetoids, getting up on a 3-foot high exam table is not fun. It brings on anxiety, which in turn, converts to a whole lot of movement and uncontrollable muscles. A whole lot of muscle movement is not fun when you are trying to relax during a gynecological exam. When doctors request you to relax, I, like many people with athetoid cerebral palsy, do the opposite and tighten up their muscles. It would be nice if some gynecologists had nitrous oxide handy for women who have cerebral palsy just to chill them out and take away their anxiety.

After the exam was over, Linda helped me ask the doctor for advice on my sexual issues I was having with Kevin. It was all about getting angles right. The doctor suggested we should come to the realization that intercourse might not be possible for us to achieve. In the fragile emotional state I was in, this was the last thing I wanted to hear. I was looking for anything to recharge my love for Kevin. I also came to the realization that if I did love Kevin, we could have been very happy without intercourse. Frankly, I could have design a myriad of things to try in bed. We were just talking creating better angles, and I was highly inventive. Kevin wasn't the man I thought I married, and he had drained me of all my happiness, all of my vigor that usually brought a constant smile to my face. I was just about tapped out of any joy in my life.

After the doctor's, we went back to my parents' house for lunch. Linda was not shy and gave Mom the transpired at my appointment. It was very evident that Mom had recognized how unhappy I was for a few months. You can't hide too much from your mother even when you try like hell to do so. It's rather impossible. I don't recall her exact comment, but she wanted me to understand that I was free to make choices. I still held onto the diluted idea that I could make it to my 20-year wedding anniversary.

That same night, I explained to Kevin what my doctor had suggested. Kevin agreed, even to the extent that we didn't have to have any kind of physical relationship at all beyond kissing. I was dumbfounded.

258

Kathy had brought on two more staff members, Mary and Arlinda. Mary was an older woman who needed time to warm up to new people. When my mother-in-law told me she welled up when she accidently broke Kevin's glass dolphin, I knew she was good people. Arlinda was good people also. She worked three weeknights with us. Kathy attempted to bring on another woman but she was too afraid to enter a house with a dog, which happened on occasion. My big, sweet Murphy could scare the crap out of people with her menacing bark, but she was all love from snout to tail.

One particular day, Mary's husband dropped by to meet us. If I had believed Santa Claus existed, I swore he was standing in our kitchen. *Holy shit, it is Santa Claus*, I thought. Okay not really, but he certainly looked like jolly Old Saint Nick. His name was Leon, and like Saint Nick, had a very big heart. He talked to Kevin and me for several minutes. Kevin wanted to say something to Leon. Kathy got out his alphabet board from his backpack and tried to figure out what letter his eyes were gazing toward. It took several minutes for Kathy to decipher his words. He asked Leon if he could do a job, I forget exactly what, on the outside of our house. Hearing this, I was appalled that he would see this man just as a handyman, and not as an actual person.

On the morning of September 11, 2001, I turned the television a few minutes before 9am. The *Today Show* was on. I had gotten out of bed and sat on the top tier of the floor. They were televising, live, the North Tower, with black, thick smoke billowing out of the top floors. Initial reports were that a small plane had crashed into it, leaving a gapping hole. I could hardly believe what I witnessed next, at 9:03am, on live television. I witnessed a jet airliner deliberately crash into the corner of the South Tower. Katie Couric immediately commented, "I don't think these were accidents." "You think?" I yelled with angrily sarcasm. I was angry with Katie. Kevin showed his discontent with body movements. What the hell was happening?!

Mary chose me to take care of that day. Like every morning since I had moved into our home, I crawled into the shower on the trail of soft, area rugs to protect my knees from the hard, tile floor. In the shower, I sat on bath mats. Minutes after I got into the shower, I heard Kevin and my mother-in-law outside the bathroom door. He was clearly exasperated. At 9:37am, another jet airliner had deliberately flown into The Pentagon. A jolt pierced my heart. Peter. Fifteen seconds later, the phone rang. It was Mom. Peter was okay. His office was in an adjacent building to The Pentagon. For the grace of God his life was spared on this horrendous day. At 10:03am, another report of a jet airliner crashing in southwest Pennsylvania. *Will it ever stop?!*

I was in my wheelchair by the time Martha stopped by. She was stunned and confused like we all were. Sarah and Thomas were already home from school. She left and no doubt hugged them throughout that day.

Much like many Americans and caring people all over the world, we were glued to our televisions. When the Twin Towers collapsed, it was almost too much to handle. Death and destruction seemed like it was everywhere; it was only a few hundred miles away. Oh the precious lives that were lost; how could anyone make sense of it all. We were hated because we were free, and that gave reason for these terrorists to kill us. How fucked up was that? The city that I had loved so much was forever changed. I remembered doing a project for my high school Oceanography class where I did a presentation on an Apple. I used graphics and text, and one of the graphics, I drew the outline of the Manhattan skyline, including the Twin Towers.

People pulled together; we were American Strong. Kevin and I experienced a few days of tranquility and reflection over the next few weeks, although I was still in a deep depression. We watched Dan Rather cry openly on *The Late Show with David Letterman*. I welled up. I was looking forward to the release of Live's new album the next week. We saw *Hearts of Atlantis* with Kathy and Mary. Still, with our independence from my mother-in-law, I remained forlorn in my silent reverie. I couldn't break free of the depression.

It felt like it had been ages since music lifted my mood. We went to Emerald Square Mall on September 18th so I could buy Live's *V* album. Initially, it was very different from Live's previous albums. It was a little hard to accept the atypical, hip-hop lyrics, and Eastern sounds embedded into rock and roll. The more I listened to the CD, the more it grew on me. I started to love it, and now it's my favorite Live album.

One of the songs off of *V*, "Overcome" became a tribute to all the victims, all of the heroes and the hope for the future of our scarred nation. Live's lead singer, Ed Kowalczyk, would appear on *Tonight Show with Jay Leno* on September 27, 2001. That particular night, I tried to be intimate with Kevin again, trying something new. Kevin was less than impressed with my efforts; he seemed bored. My motivation, how stark it might have been, dwindled in smoke.

On the morning of September 30, I got up like I normally had, sitting on the top step, watching whatever was on television. Since it was a Sunday, Kathy hadn't found staffing for Sundays, Karla and my mother-in-law would be taking care of us on this morning. It was not unusual for Kevin to turn his body around on the bed. It was certainly wasn't unusual for Kevin to express his love for me first thing in the morning, and what seemed like 100 times on each given day. A week before, I had mentioned to Kevin that he really didn't need to tell me he loved me so many times a day. He grew annoyed and told me he would only profess his love for me in the morning and before going to sleep. That wasn't I wanted, I explained. Did I know what I was trying to get him understand? It was getting so, so difficult to say 'I love you' back.

On that morning, Kevin expressed his love for me, and all I could get out of my mouth was silence. My heart dropped in my chest, as I looked vacantly towards Kevin. I quickly looked back towards the television. I imagined myself saying 'I love you', but I couldn't force any words to come out. Kevin waited, waited and waited for me return his 'I love you', but nothing would come out. Nothing. All of my reserves had dried up. I couldn't move either, knowing if I moved, the marriage would be over. Kevin kept his eyes on me, waiting to hear what he wanted to hear. Feeling so very awkward, my body movements were jerky; my mouth was dry. He waited and waited, but I couldn't say it. Kevin soon asked me if I loved him. I knew the answer; it was in my heart, screaming to be released from stifled chest. I knew I had to be happy again. I faced him, and answered his question.

I didn't leave the bedroom for hours that day. When my mother-in-law brought Kevin into the bathroom, I heard him cry. I had to take a deep breath and told myself I made the right decision. Karla tended to me throughout the day. She asked me if I wanted to call Mom and Dad. I said yes. Karla informed my mother-in-law my parents would be coming in a few hours. My mother-in-law responded, "Hope will straighten this out". Did she really think Kevin and I just had a playground spat? She certainly did.

Through my guilt, I felt a positive release that was suddenly off my shoulders. I could breathe again—I could be myself again. I worried what the immediate future held for me. I knew Martha and Glenn would be tremendously disappointed. I had to face their dissatisfaction to my abrupt end to marriage. I had to accept that other people didn't experienced what I had experienced with Kevin. I saw another side of Kevin that other people rarely saw.

I sat quietly in the bedroom for several hours with the television off. I might have eaten a half of yogurt. My parents arrived and they had to pass by very upset in-laws to find me alone in the bedroom. They gave me a big hug. Ironically, this probably was the first time in months they recognized that their daughter had returned to someone who they recognized. I didn't need to explain anything because they knew. I liked breathing again, and maybe smiling again. Mom asked Dad to go to the grocery store to buy a whole chicken, potatoes and carrots; she was going to make dinner—a very brave offering under very stressful circumstances.

I emerged from the bedroom to eat dinner. I could feel hard looks from Kevin and my mother-in-law. They blamed me for this awful mess we found ourselves in. I pulled up to the kitchen counter where I liked to eat; my back was towards Kevin. As Mom was in the kitchen, without provocation, Kevin drove his wheelchair at full throttle and began kicking the back of my wheelchair. It caught me off guard, but I kept calm. Both of our mothers witnessed his outburst, and began yelling at him. Immediately, my mother-in-law took charge of his wheelchair controls and drove him into the living room. She continued to scold him like a child. When it sunk in what had just happened, I was suddenly afraid of him, although I still understood his anger. Somehow I ate dinner.

Dad had already left to go home because he had to work the next morning. After dinner, Mom and I retreated back into the bedroom. Martha arrived, extremely unhappy, as I expected. She thought I was giving up too easily on my marriage. She suggested we try marriage counseling. I began to cry with frustration. I knew marriage counseling would be pointless. I knew how I felt; I knew I was scared to be around him. Mom tried to explain it to Martha, but Martha felt I was forfeiting the fight. It was a battle fraught with misguidance and delusions.

That night, Mom and I shared the bed that night. She overheard Kevin ask his mother why they couldn't sleep in the king bed. I guess he had neglected realize that I needed to be near my adapted bathroom to be able to use it. He and his

mother shared the pullout couch. Whether it was out of
frustration or anxiety, she spent hours cleaning out closets and
kitchen cupboards of everything she deemed theirs. By one
o'clock in the morning, she was still at it. My Mom had reached
her threshold of patience and, as politely as she could, asked my
mother-in-law to save the rest for the next morning because I
need my rest. The rest of the night was quiet and peaceful with
Mom beside me.

Kathy had already gotten 'the call' the previous evening
announcing that I didn't love Kevin and the marriage was over;
Kevin would be moving back to Kentucky. Kathy and Mary
would be walking into a house filled with disappointment and
sadness. My father-in-law, along with a friend, drove through
the night to Rhode Island. I spent the majority of the day in the
bedroom with Mom. Kathy and/or Mary sat with us from time to
time to get away from the tension. At some point, my father-in-
law asked to talk to me for a moment. I agreed. He was very
understanding and spoke in a calm voice like he always had. He
asked if there was any chance of reconciliation. I answered no.
He left me with kind words, wishing me the best for the future. I
appreciated his words.

My Mom thought it would be best if I left the house, as
Kevin's parents moved out the last of his things. Before I left
with Karla and J.J., I said goodbye to Kevin. He promised me
that he would change, as he looked sorrowfully at me. I felt I
knew him better than he knew himself. The change I needed
from him was for him to stop acting like a child, and to stop
thinking the world revolved around him. I knew that would be
difficult for him to do. I was also afraid of what he could
become if he became angry. I realized I was breaking his world
apart, but I had to save my soul. I told him I couldn't do it
anymore. With that, I didn't speak to Kevin again.

While I was gone with Karla and J.J., Mom stayed back
and witnessed the departure. Over the next twelve years, her

account of what happened next never deviated. Once again, Kevin's anger got the best of him and he charged towards my Mom. My mother-in-law stepped in and stopped him before he hit my Mom. This action sent my mother-in-law into a fit, as she tore into Kevin, screaming at him at the top of her lungs. She ordered him to leave the house. In the living room chair, she emotionally collapsed, crying without reserve. My Mom and my father-in-law sat with her, trying to console her. She continued to cry hard. Mom offered her a bit of wine, but my mother-in-law politely declined. They just sat with my mother-in-law, reassuring her that everything would be okay. Once my mother-in-law was ready to move again, Mom helped her to the tears from her face. Within the hour, they were gone.

"There's a time for the good in life
A time to kill the pain in life
Dream about the sun you
Queen of rain."

"Queen Of Rain"
Roxette
Tourism (Songs from Studios,
Stages, Hotelrooms & Other
Strange Places)

It was time Mom to go home. She missed her own house and her own bed. She was confident I was on the path to be restored to my prior self. Kathy and Mary had witnessed an overnight transformation within me. They just saw me as a quiet and despondent young woman who didn't really interact much. On October 2, 2001, I had regained life from my zombie-like state. They were simply amazed.

We all piled into Mary's minivan and drove to South Yarmouth. We had another mission that day: to retrieve my van, which Dad didn't get around to successfully selling. There was always a little voice in Mom's head that kept them selling my van. We had lunch at the All-American Pub where the majority of people from Dennis socialized, including Linda. Linda's good friend, Lisa, waitressed at the Pub. In the many years since, Lisa has become my good friend as well. I am MoJo to Lisa.

On this day, Lisa was working, and Linda just happened to be there. Mom gave Linda the rundown of what happened within the last 48 hours. Linda wasn't surprised; she saw the signs like my Mom had. Like everyone at the table, she noticed the life in my eyes had returned. I was sitting tall.

After lunch, we took Mom home. I remained in Mary's van, as Mom gave Kathy and Mary a quick tour of the house. Dad had gotten home from work, and greeted Mary and Kathy with a friendly handshake. My parents certainly liked Kathy and Mary, and they reciprocated the same feelings. Knowing much more about me and meeting Mom and Dad, Mary and Kathy had a totally different view of who I was. They would look after me like I was their own.

I had to wait for the agency to recalculate my hours, as I was going to be by myself. I was nervous; I always became nervous when decisions were out of my hands. The verdict was in: I was approved for 13 hours per day for services. I breathed a big sigh of relief. I was visited by the social worker. The reason for the visit, I still don't know. He stayed for about five minutes, probably asked me a few questions and then left. I hadn't been visited by a social worker until 2013, when my yearly ISP (Individual Service Plan) was written and renewed. I never quite understand why I needed a social worker since I never had the need to call on one for assistance. In the very few times when I asked them questions, particularly with obtaining new adaptive equipment, answers were vague and incomplete. I soon learned I had to make things happen for myself. I know there are many great social workers out there, but the great ones have eluded crossing my path, until recently. Even so, I'm my best social worker.

In the days and weeks after my marriage was over, my and Kevin's parents had many discussions over the property they had purchased for Kevin and me. Before the purchase, they had a contact drawn up that the parents agreed upon. I'm one of those very fortunate individuals who have tremendous family support, in many aspects, that I am extremely humbled by and never want to take that for granted. There are times when I talk to other people with disabilities who aren't as fortunate as I am, and I feel guilt for being so blessed for the people, knowledge, health, opportunities and support I have in my life. I wish everybody could have what I have had. I realize this is how society is. This book is a recognition of all the people who strive to be their best, every day.

During one of these phone conversations between Mom and my mother-in-law, my mother-in-law was convinced our breakup was caused by the short period of time when Kevin suffered from a sinus infection. My mother-in-law would lay Kevin over the side of the bed to help the mucus drain from his lungs. On the contrary—I wanted to see Kevin well. If it had helped, I would have gotten on the bed and rubbed his back. After all of my years at the residential school and the group home, Kevin's sinus infection didn't bother me in the least. If I was going to end my marriage over a sinus infection, then I didn't deserved the very air I breathed.

My father-in-law requested I write him a letter explaining how things went so wrong. It was a heavy task to do; I didn't want to divulge very emotional and personal matters. Mom urged me to write the letter. I probably wasn't ready to write the letter, but I wrote. It was unescapably honest. I didn't leave anything out. I never received a reply.

Sometime during the months after the marriage was over, my parents received the wedding picture proofs. I didn't want to see them, so Mom disposed of them. I don't have any regrets about not viewing my wedding photographs.

I hired my cousin, Tim, to be my divorce lawyer. I filed, and we went to court. The divorce went uncontested, and by June 2002, my divorce was final. Even today, I carry a big chunk of guilt around because I couldn't figure out a way to save my marriage. It is not in my nature not to find a way accomplish a task. My depression overwhelming through my marriage and I found it immensely difficult to do anything meaningful through that time. When I think back to the summer of 2001, it still remains very dark and blurry, almost like I was non-existent. I felt non-existent in my heart and in my head. That big chunk of guilt will not release its grasp.

I felt bad that I had taken so much away from Kevin; I broke his heart. Frequently, I thought about him and wished he was doing all right. I wondered how he was spending his days. Was he able to move on? I hope he did. Kevin passed away on September 11, 2003 from asphyxiation. I was very sad; I mourned him. I felt tremendously sad for his family.

I received a lot of support from my family and friends after my marriage ended. My Aunt Anne and Pat visited soon after. Aunt Pat had first-hand experience, having gone through a very short marriage herself back in 1982. Our marriages were eerily the same: we married men who we thought we knew but really didn't. There was only one person, a person I hadn't known for very long, second-guessing my decision to end my marriage. I didn't like to be second-guessed on such a personal decision, but I wasn't angry. I knew her attentions were coming from the heart.

I had the rest of my life to consider. I just wanted to be happy, and I have been happy ever since. I live happily single. My ideas about love and being in an intimate relationship have changed completely around. I won't seek it again; if true love is in the cards for me, it will find me. If it's not in the cards, then that is fine also. I won't grow old being bitter that I failed in love. I will never settle for less than I am worth. I know I have tremendous love in my heart and that should be the only thing that matters.

*"Time for a cool change
I know that it's time for a cool
change Now that my life is so
prearranged
I know that it's time for a cool
change"*

"Cool Change"
Little River Band
First Under The Wire

It was time to look forward. I was meeting new people and becoming more integrated with the disabled community, and so much more aware of what was available for people with disabilities. I wasn't surprised at the range of disabilities I witnessed, but services differed quite a lot depending on individual needs. I also learned that Rhode Island possessed many advocacy groups for people with disabilities. Sometimes I would participate in events, promoting advocacy for people with disabilities.

I have been also quite taken back as I met various people who manage programs for people with disabilities, and can't relate to people such as myself. Am I too intimating for them to have a regular conversation with? Sometimes I believe that is exactly the case. People like this should look inward and figure out if they are in the right field. It saddens me that attitudes such as this exist, in the field of Human Services, specifically working with people with disabilities. And to think I was intimidated by these people at one time—shame on me!

They installed the barrier-free lift in January 2002. The company installed one straight track in my bathroom and bathroom, as planned. The setup worked very well, and took a lot of pressure off knowing people were going to be safe transferring me from place to place. Having the barrier-free lift also alleviated my need to crawl into the shower every morning, saving my knees from wear and tear. I know of a few individuals who refused using the lift system. They might have thought the lift might take away something away from their independence, or they might fear change. They might also see the lift system as a sign that their bodies might not be as strong as they once were. All these thoughts ran through my mind, but I saw the big picture: when you take the physical risk out of transfers, you and your staff members will be safe. I have always put the safety of others and myself at a high priority. It is my wish that all of the big hotel chains would dedicate at least one room in each hotel fully wheelchair accessible, including lift tracks in the bathroom and over a bed.

I was fully staffed, and Kathy kept an eye out for new people to use as replacements or substitutes. There were many misses, and oh what misses they were. There were several instances where potentials just remained seated in the corner of the kitchen for the entire shift waiting for the shift to end. These are the potentials whom really get under my skin. I just want to say to them, "What the hell are you doing here if you have no interest in being here?" I chock it up to my covetousness in seeing somebody given an opportunity to capitalize and strive in new employment and letting that job escape through your fingers like water. I understand that this field of work is not for everyone, but people should have an idea what taking care of a person with a developmental disability might entail.

There have been a few delightful hits, like Terry, Melanie, Ruth, Hazel, Mahoney, Theresa, Erin, and Elizabeth. I have learned over the years that to give someone a chance to fit in, you need to give someone time to prove themselves that they have your best interests in mind. Some people prove themselves rather quickly, while others need more time. For instance, I recognized Ruth had my best interest in mind when we were at a Waterfire and she politely asked a gentleman to step aside, out of my line of sight. Then I knew Ruth had what it took. I taught Ruth how to cook.

Let me tell you, it's a long 6 or 7, or 13-hour shift when a person only asks you what you want to eat. They don't want to be there just as much as don't want them there. I give it my best to interact with them at some level, but when they don't give anything back, I become frustrated. These people don't usually last long. When Mary injured her shoulder at the start of 2004, sub reserves were low, and I got this person, who essentially wasn't a very nice person. I don't know why I put up with her for four, very long months, but I did. She was a "me" person; everything she did centered on her. She did what she had to for

me, begrudgingly. I wanted to sarcastically apologize for
breathing the same air she did. It was fortunate she didn't work
any evening shifts because she probably wouldn't have wished
me a good night. One day I listened to her on her cell phone.
She ordered a bedroom set and set up a Cash-On-Delivery on a
specific day that her husband would be home so he would have
to pay. I felt sorry for her husband being married to such a
conniving woman. I must say she was always paranoid that I
spent my days sending e-mails to her bosses, telling them all the
things that she was doing, or not doing. I didn't do such a thing;
I wasn't going to spend my valuable time on her. Funny, it didn't
seem to stop her from spending hours outside, on her cell phone,
presumably chatting with her friends. It was hard to believe she
had any friends. I breathed a breath of fresh air when she walked
out my door for the last time.

        I have also learned throughout my life that everyone has
overcome a great deal in their lives, no matter if they have a
disability or not. Ruth, a native Liberian, escaped her war-torn
homeland with a child and younger siblings, while her parents
left 8 years earlier to set up a life in New York City. Her stories
are amazing and horrifying at the same time. She is one of the
bravest people I know.

        And then I have Melanie, who just takes life as it comes,
and tries to make the best of every challenging situation. She
hadn't done this type of work before, but she wanted to try. She
spent eight days flipping burgers at McDonald's and knew it
wasn't for her. She spent her childhood defending kids in school
with developmental disabilities, because her older brother had a
mild disability from an accident. Once she learned she would be
working which a person named Maureen, she took it as a sign
from her beloved Aunt Maureen, who had recently passed away
before her employment. She is convinced her Aunt Maureen's
spirit hangs out in the little sitting area in my bedroom. Who am
I to deny it? Actually it is quite comforting to know spirits
abound.

274

Before I even met Hazel, I met her now, ex-husband. Kathy and I went into a local fish market, soliciting funds for our agency. He mentioned his wife had just started working for us. It wasn't long before Hazel was introduced to me. She probably continues to be the only person who didn't need directions to my house because she grew up around the corner. If I go sit at one edge of my driveway, I can see the back of her parents' house. They are the people with Christmas lights up all year long. I might not be able to see Russia from my house, but I can certainly see Hazel parents' from here. Jingle, jingle, jingle!

Since I had returned to Rhode Island, ORS came knocking on my door to see if they could assist me with my employment issues. Did I let them in? Of course I did. Did I have any hope that they would be successful in assisting with finding me employment? Not so much. My new ORS counselor was a very nice woman, and she tried all of her resources she had to try to find me any type of job, even suggesting I be a greeter at Wal-Mart. I never looked down on all of those great people who are greeters across this country, but becoming a greeter wasn't something I wanted to do. It might have looked good on her scorecard, but it wasn't a job I couldn't see myself in. I can't sit still through a long movie or television show without having something secondary activity to do. I can't sit still, doing nothing for more than 30 minutes. I have noticed my siblings having the same tendency. We can't sit still.

After four years with ORS trying to find me suitable employment, going so far as to hiring a private job placement firm, I wrote a letter to my ORS counselor stating I wished to end my services with ORS. I saw it as they were spending a boatload of cash on me without progress. I saw that ORS could use that money for others who would benefit from it. I was only becoming more and more discouraged with every avenue they tried, and came up short.

Between the years of 2002 and 2004, I composed my second compilation CD, *Revolutions In Time.* It had been quite a long time since I composed anything new. I renewed my love for composing music and even dared myself to come up with lyrics for about half of the songs. I'm not a lyrist, and in my opinion, I really suck at it. That hasn't stopped me from coming up with lyrics for many of my following songs. For this CD insert, I asked Sarah if she wanted to design the artwork. At the time, she was a Graphic Arts major at Rhode Island College. I let her have full reign over the design. She did a terrific job.

On April 12, 2002, my Uncle Joe Maguire, from Seattle, Washington, passed away at age 82 from complications due to a broken arm. I didn't know him very well, but on those few times he and his family visited Rhode Island, his home state, he was very nice to me. He was an Irishman through-and-through.

On September 4, 2003, Paul and Karen welcomed their second son, Benjamin Hotung, into the world. By this time, they had moved back to the states and lived in Connecticut for a time. We rented a minivan and all six of us set out to visit our new family member. It would be another Gaynor to love. When he was about seven months, he enjoyed sitting on my lap as I drove him around my house while we celebrated Sam's birthday. There is no better smell than a baby's baldhead.

Also within these seven months, I managed to lose 40 pounds. It was out of personal necessity due to my borderline high cholesterol. I did not want to take statins because I feared the side effects. I did it the old-fashion way—with diet. First thing I cut out of my daily diet was soda. For the next six months, I either ate an asparagus or a tuna sandwich for lunch. After these six months were through, I realized my unexplainable hip pain was caused by the overabundance of mercury in my system. I replaced tuna with turkey, and my hip pain vanished. I also took up drinking red wine or straight, hot cocoa at dinner, and dessert still consists of two squares of 85% dark chocolate. Within a year, my cholesterol levels dropped nearly 50 points.

By 2005, I was still sitting on my novel, *Always A Place*, wondering what to do with it. I didn't know. I think I was waiting for a miracle. In the spring I signed up for a course called, "How To Publish Your Book". Unfortunately, whether there was a mix up in initial communication with the educational organization, or my own stupidity, this particular class was on the second floor in an inaccessible building. A few months later, the class was offered again, in a very accessible building. The instructor, Steve Manchester, manned the entrance door, waiting for my arrival.

I expected there would be upwards to 20 people in the class, but there were just five of us. We were five passionate writers who didn't know where to start to get our work out to the masses, or even a small crowd. Steve, a published author of several novels, talked for a few hours about his experiences about going through the entire process, from writing and editing to marketing and promotion. Steve answered all of the questions posed to him patiently and honestly. He supplied us with reading material, which he authored and copyrighted. I asked if he could e-mail me the materials in a PDF; he trusted me that I wouldn't sell the materials for my own profit.

After class, Steve wanted to know more about my writing project. Kathy accompanied me to this class, and she explained what *Always A Place* was about. When I wanted to interject information, Kathy deciphered my clumsy speech. Steve offered to read my manuscript. He loved it, and edited the manuscript for the very last time. He thought it was a true winner. In 2007, Steve's publisher picked up *Always A Place*. It was slated to go to press, but the publishing house claimed bankruptcy before it got that far. In August 2010, I published *Always A Place* through Amazon.com's Print-On-Demand service and subsidiary, Createspace. Jean Polovchik very kindly and purposefully searched for a red barn and photographed it for the soft cover. It was perfect. I thank you, Jean!

"When they comin' home?
When they leavin' that place?
To see their lovers face again
Kid will see his daddy's face
again When they comin' home?
Oh shed some grace!
To see their lovers face again
Kid will see his daddy's face
again"

"Home"
Live
Songs From Black Mountain

In January of 2006, Peter was asked to direct Marine command headquarters in Fallujah, Iraq during Operation Iraqi Freedom. He accepted. One day, he came over to my house to do some work to something that needed attention. He told me he was going to Iraq very nonchalantly. I did a double take. In all of years in the Marines, he never been in any wartime conflicts, but now at age 47, he was entering a warzone. He would be in command of a battalion in a secure center, but Fallujah was a hot bed of conflict. I believed that this was something he wanted to do. He would be gone for eight months.

My attention soon turned to Mom and Dad; they would worry the most, along with Sue and 7-year-old Grace. I imagined Mom wouldn't sleep for eight months, and she probably didn't. Every Tuesday, she would say a Novena Prayer and lit a candle. In a time with e-mail being the popular way to communicate, if I received e-mail from Peter, I would immediately call Mom and Dad. Peter was safe and sound, and eating well. His e-mail was gold to Mom and Dad.

It would be Mom and Dad's 50th wedding anniversary in June. We would postpone the big celebration until October, when Peter returned home. The first half of 2006 was very difficult for Melanie's family, especially her mother; her mother's boyfriend of 17 years was dying of cancer. By June 23, he was in Hospice, very close to death. Kathy was away that weekend, and there was nobody else available to this very important dinner on the Cape. Martha and her family were remaining at my parents' for the weekend. I couldn't stay because I had Murphy at home. Melanie was the only one available for this short trip, and I felt horrible—her mother needed her so much more than I did.

It was a very long and tense evening, even though we were at a happy cerebration. I just wanted this night to get over so Melanie could get to her mother, to support her when the man that she loved so much took his last breath. He passed away in the early hours of Sunday, June 25. His suffering ended. I will never forget the sacrifices Melanie and her family made for me on that very difficult Friday night.

On Columbus Day weekend, we had so much to celebrate. Again, I had to call on Melanie to accompany me to this wonderful gathering. This time, there weren't any worries that kept anyone from enjoying this moment. We celebrated Mom and Dad's 50th year of marriage. We celebrated God's hands for bringing Peter back home safely from Fallujah. We also celebrated the upcoming birth of Paul and Karen's third child, due in early January 2007. We set this big family celebration in Newport over two days. People flew or drove in from out of state like my Uncle Fran and his wife, Nuala from Indiana. All had a marvelous time. It was beautiful weather in beloved Newport.

> I wrote the toast, which Paul read: *I welcome one and all to this fabulous night to celebrate our parents' 50th wedding anniversary. I was advised to keep this short and sweet. I'll do my best. Fifty years—man oh man, that's a long time to pick someone's smelly socks up off the floor. Now, that's love. Thanks to Helen and Ray Watson, these two lovebirds met. Their first date, July 4th, 1954, took off with a bang. They haven't looked back since. They have raised four tremendously talented individuals, I must say, all of who hold their values of family and the importance of being the best that you can be every day. I thought about making this little toast sappy, but who the hell wants to cry at the happiest of celebrations. The wedding is over; let's celebrate fifty years of love and...love.*

I believe there were some brief tears shed, especially by my Mom. Everyone enjoyed the toast, and the festivities that were spread over two days.

"Oh, won't you please, please
Take another picture
Please, please freeze my
features
Oh, won't you please, please
Take another
I don't wanna fade away"

"Take Another Picture"
Quarterflash
Take Another Picture

I was still in contact with Peter Falk until the last few months of 2006. He was finishing his witty autobiography, *Just One More Thing: Stories From My Life*. Always, very funny, his e-mails were little tales about what it was like to grow old. He was self-depreciating about his need to visit the men's room more than he liked, and about his short-term memory. It remains to be seen if, at this time, he had been diagnosed with Alzheimer's disease.

He asked me if I had a picture of him and myself that he could use in his autobiography. Either Peter or his assistant recalled the photograph taken in April of 1996 at the Wilbur Theater in Boston, when he and his wife, Shera Danese, performed *Love Letters*.

There is an amusing backstory behind this incredible picture Martha shot of us. It was the night before the play in Boston. We didn't know about the play. It was close to midnight on a Saturday night. Mom usually got up around this time every night to get some water. On this particular night, the phone rang; I heard the phone ringing. It was very rare that anyone called us at such a late hour. Our first thought that passed through our collective minds was *somebody died*. Mom picked up with a little angst; she said hello. A very deep voice came on the other end, "Mrs. Gaynor, this is Peter Falk." Relieved that it wasn't a midnight death call, she spoke to him very graciously. He asked to speak to me. Keenly aware that there wasn't any possible way that I could carry a conversation with him over the phone, and the other problem was that we didn't have any cordless phones in the house, Mom told Peter I was asleep. Mom talked to Peter close to ten minutes. It wasn't every day, or every night, Mom received a call from a Hollywood legend. He wanted us to come up and see the show, which was in 13 hours. He would call back Sunday morning to tell us the specific details.

The next morning, Mom called Martha to see if she wanted to go in her place. Sarah, 10-years-old, also went to this adult play. Dad enjoyed himself as well. After the play, we waited patiently for the Wilbur Theater to empty so Peter to come out to chat with us for a time. He was so very happy to see me again after 22 years. Pulling up a chair on my left side, he put his right hand on my back. I put my left hand behind his back because it was the safest place for it to be. Dad and Martha caught him up to what I was doing at that time. He said he didn't expect anything less from me. People were walking about, waiting for their chance to meet the famous actor. I watched him draw a very quick design on a top piece of a wooden lectern. He drew the design with a silver marker; his ingrained artistic abilities were apparent. Returning his attention to my family and me, Peter saw Martha had her camera ready. I tucked my left hand under my chin so I wouldn't hit Peter by accident when he pulled me to kiss me on my cheek. It's a terrific picture Martha shot, and I am very honored he put it in his autobiography.

Before his book was released, Peter sent me a signed hardcover. Inside, it reads: "Maureen – Knowing You What a Pleasure! Love, Peter". Soon after, his e-mails stopped. His assistant wrote me an e-mail message, explaining his declining condition. I continued writing Peter and Shera a letter every Christmas.

*"And we're standing on this
precipice with nothing much to
save
But the deep blue screams
Of falling dreams
With our next move"*

"The Promise"
Arcadia
So Red The Rose

When you're young, you don't know too much of what's going on in the world outside, unless something affects you directly. I believe most children in developed countries don't sit around wondering about the survival of the rain forest, whether there will ever be a cure for cancer, or whether the powers that be will wake up and realize that there is such a thing as global warming. These are adult issues, and I believe all adults should have a cause they believe in wholeheartedly and fight to make lives and society a little better before you leave this Earth. Today, children are becoming activists because many feel so passionately about a cause. Exposure to many causes, whether big or small, creates caring individuals. The world can't have too many caring people.

Of course I would like to take up many causes, but I have learned that you have to listen to your heart and realize what truly makes you tick, and I have learned that fighting for the rights of people with disabilities really ignites me. I think that is the reason I am writing this book. Yeah, my body might be a little strange and curious to many people, but that doesn't mean I am any different inside my brain or my heart. This book is my legacy.

During 2002 and 2008, I raised money for our local Leukemia & Lymphoma Society Chapter. Kathy had mentioned that she had been raising money for the charity for a number of years. The fundraising efforts culminated with a "Light The Night" walk down Blackstone Boulevard in Providence every autumn. In 2007, I raised $1430, in which I received an award from the Leukemia & Lymphoma Society and from Lt. Governor Elizabeth Roberts at the State House.

There are times when people like to take up a personal mission. In 2010, I thought it was about time I made a push to obtain a sling pool lift for my local YMCA. The facility had equipped their pool with a standard pool chair lift. Many public pool facilities have these chair pool lifts. These lifts are great for people who are able to transfer themselves, or who require little assistance with transfers. For people like myself, whose bodies flail in all directions at any given time, these pool chair lifts are inappropriate.

I tried a pool chair lift once, and it was a horrible experience. Without anything substantial supportive, or protective on my feet, executing a pivot transfer with full assistance is very difficult. I panicked my way through the pivot transfer because we were surrounded by concrete, and one false move could have resulted in a serious injury for both of us. Once seated on the chair, I was rotated straight. Even with a seatbelt, I panicked again, knowing full well if I didn't remain seated in the chair, it was a good chance I would fall straight into the pool, or onto the concrete below. I feared the concrete more. I had visions of cracking my head open, like an egg, on the side of the pool. When overwhelming nervousness kicks into a body with athetoid cerebral palsy, all bets are off trying to regain any control. As the pool chair was rotating over the water, I seriously thought this pool expedition could end in my death.

I never tried using a pool chair lift again, understandably. It was years later when I started researching alternative pool lifts. I wanted something that would operate similar to my barrier-free lift in my home. I was pleased there were pool lifts, which would lift me from my wheelchair directly to the pool via a sling. It was perfect for my needs.

The next step was to contact the facility director of the YMCA. He was receptive to my ideas and concerns, but it was my function to raise the funds for this specific pool lift. Of course I was up to the challenge. With some advice from others, I decided to run a cash prize raffle contest. I filed the appropriate paperwork with the Rhode Island State Police, and I obtained a permit from the town to conduct a gaming event. The only mistake I made was to trust the bank in which I opened up a separate account specifically for contest funds under my name and social security number. I made it a point to ask the bank associate whether or not opening this second bank account would interfere with Social Security Income. The bank associate assured me it wouldn't. Well, guess what? It did interfere, and, in the long run, I had to plead my case, with the assistance of Tim, to the Social Security Administration.

The raffle contest, itself, was extremely successful. Once the pool lift was purchased and installed, I donated the remaining funds to the YMCA. In the beginning, and at the end of the raffle, I contacted local newspapers to get media coverage. Now, I don't fear getting in and out of the pool. I have a specialized lifejacket that keeps my head above water while I exercise my body freely.

With my appointment to the United Cerebral Palsy of Rhode Island's Board of Directors in 2010 prompted the need to concentrate all my efforts of fundraising for them. I attempted to fundraise for both organizations, but I experienced serious "soliciting blues" when I asked the same people to donate their hard earned income on my causes twice a year. I had to choose main cause and put all of my energies into that. Sometimes there are a singular project or cause that lights a spark in me, such as the 2014 fundraising campaign to raise $50,000 for a film documentary called, *Best Judgment: Ladd School Lessons*. This documentary film, produced by Advocates In Action of Rhode Island, explores the long history of people with developmental disabilities through the 20th century, specifically The Ladd School in Exeter, which was closed in 1994. I felt so passionately about this film project that I even dreamt about it. On the last day of their fundraising campaign they exceeded their fundraising goal. Can't wait for the film's debut.

On January 2, 2007, everybody welcomed John "Jack" Robert into the world. Born in nearby Massachusetts, a number of us went to visit the newest member of the family. We would love him like any other one that came before him. He is very determined, very self-reliant.

\

"It's in a celebration
There's something in the air
A little celebration
There's something in the air"

"Celebration"
Kings of Leon
Come Around Sundown

Lordy, lordy—look who's turning 40! Did I have a problem turning 40? I don't think I did. I was happy. Somewhere along the line, someone leaked out about the surprise party, but I kept that to myself until weeks after. We are a typical family who love being together for almost any occasion. Me, turning 40 was just another occasion. The celebration was at the restaurant, Benjamin's, in Taunton, Massachusetts. We had a small room on the second floor that just about sat 40 people. It was a celebration to remember because my closest family and friends were in that room. All of my nieces and nephews, ranging in age from 21 years to 5 months were in that room.   Kids are just great, and they all love each other, which is the best thing of all.

Aunt Pat, Aunt Anne, her four boys and their wives came. The Morgans are very special people indeed. Mom was godmother to John, Anne's second oldest son. Tim, Anne's youngest, is 16 days younger than me. Mike, a year older than Peter, had the Marine boot camp experience, but became a Providence firefighter. And Tom, Anne's oldest, joined the Peace Corps, and forged his own direction in life, trying different paths along the way. These four men are devoted fathers and very devoted their mother. I am very proud to have them as my family.

Linda, Lisa and Linda's Paul joined in the celebration. It was always great when I got to see them. I saw them sporadically in the since 2001. When I visited Mom and Dad, we found ourselves a lot at the All-American Pub. Lisa always was working. Sometimes, Linda and/or Paul would drop by. Linda was in the midst of a long-term battle to try to assist her daughter, Jennilyn, win her fight with substance addiction. At this time, Jennilyn was in a facility. Linda had always been a fighter, and she wasn't about to give up on this fight.

After the great party, the four of us posed for a sibling picture. It came out wonderful. It was the only picture Mom ever wanted as her computer's background picture, and she never changed it.

Between the birthdays, weddings, anniversaries and holidays, reality set in that Mom and Dad might need more assistance, especially after Mom fell and broke her hip in July of 2007. It was the first time she had seen a primary care physician in several years. I believe her trust in doctors eroded after my birth. I thought it was kind of miraculous that she was only found to be anemic once she got thoroughly checked over. After she recovered from her broken hip, she did start seeing a physician regularly and began to take the usual regiment of medication for high blood pressure and high cholesterol. I was relieved she was finally receiving routine medical care.

I visited them more often, but felt helpless at the same time. I would imagine myself doing the house cleaning, cooking and all the things I ought be doing, as their daughter. Physically, I couldn't perform any of those things. I couldn't afford to have these things done for them, not that they would accept the help anyway. The best I could do was to keep their Dell computer maintained, for how seldom they used it. They didn't want to admit they might need extra help. It was even tough to get Mom to use a cane. She saw it as a sign as being older.

I had always this idea that it was my fault my parents' bodies were all distorted and hunched over. My thought was that if they didn't have to lift and carry me around all those years, would their bodies be in better shape? Mostly likely, yes. I knew that I could change our history, but the idea was still in the back of my mind.

After Mom was released from the hospital to go into rehabilitation for her hip, my lovely Linda and Lisa went to K-mart to buy her an egg cushion foam pad for the bed, and some pajamas that were easy for Mom to get on and off. When Mom came home from rehabilitation, Linda would sometimes do some house cleaning. Linda continued her battle to assist her daughter.

She wasn't giving up on the idea she could see her daughter through her disease.

Linda invited me to her Memorial Day party in 2009. I happily accepted. At this time, she and Paul were not together, but they remained friends. Also at this time, Jennilyn was still in a facility. Always a gracious host, Linda never sat down for more than two minutes at time, making sure that all of her guests had everything they needed, or wanted. This was my first time I met her son, Jeremiah, and her 99-year-old grandmother, Margaret. There was no stopping her; she was absolutely amazing. My parents dropped by for a time. Ever since Mom broke her hip, she remained unsteady when walking. I always wanted somebody to be near her when she walked. I always wanted her to settle in one place so she would be safe. There was quite a crowd gathered inside and outside Linda's garage. Mom and Linda's Nana sat next to each other, while Dad stood by, with a hotdog in his hand, ready to fetch anything that Mom desired. It was something very special to watch these two women, who had similar lives, raising children with cerebral palsy. I knew they had very different experiences due to their contrasting generations, but their ideals were the same: this was my kid and no matter what disabilities they had, they were worthy human beings; they were gifts from God.

After my parents left for home, the party moved indoors; the Cape Cod evening air was still chilly. By this time, Peter and Sue had purchased me two portable ramps, one 6-foot ramp, and 2-foot ramp. I would advise anyone who might be on the fence about what length ramp to buy. The 6 and 2-foot ramps compliment each other very nicely. Sometimes you may need just the 2 or 6-foot ramp. I find I need to use both when I visit people in their homes.

Linda's living room was sunken down a step. I settled in and didn't move until the living room became less crowded. I certainly wasn't expecting an impromptu belated birthday cake and presents from Linda's family; I was truly humbled to say to least. They knew me well from the weekly letters I wrote to Linda since early 2002. I wrote these often very humorous letters to Linda just so she could briefly be somewhere else besides the difficulties in her life. She shared these letters with her mother and other family. They knew me well.

Gradually, people started leaving. Linda's sister, Patti, stayed for the night. All of us stayed up until 2 am just catching up. I slept in the living room, on another air mattress. Two hours later, I noticed I was touching the soft carpeting below, as the perimeter of air still surrounded me. I felt like I was in a trench, looking out for the enemy: Bandit the evil cat. One time, I spotted him perched on the couch. Luckily, he kept is distance.

The plan was to go to The Breakfast Room, a small restaurant where Linda worked. Since it was Memorial Day weekend, the restaurant was jammed. We decided to have breakfast at Linda's. It was a very leisurely morning and early afternoon. I made friends with Buster, the friendliest cat I had ever met. As I sat on Linda's living room floor, Buster stretched out in front of me and allowed me to rub his chest. His personality was more dog-like and I think that's why we got along so well.

Before we left for Rhode Island, we stopped to see Lisa's new house. It was small, but cozy, with character. I loved it. I already was getting visions how I could enlarge the kitchen. It was the designer in me; it was my Mom's influence on me.

Get ready to celebrate again! Uncle Fran and Nuala were visiting from Indiana, like they did many summers. Ever since Mom had broken her hip, trips to Rhode Island were few and far between. It was her 78th birthday and she wanted to see her brother and sister-in-law. Nine of us met at Chelo's on the Waterfront in Warwick. It was a warm summer's day. Due to the fact my van was equipped with a lowered floor in its center, the air conditioning unit for the rear had to be removed so the gas tank could be relocated. The front of the van had air conditioning, but we learned if we left it on too long, the engine's heat would spike. Heat and air conditioning didn't work very well, but the van ran great.

With the front windows wide open, Melanie and I were heading south on 295. As we crossed over Hartford Avenue, an unidentified flying object came in through the driver's side window. Melanie ducked to the left and the object ricochet off my left cheek. The strong impact from the unidentified object surprised the living hell out of me. *What the hell was that?!* I remained speechless as I assessed my face. My cheek stung for a few minutes; I then supposed I would have a bruise.

When I did have the capacity to speak again, my first words were, "What the hell was that?!" Soon I was trying to look behind me; I was sure I would find a dead bird on my rear bench seat. I couldn't really see anything behind me. I was convinced it was a bird that struck me because of its strong impact. Melanie was glad I was okay.

As we got to the restaurant, Melanie came in back and looked for any evidence of a bird. There weren't any bird's remains. I got out of my van and greeted everybody with hugs and kisses. Surely someone would notice my red mark on my left cheek. Melanie explained the peculiar events of the previous twenty minutes. As we going into the restaurant, Melanie noticed some foreign debris on the left side of my neck. She excused ourselves from my family and had me follow her into the ladies' room. I had remnants of this greenish-white gook on my neck. We were slightly disgusted over this, and Melanie surmised some kind of large beetle after it impacted on my cheek. *How gross?! How gross?! Gross!*

Aside from the exploding beetle incident, we all had a very nice lunch celebrating Mom's birthday and having Fran and Nuala visiting. It was a leisurely lunch; Martha may have had to return to work afterwards. I was finishing up writing new material for my CD, *Soho Blue*. We were just happy to be together.

Once I was finished eating, some of played musical chairs. I moved to the left of Mom and Dad; Melanie was on my left now. On further inspection of my neck, she spotted more gook on my shirt collar. In a whisper, she informed me she was changing my shirt when we got back home. Mom always loved to hold my hand, and this day wasn't different. Everybody sat around the table and enjoyed each other's company. When we got outside, everybody lingered again, as we said goodbye. Mom remarked on Uncle Fran's remarkable shape at nearly 87 years young: "You are going to out live us all," Mom remarked. Fran was the oldest living sibling amongst the remaining five. We said our goodbyes, as we looked forward to more opportunities to be together.

In the back section of the van, Melanie located one half of the exploded beetle. Gook was scattered in places. Sometimes the thought pops in my head that if my face was turned one inch more to the left, the beetle probably would have flown into my mouth. Maybe I would have died, or had a really bad appetizer before lunch.

*"Till everything falls apart
Then I get to try to put it back
together Yeah, it falls apart
You can count on that
You can count on bad
Bad weather again"*

"Everything Falls Apart"
Dog's Eye View
Happy Nowhere

I was about to have my new CD, *Soho Blue*, mastered and recorded using my Roland XV 5050 sound module and CD recorder. One day, I just woke up, ready to record more, and the device driver for the Roland ceased to operate. It was one of those things that was unexplainable. I tried for a week to get the driver to work, with technical support. I couldn't get the driver to work again.

By this time, I was receiving e-mails from a company called Native Instruments. I knew they dealt with music production and sounds, but I couldn't exactly understand how their equipment worked. At this time I didn't know what VST (Virtual Studio Technology) was, but I was very curious. So, I did some number crunching and decided to take a leap of faith with some new music technology that didn't involve an external sound generator. I had many questions, and I figured the best place to visit were the people at the Guitar Center. Kathy and I went to the Guitar Center one afternoon.

I wrote down every possible question I could think of to ask. My biggest fear that this new Native Instruments called Kore 2, wouldn't work with my Finale software. I was pretty confident Finale would work with Kore 2 because Finale was VST program. After all my questions were answered graciously at the Guitar Center, I purchased Native Instruments Kore 2.

With the Kore 2 hardware connected, and its software loaded, it seemed to be working as a standalone application, although I was having issues with pairing it up with Finale. I knew was so close to making the two programs run seamlessly but there was just one little hurdle I wasn't seeing. I worked on it through the weekend. When Monday came, I e-mailed a question to the Finale technicians, and soon I would have my answer. It was quick and simple, and I was hearing my music being played with amazing quality with individual wave files recorded from real musical instruments. This leap of faith was incredibly successful.

It was a good, late, summer's day to drive down to Cape to visit Mom and Dad. Ted Kennedy had just succumbed to brain cancer and many people were saddened, including Mom and Dad. Mom identified with the Kennedys, especially Ted, because they were nearly the same age. Both came from large families, and both families endured their own tragic losses. Mom and Helen Watson loved visiting the Cape in their early 20's, when the Kennedy's were building momentum in their political lives. Mom admired the Kennedys for everything they stood for, and for their pursuit in leveling the "playing field" for all walks of life.

Mom wanted to stay home and cook us lunch so they could watch all of the tributes to Teddy on television. She remained unsteady on her feet but, of course, refused to use a cane. We had a nice lunch. Mom always strived to make every meal very special, even if it was just a Panini. It was later in the afternoon when she was doing something in the kitchen when she lost her balance and fell again. This time, it was her arm. Kathy tried to help her get up onto a chair, but Mom couldn't bear any weight on her arm to get into a position to get up. Dad was at the store, and I felt helpless. Luckily, Kirk, a Yarmouth EMT lived a few houses down and knew my parents well. While Kathy walked over to Kirk's house, I remained in the kitchen doorway, watching over Mom. I was feeling anxious.

Within minutes, Kathy returned with Kirk, along with his young daughter, Alexa. Alexa went easily to Kathy, as Kirk helped Mom up to a chair. Soon, Kirk went into EMT mode and tried to determine if Mom had a broken arm. Given the pain that she was in and the fact she had limited movement, he though it was probable. Mom was more exasperated that she had to go to the hospital and get an x-ray than the glaring reality that she had another broken bone.

After Dad returned from the store, we helped Mom get into the car. Kathy and I followed them to Cape Cod Hospital. They took Mom right into the examination area of the emergency

298

within a few days, expressing my thoughts about her Peter, and what he meant to me. I keep the picture of us, taken in Boston, on my bed shelf.

    With every low, usually came highs. It was my Mom's 80th birthday, and we wanted to celebrate it in style. She wasn't one for big, extravagant parties; she just wanted to go out to dinner with the family. Regrettably, Helen Watson was at the end stages of battling pulmonary fibrosis and could not join us.

    We all gathered at the newly renovated Pasta House in Fairhaven. It was a location everybody could get to within an hour's drive, especially for my parents. Our party of 20+ required three separate tables. Everybody was in a festive move as we enjoyed each other's company. We dined on delicious food and drank exquisite wine. Mom thoroughly enjoyed being surrounded by the people she loved so much. She asked me to bring the newspaper and the letter Shera had sent me. Both items gradually made their way around all three tables for all interested eyes to see.

    Different flavored cupcakes were brought to the restaurant, especially for the kids. Once the meal was over, we started playing musical chairs to chat with others at different tables. It was difficult for me to move around different tables because space was so limited; I stayed in place.

    As we moved outside, we lingered about, chatting and hugging. There were some picture shots taken outdoors, especially of the kids. Dad went to retrieve their car; we didn't want Mom to walk far. It was another night where fond memories were created.

    Two days later, after receiving a call from a shattered Paul, Mom called to tell me Karen just was diagnosed with breast cancer. Her voice was shaking as she tried to hold herself together. Mom told me she would call me later, knowing that she probably broke down in tears once she hung up the phone. We were all blindsided. Tears filled my eyes, as I remained motionless for a time. It was that big 'C' word we all feared hearing. The 1970's and 80's mentality suddenly came rushing back. I believe it was common for people to presume that if people were diagnosed was cancer during these decades, it was surely a death sentence. But once I pried myself out of that mentality, I began to realize that I knew far more people who had battled cancer and prevailed. I knew Karen, and I knew Paul. They would soon discover how much determination they had, both individually, and more, as a happily married couple with three young boys.

The thing I most admired about Paul and Karen's thoughtful approach to her diagnosis was they explained to all the boys what to expect during Karen's treatment: her hair loss, her fatigue and all the side effects associated with chemotherapy. I always believe that it is far greater to inform children of what to expect than not to tell them anything. Children need reassurance that everything is going as planned.

There was a moment Paul was talking to Mom sometime at the beginning of Karen's treatments. Somehow my cerebral palsy came up in their conversation. Paul was drawn to the notion that I had lived with this disorder my entire life, and thought about how much endured. I saw it as Karen being the real hero in our family. Her cancer diagnosis was sudden and life threatening. My cerebral palsy was sudden, but it wasn't life threatening after its onset. My cerebral palsy occurred at birth, while Karen's diagnosis happened at age 46. I haven't known anything else but cerebral palsy, where Karen had a healthy life before her diagnosis. I'm not the hero—Karen is.

Family and friends who wanted to lend their assistance surrounded Paul, Karen and the boys. Paul was frequently out of town on business, as the President of FirstWind, based in Boston. One of their many, many friends, Tara, set up a marvelous online tool for Karen called Lotsa Helping Hands. It is an online scheduling system, if you will, to coordinate family, friends and volunteers to help people get their needs met. For Karen, some of the needs were driving her back and forth to the hospital for treatments, cooking meals, driving the boys to various places. Tara compiled a list of people and e-mails for the purposes of fulfilling these important needs. Once people received an updated schedule, Karen's helpers would log onto her specific site, and take certain tasks, which they could fulfill.

Many times I went onto Karen's specific site and looked for tasks I could fulfill. I wanted to be of any help possible, but I realized I had to figure out my own logistics to help Karen. Many times my involvement with helping out would be more of a hindrance than an aid, especially with how I had to enter their house. This was one of those times where I used my imagination of what life could be like if I didn't have cerebral palsy. I imagined myself driving up to Boston, and driving her home. I imagined myself being in their kitchen, with the boys sitting at the island, playing or doing homework, while I clowned around as I cooked dinner. I imagined myself walking upstairs to make sure all were bathed and settled in for the night. I would do everything with so much love that I would have returned each night if I was needed. I believe my imagination gives me some comfort that I would have the capacity to do such things.

It wasn't unusual for Dad to drive to the Lexus dealership in Warwick to get his car maintained about every six months, but it was highly unusual that he became lost on his drive home to the Cape. Mom had called me around 5 o'clock, asking if Dad had dropped by to see me. He had not. Aunt Anne had called Mom around 2 pm, informing her that he dropped by her house in Warwick. Aunt Anne made him lunch. Before he left, he asked Aunt Anne what was the best way to get to I-195. This was understandable because they did extensive rerouting at the junction of I-95 and I-195 with the construction of the I-Way bridge. Aunt Anne explained it all to him, and she was very mindful to recognize signs of low and high blood sugar in people, because Uncle Tom had Type 1 diabetes. Aunt Anne didn't see any red flags.

Five o'clock came and went without any sign of him. By 5:15, Martha, Peter and I were aware of the situation, as Mom was in a state of panic alone on Cape Cod. Making Dad carry and use a cellphone instead of searching for a payphone was like making a mature writer swap out his vintage Remington Rand portable typewriter with a state-of-the-art computer. Dad refused to carry a cellphone, much to our chagrin. He even had GPS in his car, but yet again, didn't want to use it. All that we could do was pray and hope that nothing serious had happened.

An hour later, the Mattapoisett Police called Mom. Dad had stopped at the police station asking for directions home. Immediately Mom called Peter, and he was on his way to Mattapoisett. When Peter arrived, he assessed Dad. Dad had a certain degree of confusion. Peter strongly suggested he be checked out at a hospital. An ambulance transported Dad to Massachusetts General Hospital.

Martha met Dad at the hospital, as they ran tests. Given Martha's vast medical knowledge, she predicted his confusing was caused by a **transient ischemic attack (TIA)**, a mini stroke. Within four hours, all tests came back negative. He was released from the hospital that night. Dad and Martha spent the night at Paul and Karen's.

The next morning, Paul, Karen and Martha asked Dad a number of questions to what had transpired the previous afternoon. They listened carefully as he explained what roads he travelled to get home. For a man who used to make a living travelling throughout Rhode Island and Southeastern Massachusetts, it was quite unsettling to discover his inability to navigate effectively. We, as siblings, had arrived at that moment where we would become the parents of our parents.

On September 13, 2011, Mrs. Watson passed away from her progressive illness. Mom had lost her best friend of 60 years. During these last ten years, Mom and Helen talked on the phone often. I attended her wake, while Mom and Dad attended the funeral. Paul hired a car to drive Mom and Dad to the funeral and back home. They got to say goodbye to their very good friend.

Dad had a follow up appointment with a neurologist at Cape Cod Hospital. On strict orders from all four of us, he was supposed to take a taxi to and home from the appointment. He promised he would. Dad indeed took a cab to his appointment, but decided to walk to a friend's house to get a ride home. We aren't exactly sure how far he walked, but Dad thought it was about a mile. It was a warm day in Hyannis. Without a cellphone, food or water, he walked on busy Route 28, until he reached this friend's house—a friend who wasn't home. Patiently, Dad sat on the front stoop, waiting for his friend. People look out their front windows frequently, and when a neighbor saw my father lingering, they called the police. When Dad arrived home in Hyannis Police cruiser, Mom wasn't pleased, and once word got out later, neither of us were pleased with his decision-making. I read, or wrote, him the riot act, informing Dad how dangerous it was to walk, and the possibility that he could have fallen and gotten seriously hurt. I reminded him he was a diabetic and didn't have any access to food or water. It remains to be seen if my words had any impact.

In the weeks that followed, Peter strongly suggested Mom ride with Dad whenever he drove anywhere. Most likely, Mom and Dad obeyed these requirements for a short period of the time. As the weather became cooler and more inclement, it was uncomfortable and tiring for her to go out on a daily basis. Dad either went to the grocery store, went to grab a cup of coffee or went to the landfill on a daily basis. We felt confident Dad would be safe doing these activities within a few miles of their house. He was successful with completing these routine tasks.

We also visited Mom and Dad on a regular basis. It was an universal consensus between us siblings that Mom and Dad should move back to Rhode Island so they wouldn't be so far away if they needed our assistance. Martha was the first to suggest the idea. Surprising Mom wasn't opposed to the idea; it was Dad who didn't find the idea very appealing. I assumed it would be the reverse. It was Mom who loved the Cape. It was Mom who initiated their move from Rhode Island to Cape Cod. I knew this would be a monumental task for all parties. Their house was full of furniture, kitchen gear and many, many other things that were their life. I think the magnitude of figuring out where all these things were going to go was very overwhelming to Mom.

It was my first United Cerebral Palsy of Rhode Island Golf Tournament I participated in. We couldn't have had a more spectacular day for it. Jeanette, who had been working with me for over two years by this time, accompanied me to this all-day tournament. Jeanette, a force to be reckoned with, was a native of upstate New York. She started out as a farmer, turned to trucking, and then became a chef, eventually opening her own diner in Florida. In her mid 50's, she and her boyfriend landed in Rehoboth, Massachusetts to help his father with his farm. Through paths and opportunities, Jeanette found herself working with me, to my benefit. She was one of those people who I had an instant connection with.

We arrived at Valley around the same time as some of the golfers. Jeanette made our way around to the back of the clubhouse and greeted the golfers and staff members. I had assembled my own foursome earlier in the summer. The foursome included three of the Morgan brothers, John, Tim and Tommy, and Paul. Knowing Karen had chemotherapy treatment that day, I didn't expect Paul to make the tournament. To my very humbled surprise, Paul did make it. My first thought was he should be with Karen. He made this commitment and he stuck to it. Paul was able to play the entire round before he had to leave before dinner to pick Karen up at Dana Farber. I knew Karen needed a ride home that day. The next day, I e-mailed each member of my foursome, which won top prize (Way To Go, Guys!), thanking them individually for their participation. I wrote a heartfelt message to Paul, thanking him for his participation, and explaining that if Karen needed a ride home that afternoon, I would have dropped everything, and Jeanette and I would have driven to Boston to make sure Karen had gotten home safely.

Our job that day was to hang out on the Par 3 12th hole at the Valley Country Club in Warwick to urge the golfers to bet they can land their ball on the green from the tee. If they took the gamble, they would receive a free raffle ticket for the 50/50 cash pool. If they landed their ball on the green, they would receive another free raffle ticket. Ironically, the 12th hole was the furthest hole from the clubhouse, we later discovered. Aunt Pat came to spend the day with us. While Aunt Pat and Jeanette got a ride to the 12th via a golf cart, I put my wheelchair at top speed and followed behind. Of course anytime I have the chance to drive my wheelchair at top speed, I most certainly take advantage. I had a lot of fun keeping pace. Wherever there was a paved cart path, I drove on it, making sure I took in the beautiful sights along the way. After our long journey to what felt like Timbuktu, we finally reached the very picturesque 12th hole. It was glorious! Trees and the green landscape proved God wanted all of His children to enjoy the great outdoors. The beautiful sights that surrounded us were the visions of what Heaven might look like, except for the golf carts and paths.

Ready to get to work! As the first golfers came to the 12th, Jeanette always began with an introduction of who we were. Using her Grade A personality, she explained the 50/50 raffle; most all of the golfers took a chance that their ball would land on the green. Few balls did. Jeanette's pockets were filling up with cash and raffle tickets.

It very surprising how quickly five hours can fly by when you are working a hole. There were periods of down time, where we could take in the pristine scenery, including wild turkeys. Our golfers did well on the 12th.

With it being my first golf tournament, and with the sun going down, we kiddingly started coming up with a plan to survive the night on the 12th hole. Nobody had a morsel of food although we had Farmer Jeanette, who, without a doubt, would kill a wild turkey and start a roaring fire within an hour. Luckily, it didn't come to that. Bob and Karl, from United Cerebral Palsy of Rhode Island, came with golf carts. Pat was the only one who took a ride.

Back at the clubhouse, we prepared ourselves for a lavish and delicious banquet, a banquet that could satisfy the pickiest of eaters. Paul, along with Tim and Tom, had left before the banquet, leaving John to represent our foursome. I was so proud that my family foursome came out on top. I could gloat for a time. I knew the true story behind my family foursome that day.

Dad's follow-up visits with the neurologist at Cape Cod Hospital didn't reveal any deficiencies. I visited my parents shortly after the golf tournament; it was another beautiful September day. Melanie and I had a good time with Mom and Dad, as we usually did. We probably grabbed lunch at the All-American Pub, and went back to the house to spend more time with Mom and Dad. Being married for so long, they had a very common way of badgering each other—good-natured badgering. They constantly got each other cases for their day-to-day shortcomings. While Melanie and I found it endearing, others found it otherwise. I appreciated their humor.

We usually got on the road between 6 and 7 o'clock. Mom always gave me a big hug and kiss before we left, with a little tickle in my ribs. She gave Melanie the same affection. On this beautiful, early autumn evening, Dad followed Mom outside and closed the exterior door behind him. Instantly, Mom realized what he just done: locked themselves out of their own house. He had never done that before, and in all my history of being the sole hero of unlocking doors from the inside, I found myself on the wrong side of the equation. *Shit.*

We, collectively, had to find a way back into the house. Dad thought there could be a spare key in the garden shed in back. As we all went around into the backyard, I asked Melanie to hang onto Mom's arm so she wouldn't fall. Dad opened the unlocked shed and began to search the dingy and dark building. Cobwebs sprang out at every corner. There wasn't a key to be found. I asked if they might have given a spare key to Kirk. That would be a negative. *Shit.*

The best idea we had was to check accessible windows that might have been unlocked. Bingo! One of my Mom's bedroom windows was unlocked. With Mom being a stickler about locking their house like Fort Knox 90% of the time, this was a glorious occasion when something was overlooked.

It was obvious that Melanie was only person with the body mechanics to crawl through the side bedroom window. Thankfully the fence blocked anyone on the street side from seeing what we were trying to accomplish, which was doing a legal B & E. Melanie needed a slight lift up, so I raised up my Permobil seat. Melanie stepped on my footrests and catapulted herself into Mom's bedroom, glancing her sneaker's sole off my forehead. Crisis adverted. I believe Mom and Dad made some provisions if those circumstances ever happened again.

It was Thanksgiving. Paul and Karen still wanted to host the holiday even though she was feeling the effects of chemotherapy. Also, it was probably more suited for Karen to be in the comfort of her own home with her family, rather than travelling to another destination where she wouldn't be comfortable. Nobody argued.

Although I looked forward to seeing Karen, I was also apprehensive. Other than seeing people on television who were battling cancer, I had never seen anyone up close and very personal, in the same room. I fortified myself for weeks. When Thanksgiving arrived, I knew I had to be ready. When I finally saw Karen, I realized all my concern was for nothing. She was still beautiful, wig and all. She might have lost a few pounds but they remained unnoticeable. Her color was good—she looked wonderful. I believed Mom and Dad were relieved too. God is good.

Karen spent most of the prep time sitting on a stool by the curved, marble kitchen island. I sat directly across from her, in delight. Fatigue was what plagued her the most that particular day. Her sister, Toni, from Connecticut, was doing all the things Karen was unable to do that day, and many, many other days during Karen's treatment. They were the only two girls out of a brood of six. Toni was the only sibling within a driving distance to Karen. Toni had a grown son, Christopher.

When the feast was ready, we took our assigned seats. A prayer was said; I don't think there was any doubt what we were all thankful for. We enjoyed the day. It's always good when we all just be together.

After dinner, we found our places we wanted to sit. Karen lounged on the sofa; Sue took a seat on the same sofa, towards Karen's feet. Immediately, Sue started massaging Karen's feet. They had camaraderie that no one wanted; Sue's mother, Mary, battled breast cancer for a number of years. Sadly, Mary succumbed to the maddening disease in 1996. I admired Sue's mother Mary. Mary was a retired nurse, working for Rhode Island College's sports program. I found her stories of traveling with RIC's sports teams fascinating. I based the character, Eric, from my novel, *Always A Place*, on Mary's unwavering love for her profession.

Sue's knowledge and perspective on breast cancer and

the vital advances in the fight against cancer in the last twenty years have come so far was a comfort to Karen. Sue explained just the act of physical contact, such as back or foot massages, was beneficial to fight cancer. I don't know anyone who doesn't like a good back and/or foot massage. Endorphins are released during a massage, having a positive effect on the body. I could relate because I know how incredible I feel after a massage. I sat across from my sister-in-laws and just watched their incredible interaction with each other. It was incredible to witness. I knew how satisfying one of Sue's back massages were; I wanted Karen to enjoy every moment.

"Spare a little candle
Save some light for me
Figures up ahead moving in the
trees
White skin in linen perfume on
my wrist And the full moon that
hangs over these Dreams in the
mist"

"These Dreams"
Heart
Heart

Only her mother knew what surprises were coming Sarah's way on December 23, 2011. James, Sarah's boyfriend of three years, was going to propose marriage. On Sarah's 21st birthday, my Mom gave Sarah the engagement ring my father gave her 52 years prior. Ever since she was a toddler, Sarah had been enthralled with Mom's sparkly, diamond-cut, diamond ring. When she was able to talk, Sarah asked her 'Nan', if she could have it. Mom promised someday. That day came on her 21st birthday. The gift was unexpected. It was a tear-producing moment.

James had to secretly get the ring from Martha for the big night. He booked a room at a Bed & Breakfast in Newport. The next day, Sarah and James returned, engaged!

Martha, Glenn, Sarah, Thomas and I had a standing invitation to Christmas Eve dinner at their long-time friends, Rachel and Bob's house in the next town. The two couples met when they became neighbors in 1987. Rachel and Bob have two children, Jamie and Nicholas, who are very close in age to Sarah and Thomas. With two working sets of parents, somehow their schedules meshed where they rarely needed help from an outside babysitter. Today, both couples could write a humorous book about childrearing and the adventures that accompany it.

Christmas Eve dinner is always a great event, with great food, incredible Christmas decorations and all around good company, but with the surprise announcement from Sarah and James made it even more special. They didn't want to wait; soon, Sarah and James settled on a date in the summer of 2012.

It has become a family tradition to get together at the beginning of every year to celebrate the birthdays just before and just after each New Year. In 2012, we converged at the Coonamessett Inn in Falmouth. We didn't want Mom and Dad driving far. The Coonamessett Inn held had some significance to

Mom and Dad, as they had a few dates at the restaurant during their courtship. When they arrived and sat, they remarked the interior of the restaurant hadn't changed in over 50 years. Now, the family they created surrounded them.

Ten days post-op, Karen had more strength now that her chemotherapy treatment were complete. Her next stage was radiation treatments for a consecutive 8-week period. She was winning this battle. Paul and the boys were in wonderful moods, as everyone else. It was another time to enjoy the company of our family.

Sarah and James joined on this New Year's Day celebration. Everyone was excited about their recent engagement. The women at the table dove straight into a conversation about everything wedding. Sarah and James wanted a simple, but, elegant wedding. They wanted to keep it small. *I hear ya, Kid!*

Over the next six months, our family gathered a handful of times before the wedding bells rang. Sam played Long John Silver in his school's production of "Treasure Island". Sam has always been a natural entertainer, and even with a slight case of laryngitis, he didn't disappoint. About three weeks prior, Karen had finished her radiation treatment, and clearly seemed to have the energy of 100 warriors, as she was very involved with the backstage production. Instead of wearing a wig, she wore a white bucket hat; Karen had a thin, but thick layer of gray, tiny curls covering her head. It made my heart smile. I was aware what Karen endured during her radiation treatments; each week for eight weeks, Karen had to lie perfectly still, with an arm positioned above her head, for an hour at a time. I can't lie completely still for two seconds. Instantly, I considered, God forbid, if I ever need radiation treatments, I would need to be completely sedated and be bound in position.

Who says a Marine, and his daughter can't pull off a 50th

birthday surprise party for Sue? Later, Peter admitted planning this party, which was glorious, was the most logistically challenging operation he had pulled off in his life. I'm sure he was exaggerating just a tiny bit, but he said he was overwhelmed to pull off perfection. He is a perfectionist by nature. Sue was definitely was surprised.

We Gaynor folk filled up one of the large tables at a hall in Jamestown. Grace and the three boys danced the afternoon away to the music that played, while the adults enjoyed the food and chatted about anything and everything. It was another fine moment to enjoy the time with each other. *Happy Birthday, Sue!*

Five weeks later, we all gathered again for Mother's Day at The Riverway Restaurant in South Yarmouth—a three-minute drive for Mom and Dad. The Riverway had become my parents' favorite go-to restaurant when Mom didn't feel like cooking. Mom and Dad raved about the clam chowder. They knew Dad on a first name basis when he picked up take-out.

We all sat in a separate room; we filled it. Being in a wheelchair, I had formed a predisposition of sitting at the most out-of-the-way spot at a table, where I am out of the way of major foot traffic behind me. If I can squeeze myself into an inner corner, I make every attempt to do so. It was another great day for gathering. After the restaurant, we hung out at Mom and Dad's for a time. The young boys played, as young boys should. Their energy level seemed boundless. I had the first time constraint, so I had to get back to Rhode Island so my staff could get to her next shift. *Happy Mother's Day, Mom!*

Next on the docket was Sarah's bridal shower, which just happened to be on my birthday. I was pleased to give Sarah the spotlight that day. The bridal shower was held at the 1149 Restaurant in Seekonk; Martha wanted to make the drive a little shorter from Mom and Dad. As the bridal shower started on schedule, there wasn't any sign of my parents. Martha called their house several times only to find there wasn't any answer.

They must be on their way.

I continued to keep an eye out towards the entrance of the room; my apprehension increased as every minute passed. This day was for Sarah and we went going to lose our minds even though we were teetering on the brink. Aunt Anne and Aunt Pat were also getting worried about my parents' whereabouts.

As Sarah's bridal shower was winding down, Martha's cellphone rang—it was Mom, and they were home. They did make it to Seekonk, although failed to find the restaurant. Without a cellphone or the restaurant address written on a piece of paper, they were unprepared for the trip. Mom explained they stopped at a gas station to use a payphone but Dad couldn't manage to recall any phone numbers. After Mom explained everything to Martha, Mom asked if she could speak to me. I could tell by her voice she was upset that the day was an epic failure. She wished me a Happy Birthday and told me she would call me later when she was better equipped. I took a deep breath, as I felt her disappointment. In the end, they were safe.

Later on, Martha and the gang came over with burgers, hotdogs, and birthday cake to celebrate the start of my 45th year. As promised, Mom called back in a better state than earlier that day. I even was able to get her to laugh once or twice.

The night before the big event arrived. Mom and Dad agreed they would spend the night before the wedding at a local hotel. Mom wasn't a big fan of staying anywhere overnight, but she knew they had to spend one night. That afternoon, Paul, Karen and the three boys arrived for the rehearsal dinner; Jack would be the ring bearer, as James' niece, Ella, would be the flower girl.

The wedding party, along with other guests, converged on the Atwood Grill in Johnston. It was a beautiful evening as we celebrated the love between Sarah and James. Jeanette and I sat across the table from Mom and Dad. They were in good

316

spirits. There were a lot of laughter amongst the future bride and groom, and family and friends. James' parents, John and June, are extraordinarily nice people, and retired music teachers. Although not a music teacher, but rather a history and math teacher, James followed in his parents' footsteps.

The early summer sun was just going down when people were causally leaving. Jeanette and I asked Mom and Dad if they would like to follow us to where the hotel was located. Dad assured us that he could make it back to the hotel. Jeanette and I lingered for a bit before heading home. Not five minutes in the house, Martha called: Mom and Dad weren't at the hotel yet. *Shit.* All I could think about was that Martha should be with Sarah, having fun, and not a nervous wreck wondering where Mom and Dad were. Jeanette and I jumped back into my van to try to spot Mom and Dad. I just wanted to do something.

Jeanette and I mindfully drove toward the hotel, as I kept my eyes peeled for their car. We didn't spot them. Once we drove into the hotel's parking lot to meet up with Martha; my parents had just arrived. *Thank God.* My heart returned to a regular rhythm. Jeanette and I remained in my van, while we watched Martha helped Mom out of the car. Dad went to park the car. It was easy to notice Mom was upset over the situation. Dad took his time getting out of the car. With Mom safely inside, Martha went to talk to Dad to try to discern what transpired. All that Dad said was they missed the correct exit and drove another 30 minutes to Attleboro, then turned around and found their way. Martha had already had it set to have Thomas drive my parents to the wedding the following morning.

Everyone gathered at the wedding venue in Lincoln. Thomas completed his task very well, given the fact that my parents weren't fully ready to leave when he arrived. I suspected Mom was angry over the previous night's situation and had trouble sleeping. She didn't sleep well to begin with, so I presumed her frustration made sleeping almost impossible.

Let the wedding bells ring! As the guests took their seats on the covered, outside patio, Thomas was the usher. He escorted my mother, and then his mother down the narrow, concrete aisle. Once everyone was seated, the ceremony began. In the far corner, behind the Justice of the Peace, Rachel jumped up on a chair with her camcorder and started rolling. She attempted to receive technical assistance with the zoom function, but it was too late to receive help. The music started playing and Glenn walked his little girl down the aisle. It really felt like yesterday Sarah was born. That sweet, sweet baby I saw when she was a day old, was now dressed in a beautiful wedding gown, which I witnessed her tear up when she knew that was the one. Sarah was gorgeous!

The short ceremony went off without a hitch; Sarah and James were married! While the newlyweds and the wedding party shuffled off to the garden for photographs, the rest of the guests were served hors d'oeuvres and had a chance to put their green fingerprint on the tree-of-love print guests could sign as well. Kathy sponged my right, athetoid thumb in green ink, and assisted me with stamping my thumb down on the paper, creating a leaf. By the time everyone got their chance at the tree, all of the bare branches were covered in leaves.

Everyone entered the large reception room and found their designated seats. I asked Kathy to walk Mom into the huge room. Once she was seated, I relaxed a bit. I nursed a Kahlua Sombrero for most of the reception. Unfortunately, the pricey bra I bought for this very occasion was riding sky high and not doing its job, even when Kathy had a chance to yank it back down to Earth. Given my track record with bras at wedding events, it might be in my best interest not to wear a bra at such events.

Kathy and I were seated with my parents, Aunt Pat, Martha and Glenn. Aunt Anne was invited to Uncle Fran grandson's wedding in Indiana. A strong pull told her to go to

318

Indiana to see her brother; she followed her intuition.

At the next table sat Peter, Sue, Grace, Paul, Karen and the three boys. Thomas sat at the table with Jamie, Nick and their significant others. The DJ was playing music while the photo booth was being set up. Given Mom's pronounced hearing deficits and the din in the room made conversing difficult. We kept communication with facial expressions, gestures and head motions.

The bride and groom were introduced to the crowd as husband and wife. The place exploded into cheers. Over her dress, Sarah sported the official Patriots, Vince Wilfork navy team jersey. On their feet, both Sarah and James wore contrasting blue and white sneakers with their wedding date embroidered into the sides.

After the meal was served, the traditional activities such as the toasts, first dance, the dances between father and bride, and mother and groom, and the cutting of the cake. Between the nostalgic music and all these various, sweet activities, I was happily weepy. Kathy, Thomas and I took off for the photo booth and decorated ourselves in boas, funny glasses and peacock feathers to mark the joyous occasion. Everyone was having a blast!

May the dancing commence! I believe people were dancing before they finished eating. The most boisterous and lively table sat Rachel and Bob, John and Dan, and Silvia, Martha and Glenn's closest friends. They were dancing the afternoon away! Then Karen and Ben were on the dance floor. It was extraordinarily wonderful and a true blessing from God to see Karen so healthy and full of unstoppable energy. Like Jeanette reassured Paul ten months earlier behind the clubhouse at Valley, Karen's hair would grown thicker than ever before ever before following chemotherapy. She was so right!

Now, I haven't been the biggest fan of dancing, but on this day, I proverbially let my hair down at let loose. Of course,

I would rather belt out a song at the top of my lungs than dance in my wheelchair, but I don't think anybody from my generation can resist not dancing to Donna Summer's "Last Dance", or the scorn women's anthem, "I Will Survive" by my soul sister, Gloria Gaynor. I even headed up the conga line, totally sober! I drew the line when it came to the Funky Chicken.

As the music slowed, I returned to table. Mom wanted to dance with Dad. It was like pulling teeth to get him to do one dance with Mom. Paul, and then Peter danced with Mom. It finally gave Peter Mom's undivided attention, as he strongly urged her that they had to make a move back to Rhode Island before something serious happened. Mom was in agreement for that moment.

As the reception grew to its finale, many of us tried to convince Mom and Dad to stay in Rhode Island for one more night. They weren't having that. Mom had her usual excuses: not enough clothes, they only brought medications for a day, they want to sleep in their own beds, etc. We took a collective deep breath and allowed them to drive back home, but not before Peter sat with Dad to repetitively go over how to get where they needed to go. Kathy and I would lead them to the highway they needed to take. Dad assured us he knew where he was going. Once we got Mom and Dad to that particular exit, Dad remained following us. *No! No! No!* We didn't know what to do. On our left, this Nissan Murano passed us. It was Peter, Sue and Grace. He caught up with Dad and made them pull over. They took the next exit and pulled over to a safe spot. Peter pulled up behind them and got out. Kathy and I were positioned across the street. It was clear from Peter's physical demeanor that he was steeped in frustration. Two minutes later, they were back on the road. We could only hope and pray they would find their way home safely.

After going home and changing into something more comfortable, Aunt Pat, Melanie, Kathy and I headed to Martha and Glenn's for a cookout for anyone who cared to join from the wedding. I found a place to sit so I wouldn't be in the way. The kids enjoyed swimming in the above ground pool. As we all tried to relax, we all kept track of the time because Mom promised she would call when they arrived home.

My mind went to that place where it sometimes goes. I imagined myself without cerebral palsy, driving my parents home. I usually realize, after the fact, that if I didn't have cerebral palsy, my life would turned out much differently. God only knows if I would be living in Rhode Island. Life might have taken me down several different paths, but I am sure my personality and my heart would be very similar to what they are today. I would have been the same caring individual.

Two hours later, we took turns calling Mom and Dad's house every fifteen minutes. There wasn't any answer for the next two hours. We hoped they stopped for a bite to eat. We didn't show it, but we were all a bunch of nerves. Around 8:30 that night, Mom picked up the phone; they were home. We all knew we had to bring about change for Mom and Dad's physical safety.

The next day, Mom called; Melanie answered. As usual, they chatted up a bit. Mom wanted a number of local florist. I went online and found the number; Melanie relayed the number to her. The next day, all four of us siblings received a bouquet. Each note read, "It will never happen again. Mother and Father." Martha and I thought the 'Mother and Father' part was a little peculiar because neither Mom nor Dad had signed anything like that. I might have called them right after receiving the bouquet. It was about 7 o'clock that my phone rang; the caller ID signaled the call was coming from Cape Cod Hospital. Instantly I had a knot in my stomach; it was Dad—Mom had fallen and had a concussion. She was alert, but very angry. Dad was frustrated that Mom wasn't listening to him. The doctors explained to him that due to her concussion, she wasn't herself. The doctors also discovered she was suffering from a urinary tract infection, which probably caused more confusion. Feeling he wasn't any help to Mom, Dad went home, to return the next day.

Martha stepped in and became Mom's medical proxy. Mom would spend another two weeks in a rehabilitation facility. The confusion gradually decreased, especially when she refused to remain in the facility after the two-week period. Kathy, Jeanette and I went down for a visit after her first week she was in the facility. She was happy to see all of us. There were some remnants of bruising around her eye where she fell. Most of the time, Mom was lucid. Her biggest complaint, other than being at the facility, was the food they served. Dad stopped at Subway every day and brought her a chicken and avocado sandwich. She loved them.

As we were leaving, she tried to get up from her bed to escape to go home. She was alarmed so she wouldn't get up by herself. The alarm was going off. One of the aides came in to keep her seated. It was hard to leave her when she was so confused; I suddenly knew what my parents went through putting me on that bus all those years ago. I reassured Mom I would see her soon.

After unsuccessfully prodding Dad to come grab dinner with us, we dropped him off at home; he assured us he had food to eat in the house.

I hadn't seen Linda in awhile; I figured while I was in the area, I wanted to take a shot at seeing her. With her cell phone number engraved in my brain, I told Kathy her number. Kathy called it. Linda answered, but wasn't quite sure who was calling. After a brief explanation, Linda realized it was Kathy and me. At the time, she was just finishing up watching her grandson; she would be home in twenty minutes. That gave us time to find somewhere to pick up some sandwiches and meet her at her house.

I think I was aware that Jennilyn had moved back home with Linda. With sobriety comes ups and downs, and on this particular day, it was a down day. Linda was happy to see me, as she always did. We would eat and visit in the very homey garage. I was saddened by Linda's appearance; she looked physically and emotionally spent. Mother's little helper in the beach bag beside her feet, as she never tried to conceal it. Frequently, I wondered what was life was like for Linda inside of her house. I knew it wasn't easy.

Linda told us the story about how she spent ten days straight with her grandmother in Hospice. Her grandmother slept through the ten days. On the eleventh day, Nana woke up, and said, "Good morning Dear, what are you doing here?" Linda's jaw dropped to the floor. Her grandmother, almost 103 at the time, said she saw her husband and her son who had cerebral palsy on the other side. They said they were fine and it wasn't her time yet. Linda was sure she was going to outlive everybody.

Ironically, Linda's Nana was in the same facility as Mom. Linda promised she would drop by to see Mom in the following days. She did just that. Mom was happy to see Linda.

Before leaving that night, I urged Linda to come to Rhode Island for a few days, as she had the weight of the world on her shoulders. She said she would try. I knew it would be almost impossible for her to get away. Sadness filled my heart because I knew I couldn't help my friend any more than to continue to write letters to her filled with positive thoughts, support and of course, laughter.

"Come back before you leave
You shouldn't go at all
You shouldn't go at all."

"Come Back (Before You
Leave)"
Roxette
Tourism (Songs from Studios,
Stages, Hotelrooms & Other
Strange Places)

One morning, I was perusing my Facebook News Feed, as I usually do every morning. An ad caught my eye: Roxette was making a stop in Boston on their 2012 World Tour. Rarely does one of my past favorite bands other than Billy Joel or The Hooters, evoke such a need to see them in concert once again. Frankly, I hadn't listened to Roxette on a regular basis since the mid 1990's. *What have they been up to all of these years?*

Per Gessle and Marie Fredrikkson made up the Swedish rock and pop duo. They had released more albums between all those years, none of which had a big impact in the States. In Europe, especially in Sweden, their popularly still was very strong. Through all of my online "catching up", I soon learned Marie had battled a serious brain tumor in 2002. With this particular brain tumor Marie had, 1 out of 20 survive. Marie had survived, but surgery caused her to lose sight in one eye and to lose her ability to read and write. When I saw Roxette all those years ago, I wanted to be up on that stage doing what Marie was doing, jumping around that small stage, singing her lungs out, playing piano and electric guitar. Years later, I realized Marie and I more in common now: we both had disabilities that didn't have any affect on our passion for music.

I expected some sort of yanking of my chain when I mentioned to Melanie we were going to see Roxette; this time she didn't have much of a choice—we were going. She didn't mind. I thought the show had been cancelled when I went to order our tickets. My initial disappointment was soon replaced by relief after learning the show had just been relocated to a different venue.

It was a partly cloudy, Tuesday, early September evening. I was electric with excitement. Unfortunately, the crowd was thin. I hoped more people would come to the show in the two hours before the show began. For the fans who were there, they were definite die-hard Roxette fans. Melanie and I sat towards the right of the stage. I elevated my wheelchair seat to get a better view of the stage.

Finally, the concert began, and Roxette brought their A game to the very sparse Boston crowd. Marie's voice had changed to a slightly lower register, but it was still strong. The band members were very mindful where Marie was on the stage, although she stood in one central area. They were amazing to see live again, especially not knowing if they would ever play together again after Marie's serious illness. Music was her drug that healed her mind, soul and spirit. *Rock on, Marie!*

September turned into October, which turned into November. Thanksgiving was upon us, and we all decided to bring Thanksgiving to Mom and Dad's house. We all had our tasks to fulfill and dishes to bring. Martha and Sue went to the Cape the evening before to clean and to set up for the big feast. In the morning, they could put the turkey the oven early that morning. Mom wanted to help out but she didn't have the stamina to do the things she wanted to do. Since her fall in July, she had done well to rebound from her concussion. The only thing she couldn't remember and refused to believe was sending us all bouquets after Sarah's wedding. If I had gotten the Pope to call her from the Vatican to tell her that she sent the bouquets, I don't think she would have believed him. After awhile, I wouldn't allow Mom to bring up the bouquet incident.

Kathy and I arrived at my parents' in the early afternoon with a supply of cheese, crackers and soda. After giving hugs and kisses to everyone, I found a clear spot in the dining room, facing the kitchen. There was a wooden, dining room chair in front of me; Mom sat down, wearing a big smile because her children and grandchildren abound. I was very keen of what was going on in the kitchen, and when Mom became anxious to join the crowd in the kitchen, I reassured her everything was under control, but she continued to give verbal cooking cues. Dad was assisting the gang find serving plates, small appliances and other kitchen gadgets.

Dinner went off without a hitch, as we all celebrated

being together. It was an appropriate time to get a sense of what Mom and Dad's thoughts were about moving closer to any one of us. She wasn't opposed any ideas, but Dad remained quiet. A few months later, Paul and Karen included a suite for my parents in the blueprints of their new house, slated to be built in 2013.

With dinner finished, the kids watched a movie in the den, all cuddled up on the butterscotch, leather couch, while the rest of us sat around the living room. Paul and Karen had their 13-year-old Chocolate Labrador; deaf and legally blind, she had difficulties getting up to a standing position. I felt bad for the old girl, but she managed fine. Sam was the chosen one to take her out when she barked deeply.

Mom was way overdue for a hearing aid, and in a room full of quiet talkers and one slurring talker, she missed a lot. I recall one specific time I was on the phone with Mom. I distinctively heard a beeping sound—one of those beeping sounds that sound every 30 seconds to signal that a battery needed to be replaced in a smoke or carbon monoxide detector. Neither Mom nor Dad heard it. I worked with them for a half an hour, over the phone, to help pinpoint what device was beeping. Dad replaced the battery, and all was quiet. I, myself, get a little nutty when I can hear something beeping or chiming, and I have to wait for help to fix it.

People started getting to leave around in the early evening. We knew Mom and Dad were exhausted and presumed they would go to bed relatively early, but not before she knew all of us were safe at home. We were all thankful for this lovely day.

It wasn't that uncommon for Mom to call me before 4 o'clock every afternoon; if she did, it was usually had a question, wanted to chat, or had something important to tell me. On Sunday, December 2, 2012, Mom called me about noon. Linda called her; Jennilyn had passed away the day before, from

unknown causes. She would have turned 32 in three weeks.
Jennilyn died on Linda grandson's second birthday. My heart
just sank. *She had been through so much, and now this. Oh
man.* Mom sensed Linda was in shock.

I had Jennilyn as a Facebook friend, and you tend to learn
when someone is doing well or not doing well from their posts.
The more things she posts, the more that it seemed she was doing
well. Jennilyn was head-over-heels over her nephew, and
recently, her new niece. It was a tremendous lost for Linda and
her entire family.

I kept track of Jennilyn's arrangements online.
Unfortunately, I couldn't attend her wake or funeral. Mom and
Dad attended the funeral. Mom told me Linda wore a brave face,
but everyone knew Linda was crushed.

I faced the hard task of finding the right words to fill
Linda's weekly letter. I couldn't be too funny, or could I, as I
told her about my mundane life. I wanted to lift her spirits, but I
didn't know exactly how. Sometimes I pulled appropriate
prayers off the web, but soon I realized I was a writer and began
to write my lines of inspiration. My lines of inspiration usually
had something to do with Heaven. Did the letters help? I had no
idea, but I continued to write them. After the unspeakable and
horrific tragedy in Newtown, Connecticut a few weeks later, I
wrote in my letter to Linda that I was certain that Jennilyn was
helping to take care of the 20 children, now in Heaven. *Life can
be so cruelly short.*

It was a New Year: 2013. We celebrated our January
birthdays at the Barnstable Tavern. This was the first time Mom,
Dad and a few others were meeting Stephany. By that time,
Stephany had been working with me for nearly four years.
Stephany is also one of those special gems you'll find that really
get what you are all about. She's young and very interested to
learn what the world is all is about. She strives to do her best in

everything she tries accomplish. She has a tendency to beat herself up when she doesn't do something perfectly. During *Jeopardy!* she shouts out answers very quickly, and hopes the answer is correct. She does pretty well in art history, as she majored in the subject.

Stephany also has a fancy for good food. One taste of Mom's chocolate chip cookies, and Stephany was hooked. Mom made awesome Toll House chocolate chip cookies with her twist. The twists included zest from an orange peel or extra Ghirardelli chocolate chips. Stephany was convinced if she nailed down the recipe, she could sell them for $2 each.

Again, we had a nice lunch at the Barnstable Tavern. We took our time, as we had the birthday gentlemen open their gifts. Martha bought Jack a guessing game that they played for a while. The boys had a good time getting in on the fun. I watched and smiled. It was the children in our lives who brought perspective in this ever-changing world.

All shared hugs and kisses, as we went back home in different directions. I promised to come visit more, as I have been doing the past five months. I made sure someone walked Mom to the car, and she got in safely. Mom and Dad had a short ride home. I talked to her later on that evening like always. They had a wonderful day.

By this time, I had been writing steadily for this book for more than a year. On weekends, I composed music. Early in 2012, questions would arise in my mind, which Mom and/or Dad would be able to answer. Mom and I had fun conversing on the phone, and laughing most of the time. If I had more in depth questions, I usually saved those for snail mail, when technology became too cumbersome for Mom and Dad to navigate.

It was at the end of 2012, Jeanette had to endure back surgery, leaving her two shifts open. I always become a tad anxious when the hunt began for to find the right fit for me. I had a wonderful supervisor, Kris, who knew me, and knew the people who had been working years with me. The issue wasn't the issue of Kris not knowing what kinds of personalities would mesh, it was a question of what types of people Kris had available to her.

Kris' supervisors presented her with this very young woman. From all my past experiences, I knew I had to give all the newbies a fair shake, unless it was clearly evident that newbie wasn't going to work out.

As I said, Newbie One was a young 19-year-old woman, and she had a one-year-old at home. After she began taking over the shifts for Jeanette, I soon recognized Newbie One still had a 14-year-old mentality. I have known some young, single mothers who had the maturity of a 35-year-old, who have worked tremendously hard to put their kids ahead of everything else. Newbie One was not one of those individuals. Newbie One lived with her mother, and was clearly dependent on her.

People who don't even try to carry on a conversation with me, especially when they are working with me easily turn me off. Like I said, I give newbies ample time to become comfortable with me, and get to know me. Well, Newbie One was just showing up for the paycheck, and only interacting with me when she had to ask me a question. Otherwise, she texted on her iPhone for the rest of time.

One Friday, Newbie One came in and asked me if I could fax something for her to a bank. I typed on my computer screen that I didn't have the capability to fax, but if she had an e-mail address for the bank, I could send it that way. Then, she told me what she was sending to the bank. She was sending a loan application for $8000 to buy a 2005 Mercedes Benz. Excuse me for passing a quick judgment on people's actions and motives, but she drove a 2000 Audi, which looked like it was in excellent condition. I couldn't let this one pass. I thought about that little boy she had at home. I couldn't let this one go because I was dumbfounded; she had me nerved up.

I went all Suze Orman on her. I typed, "Do you have a savings account, with money?" *No.* I typed, "Have you started a college fund for your son yet?" *No.* I typed, "Why do you want a Mercedes?" *To look cool.* I nearly lost my mind. I really wanted to shout, "You have been so denied!" but I knew she wouldn't have understood me, or even wanted to understand me. She wouldn't have understood the famous Suze Orman tag line. For the next four months, I made sure she watched The Suze Orman Show with me on Saturday nights. She kept her Audi.

Things never changed with Newbie One. At age 19, getting up from a seated position seemed to be a hardship. She was quickly getting under my skin. She tried to hide the fact that she was texting while she was feeding me dinner. She really didn't know who I was. I guess she believed she could bulldoze me. One night I typed, "After three months, what have you learned about me?" Like if a schoolteacher was asking her a question, she wrestled around to find an appropriate answer. Finally she answered that I like music. I typed, "Tell me what you know about cerebral palsy?" Again, she looked perplexed. I wasn't looking for a technical answer from a textbook. She had this job, assisting people with cerebral palsy and other developmental disabilities; one might be slightly inquisitive about cerebral palsy. She was not. I helped her out with an answer. I typed, "What would you like to do for a career?" I really wanted to type what would you like to do when you grow up, but I thought better of it. She answered she wanted to be an interpreter. She was surprised when I informed her that she had to college to be an interpreter.

By the middle of March, I explained to Kris that Newbie One was making me crazy, not talking to me during an entire shift, not taking the slightest of interest in her job, and blatantly texting in front of me when she should be interacting with me. Kris understood, and was on the hunt for Newbie Two.

On March 26, Melanie and I took another drive to Cape Cod to see Mom and Dad. We went out to lunch at the All-American Pub and saw Lisa. Mom loved to tease Lisa about anything. It was playful banter. Lisa gave it right back and Mom loved it. Lisa referred to Mom as "the Mayor of South Yarmouth", because Mom knew all the happenings in town. After the playful banter, Mom asked Lisa if she knew how Linda was doing. I was curious as well. Lisa said Linda wasn't great, but she didn't have any more details. It was understandable after losing Jennilyn. I couldn't help but to wonder if my letters were helping.

We enjoyed our lunch at the All-American. We went back to my parents' house and chatted with them for a few hours. Mom and Dad were in high spirits. They always made me laugh. For the last four or five years, every time I went to visit, Mom wanted to give me some kind of item from their house. Some things were strictly off limits "until she passed over," Mom often reiterated with humor. I always tried to shoot for the nice sailboat in their front, bay window, but she always shot me down. "Oh, come on," I kiddingly replied with a smile. Truth be told, I had no place to showcase the boat since I had recently replaced my large bow window with a flat window.

It was time to say goodbye until our next visit to the Cape. Mom and Dad gave me kisses, and Mom gave me one of her ticklish hugs. Melanie and I promised to call once we got back home. Like always, we kept our promise.

"Hold on Hold on to yourself
For this is gonna hurt like hell."

"Hold On"
Sarah McLachlan
Fumbling Towards Ecstasy

Who knew Paul was such a Green Day fan? I knew he liked Green Day, but once I saw Martha's short, iPhone video of the pool of people, including Paul and Karen, in front of the stage at the Dunkin' Donuts Center, I knew he was in Green Day deep.

As they enjoyed dinner before the concert, I sent Peter, Martha and Paul a text message that went something like this: *Just talked to Mom; Dad made his second at going to the taxman in Wareham but couldn't find it.* Dad had made it home safely, although frustrated. I also sensed his unsuccessful trips to Wareham were worrisome to Mom. I suggested he find a tax preparer close to home. Dad decided he would mail everything to his taxman in Wareham.

Patriot's Day in Massachusetts: a state holiday, and the day of the Boston Marathon. I was well aware of the history of this long, sporting tradition, especially with the ongoing racing participants, Dick and Rick Hoyt. The father and son inspirational Boston Marathon cornerstones had planned for this to be their last race, as a duo after 31 marathons, but regrettably, the Hoyts along with 5,000 runners were stopped before they reached the finish line on Boylston Street.

I was not aware of the bombings until Mom called after 3 in the afternoon. I turned on MSNBC in my bedroom. Brian Williams was talking as they played the video footage over and over again. The footage was filled with smoke and rescuers doing their best. What the video footage did not show was the horrific carnage, as a results of those two deadly bombs.

I watched on but initial reports didn't change too much until later that evening. Melanie arrived, worried out of her skull because she had two friends who worked in that particular area, and no one had any contact with them. I reassured her that with all the people trying to call from their cellphones, cell towers were overwhelmed with the volume. It was a long four hours before Melanie heard that her friends were safe, although they witnessed the human carnage that would remain with them all of their lives.

Three innocent lives were lost, including an 8-year-old boy. Hundreds were injured, many critically. Again, people came together and wrapped their love and support around Boston, as they did with New York City after 9/11. Soon, we were all Boston Strong.

Mom was transfixed on this story until Friday night, when police caught the living suspect in Watertown. I talked to Mom on the phone several times a day in the days after the bombings. It was three days after the bombings when Rachel, a Doctor of Audiology, drove down to the Cape to deliver Mom's hearing aids to her. When I talked to Mom on the phone, it was a certain advantage. I didn't have to struggle to have Mom clearly hear what I was staying. I hardly needed to repeat anything because she heard it all. It was a truly amazing conversation. The next day, Mom was unable to get the hearing aids working properly.

Saturday evening, a group of us had tickets to see comedian, Bobby Collins, at a theater inside of Patriot Place in Foxboro. It was our third time seeing the very funny New York native; I guess if it was our third time seeing the man, he has to be pretty funny. He is pretty damn funny! I talked to Mom before we left for dinner and the show. We had all learned that if I didn't call Mom before going out for more than an hour that she would start calling Martha, Melanie or Kathy to find out my whereabouts. Mom knew where I was on this night.

Bobby Collins began his act with praising the Boston/southern New England crowd on their resolute to not let the horrific actions of two young brothers change the attitude of the people of Boston. Then Collins streamlined his way into humorously berating the younger brother's deplorable act of running over his brother, as he fled the police. Collins humor is centered around making fun of people's lack of common sense. I believe we all laughed throughout Collins' show. We all needed a good laugh after the horrible events in Boston.

Sunday was the official start to Melanie's week long vacation. She was going to Florida to visit some friends. Stephany filled in for Melanie's Sunday evening shift. Martha and Glenn invited us over to dinner, and to watch the season premiere of *Nurse Jackie*. It had taken a few seasons to get "addicted" to the show, but I finally saw the beauty of this Showtime series. I think the big draw to *Nurse Jackie* is to see whether or not she can get through another year clean. You root for the character "Jackie" because she's so talented as a nurse; she's a force to be reckoned with, high or not. She's fighting her own disease, a disease she thinks she has control over but never seems to have complete control. I never have complete control; I can relate.

I talked to Mom before I left to go to Martha and Glenn's. It was the third day she was unable to get her new hearing aids working correctly. Peter, Sue and Grace were returning from a week on a Caribbean cruise. I asked Mom if she had heard from them yet. My clumsy speech got her confused, as she thought I had heard from them. I clarified that I hadn't heard from them. Mom promised that she would call them in a few hours. After Mom told me to eat well at Martha and Glenn's, as always, she told me she would talk to me the next day, maybe one, two, three or four times. I smiled, and said okay. We said goodnight, followed by 'I love you'.

For a day I seemed to prepare myself for practically my entire life had come. In the early hours of Monday, April 22, Mom had passed away from a heart attack. When Kathy arrived, she had already had gotten the sad news from Martha, who was making her way to my house with Glenn. It must have been the longest walk for Kathy, to walk down my hall, into my bedroom, to break the news to me. As I was still lying on my stomach in bed, I grew emotional, as I quickly pulled it together. It was my normal response to such sad news. Instantly, I wanted to know what exactly happened, but I had trouble verbalizing. Kathy sat on my bed, very emotional, has she rubbed my back. Mom's heart gave out.

Martha and Glenn soon arrived; the came in my bedroom. Martha was in shock; we were all in shock. Peter was on his way to the Cape for Dad, while Paul had just landed in Hawaii for a common business trip. Soon, Martha gave me the details, which Dad had told to her. Once I knew the details of Mom's death, I was relieved her suffering was brief, even though the Yarmouth rescues had tried tirelessly to revive her. Mom always told me she wanted to die quickly, without suffering. She would always jokingly say, "Just take me out and shoot me out back if things get bad."

Still in bed, with half of my face was buried in my mattress and all of my extremities, hands and feet keeping the beat to each of their different drummers, Paul called from Hawaii to check how I was. I answered, "Okay." Frankly, I didn't know how was. I had all these thoughts running through my head that I could hardly keep up with. Often, I wondered who met Mom when she entered Heaven. I was comforted by the thought that her parents, her late siblings and Helen and Ray Watson would all greet her. I speculated that Mom was finally going to meet her daughter, Mary Ann. Oh, what an encounter that must have been. I used all these images to comfort myself. I knew, from that day forward, life would never be quite the same; it would have an empty space that no one or anything would ever fill.

Martha had already called Aunt Anne and Aunt Pat. Quickly, they were calling Uncle Fran, Uncle Bill and other close family members. Uncle Fran was scheduled for knee replacement surgery the following day; he decided to go through with the surgery. Aunt Anne and Aunt Pat would be arriving shortly; I needed to get up and shower.

My stomach was churning; I didn't quite know if I could eat anything. My aunts were already here before I emerged from the shower. Everything felt just so surreal; I didn't have any benchmark to gauge myself. I was keenly aware that everybody's focus might be on me. I didn't want that focus; I remained strong. My aunts greeted me with hugs, kisses and condolences. I couldn't help but to think they had just lost their little sister; a sister they have loved for 81 years. After I ate the first spoonfuls of Cheerios, my stomach felt calmer.

Martha returned; Thomas left work early and Sarah would be doing the same in a few hours. As I ate breakfast, everybody was talking, which helped immensely. When it came to a question that only I could answer, I answered it with a pride and conviction, knowing, besides Dad, had talked to Mom the most over the last few days. I could share something with everybody that they wanted to know.

I didn't know what to do with myself that day; I wasn't sure what I would occupy my time with until my focus returned. I didn't know when it would return. I thought back to the night before, as I was finishing up Mom and Dad's latest e-mail message, I was unable to complete the last line because the laptop battery begged for a charge. I ended each evening e-mail message with, "I will talk to you tomorrow." Since that very night, that particular file still has a modified tag: "April 21, 2013, 11:26PM". I often wondered if I had finished that last line, would Mom have lived another day.

Pat stayed with me throughout the day. I waited for Dad to call. I knew I had to call Melanie; I knew I had to call Linda and Lisa. Kathy helped me make all of these calls. I was very grateful to her. The only person I talked to directly was Linda. Of all the days I could bring this horrible news to her about Mom, Patti, Linda's sister, was about to arrive with the autopsy results on Jennilyn. *This woman can't catch a break.* I was about to compound her sadness on this very sad Earth Day. I was already accustomed to her sadness. Linda, tearful on the phone, expressed her condolences over Mom's passing. My eyes filled. She offered any assistance she could give to my family and me. Kathy and I would keep her apprised of Mom's funeral arrangements when they were known.

Not long after, Dad called. He repeated, in a calm and collected voice, exactly what had transpired early that morning. No new revelations came about. Peter was with him. He worried about me; I reassured him I was doing okay. I worried about him. This was going to be a dramatic change for him. I wondered how would he spend his time now that he didn't have Mom to help with what she needed. We needed to do the right things by him.

As Melanie was on vacation, Newbie One was slated to cover that particular evening shift. It was already set to be her last. Dealing with her was already cumbersome for my normal psyche; it would be much more difficult to deal with her with a weakened psyche. I decided the best way to cope with Newbie One was to ignore her the best way I knew how. Newbie One was not comfortable in social situations; her social difficulties became glaringly apparent, as we went over to Martha and Glenn's for pizza. I should have given her a bit more slack given the difficult day, but Newbie One hardly said many words to me during her last six hours.

Emotionally and physically drained from the day, I did manage to sleep. When I was awake, my mind was constantly on Mom, and what Heaven was like. I had no doubt in my mind that she was looking down on all of us. I knew the next days would test me in ways I hadn't been tested before.

It was easily determined that Dad wanted Billy Watson to preside over Mom's funeral, even though the funeral would be on the Cape. Tuesday, Paul e-mailed me with two requests: to assemble the pallbearers and to assist him with writing Mom's eulogy. Physically and mentally, I was engulfed in a thick haze of sadness, but my undying drive to have a purpose, the drive to be useful, did not waver, especially when it came to my family. I did what I was asked. All of the Morgan men, and my other cousin, Paul McDermott graciously answered my e-mails, and told me they would be honored.

Through my sad haze, I wondered where I might find the focus to be able to write anything. My daily routine had been turned upside down, and inside out. My attention span resembled the attention span of a gnat. Once I opened up a blank MS Word file, I had a focus. As the words began to appear on the screen, I felt the sadness melt away for just a little while, although tears welled up in my eyes often. After a few hours, I had written about three or four paragraphs. I spent a long time re-reading them over and over again. It was something to occupy my time. Everything was how I wanted it to be and I e-mailed to Paul to use whatever he wanted. I cannot recall too much I did during those first few days, other than hearing from Aunt Pat to keep abreast how Uncle Fran did after knee replacement surgery. He did well.

Wednesday, Mom's obituary ran in the Cape Cod Times. It brought it all home. I steadied myself as I brought it up online. The picture Martha had chosen was a black and white picture she had taken of Mom at Sarah's 21st birthday, and one of the best pictures of her. It was a good choice. Other than it being a typical obituary anyone would see in the average, American newspaper, it was our mother's obituary, with our names all listed. Even though I prepared myself for the day I would lose my parents, I don't think I ever thought about what their obituary should say. Suddenly we were the children and the grandchildren of our late mother. Contributions would go to the Rhode Island Chapter of United Cerebral Palsy in Mom's memory. The unwanted focus turned to me once again. The generous offer moved me to tears.

340

As I processed reading Mom's obituary, I knew I had to share the link with some people on Facebook who would want to know the arrangements. I copied the Cape Cod Times link and posted in private messages. I was coping by having a sense of purpose. I always needed a sense of purpose.

Melanie bought a Florida scratch ticket and won $1200. She looked far up into the Florida sky and thanked Mom for the win. Melanie decided early on to fly back early to attend Mom's funeral. I wasn't surprised by this gesture; she loved my parents. She would do anything they asked, even breaking and entering their own house when the need was there.

Martha soon was on the Cape, as she stayed with Dad and handled the rest of the arrangements. Mom always mentioned she wasn't going to have calling hours. Not knowing her exact reason, I personally believe she didn't want to put any of us through any added on solemnity. I had never attended a wake until 1998 when my Uncle Tom passed. Not knowing what to expect made me very anxious; I had never seen a dead body in my life other than what was displayed on television, with 90% of that made up for television and film. I recall before I entered the room where my Uncle Tom laid, I positioned myself to look in to see what to expect. I saw the open casket with my uncle in a peaceful state. *I can handle this,* I told myself. I still hung onto some of my anxiety as I approached his casket. Quickly, I got past the idea that I was looking at a deceased person. It was my Uncle Tom lying; his body was asleep for eternity. I said a little prayer in my head and moved onto the receiving line. I had no clue what the protocol was for a wake. I thought that people sat quietly in the chairs provided. Instead of people remaining quiet, people actually had conversations, they laughed, they talked about their lives, as they caught up with their family. At first, I thought it was a bit odd that people were carrying on chummy conversations while there was my Uncle Tom lying in a casket. As soon as I realized this was the norm, I kind of embraced the atmosphere of it all. People were there to celebrate his life by being alive and grateful they had known this man.

Uncle Tom also was the first I accompanied to a cemetery. Again, I expected the mourners to gather around an opening in the ground, as the priest said the last words, the casket would be lowered into the ground. For Uncle Tom, the mourners gathered in this small chapel. We gathered around his casket and listened to the final prayer. Everyone filed out of the chapel, leaving the casket alone. My first instinct was to wonder who was going to remain with his casket until he was taking to his burial spot. I didn't want to leave him alone there. I was learning as I went. I learned it was okay to leave his casket alone; I learned to have faith in the caretakers of the cemetery that this was their business and they knew their function. This idea didn't lessen my need to wait with Uncle Tom's casket until an official tended to it.

Sleep was very hard to come by in the days that followed Mom's passing. I was feeling anxious, very anxious. I desperately wanted my body to be calm during Mom's services. I obtained a Xanax from a kind soul. It was Friday, April 26, exactly one month since I last saw Mom, five days since I had spoken to Mom, and on this day, we were laying her to rest. Kathy, Melanie and I left Rhode Island early to make it to South Yarmouth's Saint Pius Church in plenty of time. Linda asked us for a wake up call; we completed that task. The drive down was quiet, but we still chatted during the ride. We parked in the church's lot, as we waited for people to arrive. My nerves remained at a level, which I could handle. I was still in that hazy fog I had been in for the previous four days; it wasn't going away anytime soon, I thought.

As the time on the clock approached 9:50 AM, we got out of the van and began to greet my aunts, cousins and family friends, most of who travelled in from Rhode Island and Connecticut. There was a cool, April breeze that chilled the sadness. Linda arrived, with her now auburn her, which was a certain change from her constant blonde hairstyle. Two deaths had occurred since I saw her nine months earlier. She looked worn and broken but amazingly her energy level didn't seem to lessen. I was glad she was there.

The hearse and limousine pulled up to the entrance to the church. I took a deep breath as I looked on. My family got out of the limousine one by one. It was the first time I saw my Dad, now a widower. He came over and gave me an emotional kiss. I held it together somehow. When Paul came over to kiss me, I began to cry, as my hand automatically grabbed the back of his arm. "Be strong. I need you to be strong," he whispered. His words instantly calmed me. *I can do this.*

I saw a familiar face, Billy Watson, as he took charge. The rear hearse door opened, displaying Mom's pastel gold casket. The pallbearers guided Mom's casket on the aluminum bier. Billy conducted his employees to position Mom's casket in the entrance of the church. He directed Dad, Peter, Martha, Paul and I to line up following Mom's casket. It was a crash course on funeral etiquette I was lacking. Billy was great, as he told me where to position myself. Once we reached the front of the church, Billy directed all of us where to sit; I pulled up next to Dad, on my left. Mom's casket sat about two feet to my right. It was all so surreal. As I never found myself inside this church before, I familiarized myself with it. Inside, it was a contemporary church, a contemporary church fooled by its average exterior. The interior was inviting and soothing.

The Mass began. Often, I would look to my father; he knew what he was doing. I knew the basics. I focused in on the young priest; if I concentrated on him, I knew I would be okay. I kept to the task, listening to his every word. Occasionally the organist would play and sing, giving me a chance to adjust my physical stability. When Paul walked to the pulpit to give the short eulogy I helped him prepare, I recalled his words: *Be Strong.* He never did anything like this in his life. His voice remained strong and steady, as he recited his tender words about our loving mother. Later, Paul revealed he was looking for Martha's friend, John, amongst the mourners. John had given

Paul some words of wisdom over the phone on how to steady focused speaking. Unfortunately, John and Dan were unable to attend Mom's funeral. Paul must have found someone or something to draw his focus on, because it did waver. It seemed like more than one of us were searching for a focus point that difficult day. Mom would have been proud of us. She was proud.

I breathed again when I knew the Mass was drawing to its conclusion. Mom's casket exited the church in the similar fashion as it entered. It was guided back into the hearse for the 30-minute ride to the Massachusetts National Cemetery in Bourne. Linda joined us for the funeral procession. The atmosphere in my vehicle was more relaxed. Linda sat directly behind me. Kathy was annoyed with the inconsiderate drivers coming on and off of Route 6 West. Despite the difficult tasks taking place that day, I felt glad Linda was with us.

Soon, we were at the National Cemetery. Mom remarked that the cemetery was a beautiful place, and it was. Linda was familiar with this cemetery; for years she took care of a man buried amongst the many. He was a military man. Dad served in the Army for five months during the Korean War. Dad served in the supply maintenance division. His service qualified him, Mom and myself to be laid to rest at the National Cemetery.

Mistakenly, I was told to get out of my van only to be asked to get back in to drive to a different location of the cemetery. We followed the other vehicles to the correct location. Everyone parked where they could and walked a short distance to the small portico where Mom's casket was already positioned. I drove myself in between the only two benches. Dad was on my left, and Aunt Pat and Aunt Anne sat on my right. The rest stood in a half-circle, as the military pastor prepared to speak. He was an older gent, dressed in a dark wool overcoat and a red military cap. He was a lively soul with an engaging personality. It was easy to see he had done this hundreds of times; he was very comfortable in his own skin. Instead of being somber, his words were uplifting. He took an interest in me. I guess it was not a common occurrence to see someone with athetoid cerebral palsy. He said a few prayers for my Mom, and for those who were saddened by her passing. We were all saddened.

We lingered for several minutes until the officials politely asked us to take our leave because they had another burial service to conduct. Before that time, some of us gathered around Mom's casket. Many of us took some flowers atop. Aunt Pat kissed the top; she wanted to know if I wanted to do the same. I just put my hand on the corner and created a little prayer in my head. I knew Mom would always watch over me, until my dying day. We would be together again. Unlike the ending to Uncle Tom's burial service, I didn't worry about leaving Mom's casket. I knew she was in good hands.

The luncheon would take place at a nearby country club. Hazel and her older sister, Gloria, attended the Mass and burial. I was quite touched they had made the trip. With all of my friends who came, we filled up almost an entire, large, round table. Aunt Pat joined us. We were ready to eat. Some of us were ready to drink. It was a lively atmosphere despite the reason why we were all together.

I usually take longer to eat because of my cerebral palsy. People began to mingle amongst the different tables. Sam blessed us with his presence, as he began telling us this story that only a 12-year-old's imagination could conjure up. He had a captured audience for about 15 minutes. As this strange story continued without a foreseeable ending, his audience attention started to wane. Jack joined in and added his own twists to his brother's story. I thought about what Mom's reaction would be to this never-ending tail about monsters built like blocks. She would have given Sam her attention for a good half an hour, and then politely urged him to come up with an ending. Although his story may not have been a blockbuster, there wasn't any doubt Sam entertained us all.

Once I finished my meal, I mingled with our guests. Some people had to leave to pick up their kids from school. Dad was sitting with the Watson daughters, and their uncle. His former boss from Cape Air, Barbara, attended Mom's services, along with our cousin, Elin, and her daughter, Annie. Elin is the daughter of my late Uncle Matt, Dad's brother. I believe he was very grateful for the people who attended. Dad seemed tired but he fed off the energy of others.

Hazel, Melanie and Linda wanted to go outside for a quick smoke. Melanie had quit a few years back, and only indulged on certain occasions. Through the luncheon, I noticed Linda was wearing a necklace with an electric blue pendant attached. She grasped it between her index finger and thumb a number of times. I had the idea that it held some of Jennilyn's ashes. Linda was never shy explaining things, such as the pendant came to be. Anyone could see how precious this blue pendant was to her. She always had a piece of her daughter close to her heart.

We thanked Hazel and Gloria for coming; they had to get home. I would see Hazel the next morning, which brought me comfort. Melanie, Linda and I went back inside. Along with my immediate family, we thanked the rest of our guests for coming. Outside again, Kathy went to retrive my van that was parked in an inaccessible position. She drove it up curbside. This time, we had an additional passenger coming along for the drive back to South Yarmouth. It was Thomas. He was our comic relief for the afternoon.

Thomas has this wonderful gift of humor that we all possess in some shape or form, but Thomas' is two notches up from the rest of us. Along with his gigantic sense of humor comes his facial expressions and his vocal nuances that make him that much a comic. He wasn't troubled he was in a vehicle with all women. I think he feeds off a female audience. Like myself, Thomas really enjoys making people laugh, especially his mother. Our ride was a little bit longer because Kathy wished to drop by her cousins' home in the area. I just listened to the humorous banter going on in the backseat. I was almost positive that a great deal of time past since Linda had a good laugh out loud. Thomas was supplying the laughs, whether or not the jokes were raunchy or just plain funny. His funniness lasted through the drive back to South Yarmouth.

We returned to the church parking lot so Linda could retrieve her black Chevy Tahoe. She remarked she had rarely driven it in a number of weeks. This was when I realized how fragile she was. Linda followed us back to Mom and Dad's. Except for Peter, Sue, Grace, Sarah and James, our family was gathered, winding down from the day. The only ones who had any substantial energy left were the three boys. We were eating and drinking what was available. Dad was comfortable sitting on the faux leather couch in the outer room. Sometimes, his tired eyes would close in intervals. Martha and Paul would keep him engaged with having him tell funny stories from the past.

I stayed in the outer rooms; I knew people were coming in and out of the kitchen. I didn't know if my psyche was strong enough to go in the kitchen and not see Mom there. I remained where I sat. I laughed at Paul when he jokingly mentioned that I saw the lands where my body would lie after I passed on, but not for many, many years, God willing. I imagined myself giving Paul a geeky, goofy smile, along with two thumbs up in sarcastic body comedy, but of course I could not pull off the thumbs up action, so I just laughed very hard. It was our kind of humor.

Like myself, Paul was content where he sat at the oak table. Linda was in front of him, and I was beside Linda, on her left. It was then Paul inquired about her electric blue pendant. Linda told him straight out that she lost her daughter, Jennilyn, to a brain aneurysm four months earlier. Paul didn't expect to hear such tragic news. Linda explained Jennilyn had some underlying conditions that most likely contributed to her early death. Linda also explained to Paul that she was the one who found Jennilyn's lifeless body in her bed. I knew all of this, but I think Paul was

still blown away. He gave Linda his sincere condolences over
the lost of Jennilyn. She appreciated his kind words.

It was getting on to be going home to Rhode Island.
Melanie, Kathy and I would say our goodbyes to everyone.
Linda was very pleased to see her, and I, as well. She remained
in good company with my family. The ride home was quiet;
more sadness crept into my soul, as I stared out to the spring
glow of the setting sun. Somewhere amongst that Heavenly,
orange glow, Mom was looking upon us all.

It was a few years back that I reconnected with Debi, who
worked at the residential school as a registered nurse. When she
found me on Facebook, it was a very happy and exciting
occasion. I had tried several times before to find her address.
Come to find out, I was spelling her last name wrong. What a
dope. Before reconnecting via Facebook, we hadn't spoken in
nearly 20 years. Since Facebook, we have talked several times
on the phone, and we even met up in Boston one day. The day
was spectacular in fabulous Boston!

On the Sunday following Mom's burial, Debi phoned.
Sadly, her mother passed away just the day before from ovarian
cancer. Tears welled in my eyes, as she explained how rough the
last few days had been, watching her Mom pass. Debi spent a
number of years as a Hospice nurse. Her experiences of helping
others get through their final days and hours of life didn't
compare to her own mother's passing. During the last few
months, Debi would make weekly trips to her parents' home to
give her Dad support in the daily, physical care of her Mom.
Debi and I were 'sister-in-grief', as I referred to it, after we both
lost our dear mothers within a five-day span. We talked a lot via
Facebook.

It was a period of a few weeks that I had many
acquaintances losing loved ones. I thought to myself, *this is*

crazy. Make it stop.

Paul had Dad move in with him, Karen and the boys. Paul bought a number of items from the house so Dad would be comfortable at Paul and Karen's. Besides being the financially sound decision, we all knew that he needed some supervision, mainly with making sure he ate meals on a regular basis. We also knew he wouldn't be able to keep up with the housekeeping. My parents' home would be sold.

For the ones who weren't cleaning things out at my parents' house, we spent Mother's Day brunch at TPC Boston. We had dined here a handful of times before, but this day felt very different without Mom. The loss of her was still fresh in our hearts. Mother's Day will never be the same.

It only was three weeks; Dad seemed content living with Paul, Karen and the boys. They were waiting on him hand and foot. I began trying to get in the routine of writing him letters. I was still in the state where my focus was diagnosed with Attention Deficit Disorder. Time was the only prescription necessary. I don't know if Dad enjoyed my letters as much as Mom, but I continued to write them.

For so long I resisted Facebook requests to play Candy Crush Saga. I saw other people playing it and I didn't see the appeal of it. After Mom passed, I inherited her Apple iPad. It was very difficult for me to direct my focus on doing anything meaningful. When I needed to get away from the computer, Candy Crush, or as we like to refer to it, Candy Crack, it was a mindless game that passed time until I was able to find my rhythm of life. I would like to also believe that playing Candy Crack gave me the opportunity to fine-tune the best methods to use the iPad with my headpointer. I spent months trying to find appropriate conductive tips and the right angles to use the iPad with my headpointer.

349

The iHome pens with the stylus on the ends of these pens worked particularly well because the stylus caps were removable and hollow so that they contoured well onto the end of my headpointer. The only drawback was the rubber tips on the iHome pen styluses would fail over a month's time. I found a stylus cap for use for a pen. The stylus is constructed out of high-strength steel with dense rubber, replaceable tips. The tips lasted far longer than the iHome pen stylus tips, but I had difficulty keeping the stylus cap on the bend of the headpointer due to its wide diameter.

Finally, I found these conductive tips, handmade, on Etsy.com. The conductive tip slides onto the end of my headpointer and is very secure. These conductive tips work extraordinarily well, with the iPad at the correct angle so the user has the ability to apply some pressure to the iPad, or similar tablets. These handmade conductive tips last a very long time.

In the healing times when I wasn't playing Candy Crack, I managed to continue to compose new songs for my 2014 CD entitled, *Iron Horse*. In this album, I just did what I loved to do, and that is creating music. My lyrics seem to reflect what was pouring out of my head and my heart. Of course, they aren't fabulous lyrics, but they are my lyrics all the same. Especially towards the latter part of 2013, I was banging out songs left and right, as my soul strengthened, as I saw life in a brighter light.

That strengthening took some major setbacks along the way. By the beginning of June, Dad was growing more and more frustrated with his new living arrangements. We all agreed that Dad should not have his car in a town and area he wasn't familiar driving in. Dad grew frustrated because he couldn't come and go on his own. Martha and I took turns going to get Dad on weekends to bring him to Rhode Island. We lined up different odds and ends we needed help doing around our homes. It gave him something to do; it gave him a purpose.

Dad's weekend trips to Rhode Island didn't lessen his desire to have his car, which was still on the Cape. The more we kept stalling to give him his car back, the more Dad obsessed over the car. There were times Dad didn't talk to Paul for a few days because Paul didn't allow to have his car. My heart just broke for Paul and Karen. They were trying everything possible to get Dad comfortable in his new surroundings, and Dad was viewing them as his 'caregivers' keeping him from his freedom. It also broke my heart that Dad didn't understand Paul and Karen's true intentions of trying to keep him safe. Through my weekly letters to Dad, I tried to reinforce the idea that we were concerned for his safety driving in an unfamiliar area.

Things came to a head on Father's Day. I was already was planning on going up to get Dad at Paul and Karen's to take him to dinner. Earlier in the day, I heard rumors that he was planning on going home with me. I kind of brushed off the rumors as just that, rumors. Melanie and I arrived at Paul and Karen's, and sure enough, Dad had a few small bags packed up; he was coming back to Rhode Island. Immediately, I thought about all the boxes and a few extra pieces of furniture I had inherited from the Cape. The sleeper sofa didn't have room to expand out that night. *Just go with it,* I thought.

Dad got into the back seat of my van. Paul and Karen eyes signaled 'peace' and sincerely wished me the best. I was relieved that I was able to come give them the breathing room.

Early the previous week, I had already made reservations online for the Sherborn Inn for three. We sat at the table. Dad was consumed about his lack of freedom living with Paul and Karen. He vented throughout our delicious meal. All I could think about was if Mom was able to hear his displeasure, she would surely put Dad in his place. I had to realize that his thought process was different that it once was.

We were on the road to Rhode Island. An hour later, we stopped at Martha and Glenn's. Martha wanted to gauge his

351

overall mood. We all went inside. There was tension. All he wanted was to get his car at the Cape. Martha explained to him that his car was an hour and a half away. He believed it was ten minutes away. Dad also believed his car was ten minutes away when he lived with Paul and Karen. If we were in Hartford, he would have believed his car was ten minutes away. Martha brought up a map of Southern New England on her laptop to show Dad. Again, he didn't agree. Thomas, Melanie and I all backed up Martha's explanation, but, again he disagreed. Martha offered to drive him to the Cape to prove how long the trip would take. Dad declined. I believed somewhere in the back of his mind, Dad knew it was true. He didn't want to accept his thought process might have declined.

As we tried to convince Dad we were being truthful, we remained calm, although the stress level in their dining area was palpable. He asked Melanie and I to take him to his car. It was nearing 10 o'clock at night. Again, in a calm manner, we explained that Melanie had to help me to bed, and she had to go home. In his eyes, everybody was against him. He proceeded to get up from his chair, grab his bags to head out the front door. Dad said he was going to get his car.

If one of us forced him to stay, Dad would have become even more frustrated. His safety was our top priority, and it was our consensus to call the police for their assistance. *I can't believe we are calling the police for our father on Father's Day.* Glenn followed Dad at a fair distance just to make sure he didn't lose his step and fall. Dad was 85 by this time. A few minutes later, the police pulled up alongside of Dad, and started a polite conversation to judge his competency. They asked him several questions and Dad's answers were nearly entirely correct. The only question that he stumbled upon was defining the current date. Gradually, the very nice police officer coaxed him back to Martha and Glenn's. On Dad's return, he sat quietly, with his head bowed, in a defeated stance. Again, everybody remained calm, as Martha had an open conversation with the officer. We supplied the officer with the total picture. The officer gave Dad two choices: either stay at Martha and Glenn's that night, or spend the night at a local hospital. Dad chose to remain where he was. Martha already had it set to have Dad evaluated at the VA Hospital the following morning.

What a difference a day makes. After Dad's evaluation at the VA, his mood had changed 180°. Martha and Dad dropped by my house, and he couldn't stop raving about how nice the doctors and staff were to him. He told me everything they did that particular day, and what they plan to do in the near future. Nobody was the bad guy anymore.

Now came the question of where he would like to live. Over the next ten days, Martha located an apartment in an assisted living facility just walking distance from both of us. During these ten days, he stayed several days with me, and a few days with Peter, Sue and Grace. We strongly encouraged him to take the apartment. Time was nearly up when he finally agreed. Dad wanted to talk to Paul about his decision to move to Rhode Island. We all thought that this was the right decision for Dad. He needed to be settled and content.

I was breaking in Newbie Two. Her progression curve plateaued at a very early stage, to my dismay. Her maturity matched her age, which I was pleased about, but like Newbie One, she wasn't talkative. Unlike Newbie One, Newbie Two had a serious nodding off issue. On one of the days Martha, Peter and I were encouraging Dad to take the apartment, as we sat in the living room, Newbie Two was leaning on the kitchen counter with her eyes closed. *You have to be kidding me?*

It was early in the game, and I wanted to give her a chance to grow and become more comfortable, and interested, in working with me. On a few occasions, I asked Newbie Two if she really liked working with me. She promised she did, and she wanted to talk, and engage with me more. I knew she was very involved with her church, so I invited her to listen to my

Christmas CD. On my computer screen, I explained to Newbie Two how I did the Christmas CD, and we talked about other things. I really thought we had progressed into a more sociable stage, but a week later it was back to just asking me what I wanted for dinner. When I can predict with precision when a person only asks me what I want for dinner and that is the main question of the total shift, I get so discouraged with that person, I cannot expend more of my energy to make them realize there is so much more to this job than feeding me, helping me to the bathroom and putting me to bed. It was time to be on the lookout for a replacement for Newbie Two.

In June, our oldest cousin, Carol Ann, had passed away unexpectedly. She was 69, and the daughter of my late Uncle Joe Maguire. Her family lived in Washington State. Over the many years, she and her family visited New England a few times. I didn't know her very well, but we were all saddened by the lost.

While Aunt Anne was making a recovery after her stomach surgery, Uncle Fran was failing after his knee replacement surgery. He developed renal failure, and was in and out of the hospital. We all were praying his condition would improve. We all knew how strong and determined he was throughout his life. Surely he would pull through this.

In the early hours of July 23, 2013, Francis Maguire passed away surrounded by his loving family in Indiana. It was three, very short months since Mom had passed. I thought about how Mom would have reacted if she had lived to see this sad day. She would have been heartbroken and inconsolable. She used to tell us stories about when she hung out with her older brother, driving around in his car, which had a rumble seat. Once, Fran didn't want attention drawn to the car, especially by a cop. Mom, in the rumble seat, precocious, did a queen's wave to a beat cop, resulting in him pulling Fran over for an outdated sticker. I think that was the last time Mom got to ride in the rumble seat. I had no doubt that Mom welcomed Francis into

Heaven.

I don't think there was one single, family member Uncle Fran did not influence. Every time Uncle Fran visited Rhode Island, all of his siblings, nieces and nephews made a point to meet up with him. He loved everybody and we just loved him. I cannot imagine anyone saying anything negative about this kind and gentle man. In the 1990's, Uncle Fran went out of his way to obtain an autographed CD from John Mellencamp for me, through Dutch Mellencamp, John's father, who was one of Fran's electrician apprentices, I believe.

I had the unfortunate task of telling Dad about Uncle Fran's passing when Melanie and I brought Dad to the DMV, and to Chelo's for a well-deserved lunch. He already knew Uncle Fran was very ill, so it wasn't quite a shock. Dad felt very bad; he would send a donation.

Two steps forward and three steps back. Mom's passing was still fresh as it was in April. Uncle Fran's passing was another jolt to every day life. The next lost I would endure was unfathomable on the surface, but understandable in the deep, deep recesses of my soul. Linda unexpectedly passed in the early hours of August 19, 2013. Linda's obituary stated she died of a broken heart. It was spot on. She was 57. I was completely stunned when Kathy answered the phone to hear Lisa tell her the devastating news. *This can't be happening again?* Instantly, I thought of her family, especially her son, Jeremiah, who had endured his sister's death only nine months earlier. Now, he lost his mother; Jeremiah's young children lost their grandmother; her mother lost her daughter; her siblings lost their sister; her grandmother lost her granddaughter; a great number of people lost a tremendous friend in Linda. Again, if Mom was still with us, she would have been heartbroken and very sad. Mom would have been heartbroken for me. God was merciful because He chose Mom as one of the ones to welcome Carol Ann, Uncle Fran and Linda into the Kingdom of Heaven.

With Dad in possession of his car again, Martha, Peter and I made it a priority to bring Dad to his medical appointments at the VA. On this day, Kathy and I were taking him to a podiatrist appointment. Earlier in the day, I was prepared to tell Dad about Linda's passing. As every sinking moment drift by that day, my resolve to tell him unraveled. After his appointment, we found ourselves back at Chelo's. It had been a month since I told him about Uncle Fran's passing. I didn't want to associate Chelo's with the 'death talk'. I was not prepared to tell him because everything was so raw; I couldn't get my head around it. Given all happened during the year, I chose to spare him anymore sadness. Peter, Martha and Paul concurred with my decision.

Kathy and I drove down to First Church of Harwich, where Linda's services would take place. It was the same church Mom and Dad came to mourn Jennilyn. The church was a stone's throw from Linda's home—a minute's walk. Kathy and I entered at the rear entrance, which bought us near the altar and near the beautiful walnut casket where her body laid. Flowers surrounded the casket. Propped up below the casket was an enlarged photograph of Linda, with her jean overalls, a white tee shirt, sitting sideways on a Harley-Davidson motorcycle. She thoroughly enjoyed being the passenger on Harleys. The photograph spoke to her adventurous personality.

I chose to sit on the far right of the church, about four pews back. I wouldn't be in the way of people walking in or out. I still couldn't believe I was here, at Linda's funeral. I looked back and saw Lisa, Paul and many other familiar faces enter and solemnly take their seats. I couldn't believe we were all here, but we were. Jeremiah, his wife Leah, and the little children sat in the front row; Linda's Mom, Martha (Marty), Patti, and Linda's brother, Scott, sat in the front row, on the opposite side.

It was a sunny, Cape Cod Friday. The tall interior of the church was bright and airy. Sometimes I would gather myself by looking out the double-hung window on my right. If I dared to contort my body just right, I might have caught sight of a small portion of Linda's house.

The pastor began his sermon, and began to speak about Linda, especially about her recent loss of Jennilyn. Jeremiah was filled with sadness, as he cried openly. I imagined everybody in the church wanted to give him a collective embrace because he lost just so much in the past nine months. We hoped the best for him and his beautiful, young family.

There were intervals of prayers, eulogies and a woman playing the guitar while singing songs. Patti was the first to step to the altar. She read an acrostic poem Linda had composed. The vertical word was 'friendship'. It was a beautiful poem, which Patti read fearlessly. I imagined the original copy of this heartfelt poem had Linda's bold signature, in red of course, somewhere on its paper. It's a family trait—bold, red handwriting.

After another wonderful song was performed, Leah stepped to the altar. She was one of the people who spent the most time with Linda during, what turned out to be the last months, weeks and days, of her life. Leah clearly spoke from the heart, while Jeremiah wept. She spoke about Linda's overwhelming sadness over the loss of Jennilyn. The sadness, like the fury of a rough sea, drained Linda's verve. I don't know how I held myself together listening to Leah describe the way she kissed her grandchildren goodnight after spending her last day on the beach with them. Linda was here one day, and then, gone the next.

Another song was performed before the beautifully sad service ended. Kathy and I lingered for a few minutes while the crowd retreated out of the church. Three or four other people lingered around Linda's casket. Soon, she would be cremated. One of the people who lingered was Linda's friend, Deanna. I met her a few times. In the summertime, Linda would sneak into Deanna's garden to help herself to her luscious tomatoes.

Sometimes I was the lucky recipient to Linda's haul. We couldn't have foreseen Linda would leave this Earth so early.

Before the funeral home took Linda's casket, in the exact manner I did with Mom's, I touched the casket on the top, left corner and recited a little prayer. As I slowly made my way to the front foyer of the church, I watched the funeral home ushers wheel the casket out of the side entrance.

Several collages of photographs were placed on easels in the front foyer. The pictures were all of Linda, at different ages in her life. I hadn't seen any of them before. I enjoyed looking at all of them, as Kathy and I waited to go through the receiving line in a room off the foyer. Marty, Patti and Patti's son, Christopher, all gave me tremendous hugs, and thanked us for coming. It felt very strange to be in the company of Linda's family without Linda. I imagined Linda popping into the room with that boundless energy she always possessed. Reality was so, very harsh. Kathy and I sat and talked with Linda's family for a few minutes.

The luncheon was held at The Riverway—a very familiar place. It was there that Lisa, Paul and a few of Linda's friends embraced me. It was clear to see Paul was a broken man, even though he and Linda had ended their relationship years before. It was very obvious he still loved Linda. He reiterated what we all believed to be true: Linda missed Jennilyn so much.

It was a nice lunch. Kathy and I sat with Linda's brother and sister-in-law. We also sat with a young man and his mother. This young man knew Linda when he began working at a restaurant. It wasn't surprising when he told stories about how helpful Linda was teaching him the restaurant business. Kathy shared my stories with Linda with these very nice people.

As we ate the dessert, Kathy and I knew we had to leave for Rhode Island soon. I made it a priority to weave my wheelchair through the tables and chairs to say goodbye to

Marty, Patti, Christopher and Jeremiah. I also made it a point to place my right hand on Jeremiah's shoulder to signal to him that things will be okay. By reading this book, he will realize exactly what I meant. I promised Marty and I would write frequently; they enjoyed the hundred of letters I wrote to Linda.

Lisa and Paul walked Kathy and I out to my vehicle. They gave us big hugs, and wished us a safe ride home. In my open glove box was the small, blue box of 40 count of tissues Linda left in my van four months earlier, after Mom's funeral. They still remain.

"Oh carry on, carry on sweet child
And break on through
You'll never save the world
From behind the glass
Just take your time
Between the lines sweet child
You'll find the answer
Balanced on a razor
You'll be dancing with angels"

"Angels On A Razor"
Ed Kowalczyk
The Flood And The Mercy

I desperately wanted to get passed the sorrow of 2013 had left, permanently, in my bones. I had to learn a new reality; I knew I had to make a plan to live with an intensity that I never felt before. I had to produce something that would be my contribution to society, and leave a proud legacy to my family and friends. I set a goal to write this autobiography, and do very little of anything else, including compose music. I wondered how I would make it through a year without composing any music. I had to strive for something; I knew if I rewarded myself with a "musical prize" once I completed my autobiography, I knew I would be able to stay on track.

The last three month of 2013, I was able to find some kind of rhythm again, as I prepared myself to strictly write my autobiography in 2014. Frankly, I stepped back a little bit and enjoyed not knowing what I was going to do every day.

One of the few highlights in 2013 came on October 24th, when I saw, and met, Ed Kowalczyk, the former lead singer of the band, Live, on his U.S. Acoustic Tour. He stopped in Natick, Massachusetts, and played a great show. After a few attempts of meeting him at past Live shows in the past, I was lucky enough to score Meet 'n Greet passes through Facebook. I was never one to get all school girl giddy when to meeting famous people. I was excited but never giddy. He is a human being just like I was. After shows, Ed likes to snack on Tostitos, Tostitos Salsa and Heineken beer. My kind of man! He was a family man now with four children, the last child, his first son, being born on August 5th, what would have been Mom's 82nd birthday. The son was named Paul Edward. I appreciated how God worked various things out, to give the woeful people signs that life will definitely carry on. Ed's music reflects that ideal.

This was the first time I have ever been backstage with a rock star. Surprising it was quiet and orderly. We were told we could enter his dressing room of the venue. It was about the size of my living room, maybe a little bigger. Kathy and I moved in

and situated ourselves where other fans could enter. He had a
female percussionist, Jen, accompanying him on some of his
dates. As the other fans had his attention, Kathy started a
conversation with Jen, and introduced me. She was very nice
and very cordial. My attention went between Jen, and then,
watching the other female fans clamor for Ed's attention. His
manager was the designated photographer for who wanted their
picture taken with Ed. I finally got my time with Ed. Earlier in
the day, I had written a quick note for him. In it, I explained to
him that I have been big fan since *Throwing Copper* was
released in 1994. I wrote him that Live's *V* was a very unrated
album, referring to it as "genius". In my second paragraph, I
quickly explained that I have been writing songs with the aid of
my computer. I think he thought that was cool. Lastly, I asked
him to sign my copy of his CD, *Alive*. He did. He urged me to
keep composing. I think what excited me the most was Ed took
the time to read my letter. Before leaving, he posed with me for
a picture. It was a very cool experience. Thanks Ed.

        Our family closed out the year with celebrating
Thanksgiving and Christmas. It was a glaring reality that we
were missing Mom at these holidays, but she was with us in
spirit. I could feel her presence and I always will. In Paul and
Karen's new house, before dinner, Karen gave a number of
toasts, one of which toasted Mom.

        In the week before Christmas, I found the passion to
write a fictional, short story about embracing the Christmas
spirit, embracing the idea of hope is always around the corner,
despite what has happened through our existence on Earth. Let
all of our lives truly mean something. Help the ones who might
need a little more assistance. Don't judge the people who might
look a little different; people are people no matter who they look
like, what disabilities they might have, what God they worship,
who they choose to love or what their life experiences are.
Every person alive possesses a brain to think, lungs to breathe
and a heart to love.

Never underestimate the will of any human being.

Made in the USA
Middletown, DE
10 April 2023